60 Days for 60 Years

Israel
A Commemoration and Celebration

60 Days Series Editor
Rabbi Andrew Shaw

60 Days for 60 Years: Israel Editors
Fiona Palmer
Rabbi Aubrey Hersh

YOUNG UNITED SYNAGOGUE

First printed in Great Britain 2008 by Tribe
Adler House, 735 High Road, London, N12 0US
Charity Number: 294847
Enquiries: info@tribeuk.com
Website: www.tribeuk.com

UK edition   ISBN – 0-9549397-5-1

Produced by Ethical Communications, London +44(0)20 8201 9984
info@ethicalcommunications.co.uk

This book Is dedicated to
Chief Rabbi Sir Jonathan Sacks
in appreciation of his inspiration and support for
Tribe and the United Synagogue.

In memory of those whose lives have been lost
in times of war and terror.

Arnold Ziff zt"l

Arnold Ziff zt"l with his beloved wife Marjorie

THE LATE ARNOLD ZIFF was one of Anglo-Jewry's most unforgettable characters: down to earth but driven by high ideals, brisk and bluff but with a wonderful sense of humour, a man of action who not only built a highly successful business but contributed hugely to the Jewish community and to the civic life of Leeds. I counted myself privileged to know and admire him – he was a cherished friend.

Born into a hard-working middle-class family in the Chapeltown district of Leeds, Arnold took over a small family business and turned it into a large concern. He was active in Jewish affairs, becoming President of the Leeds Jewish Welfare Board and the local housing association. He worked tirelessly for Israel, a country he loved. He devoted much time and energy, as well as philanthropic support, to the wider community of Leeds. He was active in supporting its art gallery and the Yorkshire cricket school. He brought the Royal Armouries Museum to the city, and helped create the Leeds International Piano Competition. He built the Tropical World Garden in Roundhay Park, and was responsible for providing the St James' Hospital Leeds with its first body scanner in 1979.

These last two projects, both close to Arnold's heart, exemplified his passions and principles. His condition for both was that they would be available to everyone free of charge. He believed that everyone should have equal access to the things that matter, from health care to public galleries and gardens. He never lost his Jewish sense of social justice and human dignity, believing that one should be true to one's faith while at the same time being a blessing to others, regardless of their faith. I thought of him as a perfect exemplar of the teaching of the prophet Jeremiah, "Seek the peace and prosperity of the city to which I have carried you into exile; pray to the Lord for it, because if it prospers, you too will prosper." That sense of pride in your own traditions, combined with social responsibility, made Arnold a role model for others to emulate, though he was far too modest and self-deprecating ever to see himself in that light.

Arnold was a leader, not because he thought he had unusual gifts – which he did – but because this role came naturally to him. This was, he assumed, what we were placed on earth to do. He had no ego; he sought no honour or recognition. Yet honours pursued him. In 1991 he was made High Sheriff of West Yorkshire, and was nominated in 2002 as the "greatest living Yorkshireman". Shortly before he died, Leeds Metropolitan University created a professorial chair in his name.

In all he did, Arnold was supported and partnered by his beloved wife Marjorie, an exceptional character in her own right: gracious, determined, overflowing with energy and a sense of delight in life. They made a wonderful couple, and were devoted parents, taking joy and pride in their children, Michael, Ann and Edward, and their 13 grandchildren. In my last conversation with Arnold, just a few days before he died, I congratulated him on the barmitzvah of one of his grandsons, the last great joy of his life. To the end his mind was lucid, his voice strong and his character as robust as ever.

Psalm 92, entitled "A psalm, a song for the Sabbath day," contains the following verse: "The righteous flourish like a palm tree, and grow tall like a cedar in Lebanon." I long wondered why the psalmist felt compelled to compare a good life to two kinds of tree. Then I realised: we enjoy the palm tree while it is alive. We sit under its shade and enjoy its fruit. A cedar of Lebanon, however, is a tree we appreciate fully only after it is cut down. Then we see how tall it was. We who were privileged to know Arnold Ziff were lifted by his presence when he was alive. Only now, though, do we appreciate fully how tall he stood and how towering were his accomplishments. He gave to life so much more than he took, and he left all who knew him enriched and inspired. May the *60 Days for 60 Years: Israel* project perpetuate his memory, so that it, like his life, becomes a source of blessing; to Britain, particularly his beloved Leeds, to Judaism and the Jewish people.

Chief Rabbi Sir Jonathan Sacks

Contents

Arnold Ziff zt"l   iv

Preface   x

Acknowledgements   xii

Letters of Support   xv

Commemoration and Celebration

Divesting From Morality: An Academic Hijacking
                                        Alan Dershowitz   xxxvi
The Jewish Homeland   *Sir Martin Gilbert*   xxxix
The Rebirth of Jewish Life   *Lady Jakobovits*   xlii
Photo Gallery: Israel's Many Faces   xliv

60 Days for 60 Years: Israel

1 The Miracle of Israel. *Chief Rabbi Sir Jonathan Sacks*   3
2 Tiberias: A Tale of Romans, Rabbis and Renewal.
                                        Dr Raphael Zarum   7
3 Tehillim: The Ultimate Connectivity.
                                        Mordechai Ginsbury   11
4 From Rosh Hashanah to Yom Kippur:
   Actualising Your Potential.   *Sara Yoheved Rigler*   15
5 A Journey Through Israel.   *Simon Goulden*   21
6 Our Holy Language: The DNA of Creation.
                                        Yehudah Silver   25
7 Touching Every Human Need.   *Shalom Verrilli*   29
8 The Holiness of the Land of Israel. *Mordechai Becher*   33
9 Jewish Medical Ethics.   *Dr Kenneth Collins*   37
10 Rabbi Kook: Chief Rabbi of Israel.   *Joel Zeff*   41
11 Living Peacefully: A Simple Guide to Life.
                                        Dr Abraham Twerski   45
12 Living in Israel.   *Binyamin Tabory*   49
13 The Essence of Purim.   *Zev Leff*   53
14 When Breaking the Law was Breaking my Word.
                                        Sarah Shapiro   57

15 The Mystical City of Tzfat.   *Ari Kahn*   61
16 Some Thoughts About Jewish Memory.
                            Professor Dovid Gottlieb   65
17 Esther Cailingold (1925 – 1948): A Jewish Heroine.
                                    Yehuda Avner   70
18 Science and Religion: Partners or Adversaries?
                                Professor Cyril Domb   75
19 The Nobel Prize for Literature (1966). *Samuel Y Agnon*   79
20 Yom Kippur, Repentance and the Land of Israel.
                Yitzchak Schochet & Chaim Kanterovitz   83
21 The Tzaddik Reb Aryeh (1885 – 1969). *David Mason*   89
22 What Does Shema Yisrael Really Mean?
                                Dr Shlomo Riskin   93
23 Luggage Versus Baggage.   *Aubrey Hersh*   98
24 Jerusalem: Peace and Beauty.   *Shaya Karlinsky* 102
25 The Blooming of Israel.   *Samuel Green* 106
26 Love, Relationships and Parenting.
                        Gila Manolson & Danya Ross 110
27 An Inspirational Shavuot.   *Yitzchok Rubin* 114
28 Coincidences: God's Way of Saying Hello.
                                Yitta Halberstam 118
29 A Diaspora Yearning.   *Harvey Belovski* 122
30 Rabbi Shlomo Zalman Auberach (1910 – 1995):
    Torah Leader of the Modern Age.   *Jason Kleiman* 126
31 Successfully Meeting Life's Challenges.
                                Esther Jungreis 130
32 A Divine Document.   *Daniel Rowe* 135
33 Pride in our Judaism.   *Chief Rabbi Sir Jonathan Sacks* 142
34 A New Look at the Shemoneh Esrei.
                                Emanuel Feldman 146
35 Delivering in Dallas.   *Paysach Krohn* 150
36 Chanukah: Accepting Others.   *YY Rubinstein* 154
37 King David: Our First and Greatest C.E.O.
                                Menachem Leibtag 157
38 Jewish Identity: Let's Make It Positive! *James Kennard* 161
39 The Land and its Unique Mitzvot.
                            Dayan Yonason Abraham 164

40 To Listen and to Do. *Naftali Schiff* 169
41 The Jewish Family. *Malcom Herman* 172
42 Black Fire on White Fire:
The Sanz-Klausenberger Rebbe. *Chaim Fachler* 176
43 Pesach: One Great Jewish Community.
Chief Rabbi Dr Warren Goldstein 180
44 The Kotel and the Gate of Prayer. *Sara Yoheved Rigler* 184
45 Hide and Seek. *Chana Weisberg* 187
46 Destination and Destiny. *David Blackman* 190
47 Rabbi Menachem Mendel of Vitebsk (1730–1788).
Dr Naftali Brawer 194
48 Making It Happen. *Yaacov Haber* 197
49 My Name is Esther Wachsman. *Esther Wachsman* 200
50 Succot: The Joy of a Restored Relationship.
Yossi Michalowicz 205
51 Aliyah: Making the Move. *Gideon Sylvester* 209
52 Mezuzah: Faith and Conciliation. *Daniel Levy* 213
53 Chesed and Gemachs. *Yoni Sherizen* 217
54 Behind the Mask. *Dr Akiva Tatz* 221
55 Chevron: Connecting Heaven and Earth. *Holly Pavlov* 225
56 Kids: A Public Commodity. *Yaffa Ganz* 229
57 A Modern Day 'Dayeinu' Song. *Laurence Perez* 232
58 Listening to our Inner Voice. *Tziporah Heller* 237
59 Doña Gracia: An Inspiring Example. *Aubrey Hersh* 241
60 Our Israel: A Youth Perspective.
Judith Flacks, Gideon Glass & Ben Gross 247

Afterword 251

**Prayer for the Welfare of the State of Israel,
and its Defence Forces** 253

Prayer for the Missing Soldiers 254

Supporting Israel 255

For more information 257

Biographies 258

Glossary 269

Remember the Past to Build the Future 279

Preface
60 Days for 60 Years: Israel

Just over 60 years ago who would have believed there could be any positive future for the Jewish people? Entire communities wiped out, historic synagogues destroyed, hundreds of years of Jewish life eradicated as if they had never existed, and six million of our people lost.

However, just as we did in days of old, we rebuilt. After the ashes of the Holocaust, the State of Israel was formed, communities were recreated and the vibrancy that had been part of our history began to flourish. Now as we stand at the beginning of the new century, we can marvel at how far we have come in such a short time.

So began the final essay of the first 60 Days for 60 Years book, the worldwide initiative where Jews from across the globe learnt one essay a day in memory of victims of the Holocaust. Internationally, over 100,000 Jews participated providing a fitting memorial to the six million souls, by remembering the past and building the future. They did this by learning what it means to be a Jew in the 21st century.

Three years on, it is time to remember another 60 years. This time it is not only a commemoration but also a celebration – celebrating the miracle that is the State of Israel. A state that came into being in 1948 and is now 60 years old. For 60 years it has defied the odds not only to survive but to thrive. This project celebrates the immense achievements of the young state.

However, our state came and continues to come at a high price: the loss of thousands of men and women who gave their lives so that Israel could be born and continue to live and breathe. Their sacrifice allows us to celebrate 60 years of the modern State of Israel, a state that has from its inception wanted peace above all else, a peace that has so far eluded her.

60 Days for 60 Years: Israel is a commemoration and a celebration. A brand new book with 60 essays from internationally renowned educators, scholars and Rabbis. They have come together to cover a wide range of topics celebrating three aspects of Israel – *the Land of Israel, the heroes of Israel and the Torah of Israel*.

We will be learning in memory of those individuals who fell defending Israel from its enemies and in memory of those men, women and children who have been victims of the terrorist attacks, that have been all to frequent over the last decade. It is in their collective memory that we learn.

To accompany the book there is a learning card for those taking part in the project. For each of the 60 days of learning running up to the 60th Yom Ha'atzmaut the card lists a key event in Israel's history. Each essay will be learnt in memory of those who lost their lives in that tragic event. For those who wish to do more, for each essay we have also provided a selection of Psalms that can be recited.

As you begin the 60 days of celebration and commemoration, realise that you are uniting with hundreds and thousands of Jews across the world in Australia, New Zealand, South Africa, Great Britain, USA, Canada and of course Israel. Uniting in pride and affection for the Israel that we love.

60 years ago on 5th Iyar 5708 David Ben Gurion declared Israel a state. 60 years on we are gathering together to learn in memory of those who gave their lives so that Israel could live and breathe. 60 years on we are gathering to celebrate the remarkable achievements of Israel, how after 2,000 years of wandering – we finally came home.

Rabbi Andrew Shaw
March 2008
Adar II 5768

Acknowledgements

There are so many people to thank for making this inspirational project a reality. It is impossible to thank everyone who has contributed to making *60 Days for 60 Years: Israel* a success. However, the following people deserve special mention:

Chief Rabbi Sir Jonathan Sacks who has been a wonderful friend and supporter of Tribe and the United Synagogue family

Marjorie, Michael and Edward Ziff, true supporters of Tribe, for their generosity – without which much of this project would have been impossible

Melissa and Mark Shooter for sponsoring the closing event

Stylo-Barratt Plc and Town Centre Securities for their sponsorship of the 60 Days website

Syma Weinberg for her ideas and hard work on our behalf

David Kaplan for his continual support and advice

The Israeli Embassy and the Israeli Government for their support

Sir Martin Gilbert for his continued support

All the authors for their inspirational essays

All our donors and supporters for making this project a reality

All our overseas partners for making this project an international success

Chaim Fachler for his work to bring this book to as many overseas audiences as possible

The Shabbaton Choir for their performances at our events

The Yoni Jesner Foundation for its sponsorship of the 60 Days books for students on their Gap Year in Israel

Our sub-editors: Gila Shaw, Leigh Gower, Vicki Belovski and Jonny Lipczer

Kellmatt for printing and distribution

Totally Jewish for the promotional video

Bracha Erlanger and all those at the JLE for their invaluable assistance

David Brinn at Israel 21C for his assistance with 'In this Year' - A Focus Beyond, www.israel21c.org

Susan Lightman for all her legal advice

Johnny and Mandy Mitchell for their incredible patience and marvellous artworking

Ethical Communications for all their marketing and creative input

Dina Brawer and the whole 60 Days team who made this project happen.

Letters of Support

office of the
CHIEF RABBI

60 years ago, the State of Israel was reborn after a lapse of almost two thousand years. There has been nothing like it in history. No people has survived so long in exile and dispersion. None has placed a land so deeply at the heart of its collective consciousness.

Wherever Jews were, they prayed about Israel. When they prayed, they physically turned toward Israel. They lifted their eyes to its hills, they remembered its language and landscape, they carried it with them as a memory and a hope. And finally they returned.

This would have been astonishing, miraculous, even if there had been no Holocaust. But there was. This makes Israel more remarkable still. How so? Israel's national anthem is called *Hatikvah*, "the hope". It contains a phrase, "*od lo avdah tikvatenu*" "our hope is not yet lost", that refers back to the most haunting of all biblical prophecies.

26 centuries ago Ezekiel saw, in a vision, a valley of dry bones. God told him that they symbolised the Jewish people, devastated by the Babylonian conquest and exile: "Son of man, these bones are the whole house of Israel. They say, 'Our bones are dried up and our hope is lost (*avdah tikvatenu*); we are cut off.'" God then showed Ezekiel the bones coming together. The people lived again. God then said to Ezekiel: "Prophesy and say to them: This is what the Sovereign Lord says, O my people, I am going to open your graves and bring you up from them; I will bring you back to the land of Israel" (Ezekiel 37: 1-14).

There is no more powerful image than this to describe what happened to the Jewish people after the Holocaust. Because of Israel, the Jewish people lives again. Let us, for 60 days, learn in the memory of all those who made it possible. Their memory is our blessing. Their courage restored our people's hope.

Chief Rabbi Sir Jonathan Sacks
Chief Rabbi of the United Hebrew Congregations of the Commonwealth

It gives me great pleasure, on behalf of the people of Israel, to compliment you on your initiative in compiling the *60 Days for 60 Years* book.

The idea of Jews throughout the world uniting to celebrate the 60th anniversary of the establishment of the State of Israel by contributing to, and participating in, the creation of a book is indeed inspiring and moving.

60 years in the history of the Jewish people is but a short period and yet the State of Israel, since its creation, has much to be proud of. Despite the wars, intifadas and much strife. Israel has carved out a global role for itself in the spheres of science and technology, culture and academia, and serves as a pioneer in the search for solutions for global challenges.

The Jewish people throughout the world, including the Anglo Jewish community, have been, and continue to serve, as a backbone to these achievements. The unwavering support of the Jewish people is crucial to the continuation of Israel's positioning itself as a model society.

"Behold, how good and how pleasant it is for brethren to dwell together in unity." (Psalms 133:1)

Wishing you every success in your significant undertaking.

Shimon Peres
The President
State of Israel

60 Days for 60 Years: Israel is a powerful expression of a core United Synagogue value – the centrality of the State of Israel in Jewish life.

Israel holds a special place in the hearts of Jews the world over. Whatever their politics, level of religious commitment or ideology, when Jews travel to Israel they return home.

The essence of the United Synagogue can be expressed in the well-known saying – *Kol Yisrael Arevim Zeh Ba'Zeh.* (All Jewish people are responsible for one another.) We are at our core one people united by history and destiny and nowhere else on earth do these twin themes come together as they do in Israel. This is why Israel is so important to our peoplehood and our religious identity.

As you study the essays in this book please reflect not just on Israel the Land but also on Israel the People. The two are so intertwined as to be inseparable. Indeed, one can not love one without the other. It is my fervent hope that this book serves to deepen our appreciation of Israel and of each other.

Once again, the United Synagogue has taken the initiative of providing the international Jewish community with a most valuable resource. In so doing we have taken our place amongst the rank of world-class Jewish organisations. This for us is a source of much pride and satisfaction. It means that, in addition to the sterling work we do in the United Kingdom, we also have a role to play in the wider Jewish world. We look forward to developing this role in the years ahead.

I would like to express our sincerest thanks for the magnificent work that our Tribe team has performed in putting together *60 Days for 60 Years*, and for all their efforts in support of celebrations for Israel's 60th birthday. I also wish to thank our dear friends the Ziff family for their generous sponsorship of this project enabling the Tribe team to turn vision into reality.

Dr Simon Hochhauser
President
United Synagogue

Orthodox
Union תורה ומצוות

We are all living in historic times – times which often cause us great sadness and considerable anxiety, but also times which call for celebration and gratitude to the Almighty.

This year is a year for such celebration and gratitude. It is the 60th Anniversary of the State of Israel. How fortunate is our generation to witness what our ancestors prayed and wept for.

60 Days for 60 Years: Israel is a publication and project that helps us celebrate in an educational and enlightened manner. Those who make use of this work will be able to prepare properly, step by step and day by day, for a celebration based on an informed understanding and profound appreciation of this momentous event – 60 years of Medinat Yisrael.

Those who initiated this project and who contributed to its publication and dissemination are to be commended and thanked for their role in preparing us all, intellectually and spiritually, for Yom Ha'azmaut 5768.

Rabbi Tzvi Hersh Weinreb
Executive Vice President
Orthodox Union

I was delighted when Rabbi Andrew Shaw, Tribe's Executive Director and a good friend, called me regarding this magnificent initiative – editing a book which will celebrate every year of the Third Jewish State in the history of the Jewish People: the State of Israel. I collaborated with Rabbi Shaw distributing thousands of books of his former project to the 7,400 participants of the Maccabiah Games 2005 in Israel. This previous book, *60 Days for 60 Years,* was a memorial to the 6 million Jews assassinated during the Shoah, the most horrific tragedy in humankind's history. I felt that this new project, a celebration of the main achievement of the Jewish people since *Galut* (exile), would complete the first one.

The creation of the State of Israel brought relief and a physical solution – a *refuge* – to the systematic persecution of the Jewish people in the Western world. It was and it is the glorious co-production between God and His People. An accomplishment with the very heavy price of 22,305 men and women who have been killed defending its borders since 1860. This was the year that the first new Jewish neighbourhoods were established outside the old Jerusalem.

In addition to this, the new State of Israel was the divine reparation to the Children of Israel that provided a renovated hope in their future. It retrieved the concept of *Ge'ulah,* salvation, to a people who had known only the yoke of oppression, persecution and death for 1,800 years. It was the historical reparation of a Nation expelled from their land – a right finally recognised by the Family of the Nations.

Today, with 7,150,000 citizens - 5,415,000 of them Jewish (my family and I amongst them), the State of Israel and its many heroes will be honoured with this collection of essays. May God bring His blessings to this book, dedicated to the memories of the fallen *k'doshim* who made possible the glories of the present.

Rabbi Carlos A. Tapiero
Deputy Director-General and Director of Education
Maccabi World Union

60 YEARS IS A SHORT TIME in the history of a nation. It is even less time when one considers the history of the Jewish Nation which was persecuted throughout the ages, but did not give up its belief in the Almighty as the saviour of mankind. Every nation has a history of heroism and suffering. The Jewish Nation even more so. The story of our survival as a nation should never be forgotten.

Haman and others wanted to destroy us. But we survived. Earlier in the 20th Century the leadership of the German nation wanted to destroy the Jewish people. With the help of Hashem we survived. A few years later hundreds of thousands of our people were murdered in the concentration camps. Many of those who survived became the builders of our new home for all those who were tired of being "displaced". They wanted their own "home".

Together with those who saw in the establishment of a Jewish State in the Land of Israel the answer to Jewish suffering, they succeeded, with the assistance of those of us, who were all to be a part of those rescue activities – initially in saving many, who the Nazis were about to kill, before war broke out. In the following years millions were killed. But the Jewish people survived.

Those of us present, in the Hall in Tel Aviv 60 years ago, when, after many discussions the Jewish State of Israel was formally established, realised that now the time had also come to save the remnants of our people elsewhere.

The suffering Jews in North Africa - in Morocco, Tunis, Algeria and Tripoli - became the builders of our country. The suffering Jews of Soviet Russia were given new hope and a new home: Israel. Millions came and joined them. Nor did we forget the suffering Jews, *Falashas*, in Ethiopia.

Today, many of our brothers and sisters, in the free western countries, have decided to participate in building up our country. They are those who have, since and prior to the formal establishment of the State of Israel, also become builders of the State. And they, together with Israel as a whole, have benefited from the generosity of the Jewish communities and many individual Jews.

The knowledge that many of our young people are today builders of Eretz Israel is a great encouragement to all of us. May their numbers in Israel grow to many more in the coming years.

60 Days for 60 Years: Israel is yet another example of international activity in support of Israel and the Jewish people. Learning an essay a day in memory of the tens of thousands of soldiers who died defending the Jewish state and the thousands of civilian victims of terror – this is truly inspirational. May the Almighty continue to give us strength to build a country with justice and honesty to ourselves, and to mankind.

Arieh Handler
Last surviving attendee at the signing of the Declaration of Israeli Independence

The American Jewish Joint Distribution Committee (JDC), which serves as the overseas arm of the organised North American Jewish community, is pleased to offer its strong support for the educational initiative you have embarked upon to mark Israel's 60th anniversary. Participants in this project will come away with a new appreciation for the heroes, heroines, and ordinary citizens whose collective accomplishments – amid grave hardships and recurring conflict – have made the Jewish State the strong and compassionate nation that it is today.

JDC's own history is inextricably intertwined with the history of Israel. We came into being in 1914 to help sustain the members of the *Yishuv*, the Jewish settlers, in what was then Ottoman Empire Palestine. These settlers were cut off from their normal sources of support by the advent of the First World War. In the decades that followed, the generosity of North American Jewry enabled JDC to take part in *"hakamat hamedina,"* the building of the Jewish State, and to come to the aid of those who were most in need of assistance.

Since the establishment of the State of Israel, JDC has been involved in developing services and pioneering initiatives that have enriched the lives of the country's most vulnerable populations – in times of peace and in times of crisis. JDC's accomplishments in this regard, and that of its partners – the UJC/Federation system, UIA Federations Canada, UJIA, and numerous foundations and individuals – were recognised in 2007, when our organisation proudly received the Israel Prize for Lifetime Achievement and Special Contribution to Society and the State.

While the JDC has a presence today in 66 countries, the professional expertise garnered through our uninterrupted years of activity in Israel has infused our global operations, and the programme models developed there have enabled us to strengthen Jewish communities worldwide. We acknowledge with thanks our UK partner in these efforts, World Jewish Relief.

Israel is the dream that unites us all – for it is at the core of our identity as a people. As such, we heartily applaud your efforts to celebrate its 60th anniversary by enlisting a new generation in the ongoing communal endeavour that has made this dream a shining reality.

Steven Schwager
Chief Executive Officer
American Jewish Joint Distribution Committee

UJIA The heart of
Jewishlife

Since its establishment in 1948, the State of Israel has
become a safe haven for persecuted Jews, absorbing millions
of immigrants from throughout the world. It has turned
barren desert into fertile soil, producing crops that are sold in
every corner of the world. It has created world-leading
universities, enabling students to contribute to every possible
field and discipline in the world. It has established yeshivot
and learning institutions, offering the highest quality of
Jewish education in the world. It has founded non-profit
organisations, offering help and support to Jews and non-
Jews in distress across the globe. It has created industry and
technology, enabling innovation and advancement to occur
in every continent. And after all the tragedy and traumas of
the past, it has given Jews new-found hope, meaning and
purpose in every community of the world.

It has done all this in spite of being one of the smallest
nations in the world, and one of the most besieged nations in
the world. Its successes have not come without loss, without
sorrow, without war, without suicide bomb, without rocket
attack. As much as we celebrate 60 years of achievement, we
also mourn 60 years of conflict. As much as we celebrate
those individuals who helped to build the State of Israel, we
also mourn those individuals who died in the service of our
shared dream: to be, finally after two thousand years of exile,
a free people in our own land.

This book celebrates all those individuals who helped to
establish and build the State of Israel, and honours the
memory of all those who died trying to defend, or simply
live in the State of Israel. This is one of the greatest projects

the Jewish people have undertaken. It is not yet complete and the UJIA is privileged to be associated with it – and is proud to be supporting young people and education in the on-going task of building Israel's future.

Mick Davis
Chairman
UJIA UK

This year thousands of Jewish students across the UK will commemorate Israel's 60th Yom Ha'atzmaut.

Like the rest of the Jewish community they'll celebrate six decades of wonderful achievement whilst remembering the many lives that have been lost. Unlike the rest of the Jewish community they face vilification for doing so. For young Jews, life on campus is not what it once was.

Sadly, Jewish students today often face hostility for daring to show a pride in their Judaism, in their heritage and in Israel. This hostility shames the campuses of the United Kingdom and is something which Jewish Chaplaincy refuses to ignore.

There is so much in this book that will give strength and pride to young Jews; which is just what Jewish Chaplaincy is all about.

We're honoured to be a part of this project.

Ian Myers
Chairman
University Jewish Chaplaincy

As we approach 60 years of Israel, it is an exciting landmark for all Zionist Jewish organisations. The multitude of events will bring so many British and Diaspora Jews together. It's is an electrifying time for us all. Not only do we see a country that has developed itself so much over just 60 years, through media, technology, medicine, literature, music, theatre and the arts, but at the same time, we also see a country that has experienced some of the toughest situations, events that many countries have not had to face in the hundreds of years since their creation.

And yet the youth of the world have never been more ready or prepared to embrace the challenges and opportunities that issues surrounding Israel throw at them.

The Union of Jewish Students, (UJS), is a true leader with regards to Israel advocacy. Students defend and protect Israel's right to exist daily on campus. They successfully educate Jewish and non-Jewish students about Israeli successes, politics and more.

With the work that Tribe are doing to make this book, I am excited that Jewish students all around the country will have these texts available to them to study and to use as tools when advocating for Israel. As the national umbrella organisation for all Jewish students on campus, UJS is exhilarated to endorse the educational and celebratory opportunities that Israel 60 presents. May this year be one of peace, and celebration for all.

Jessica Truman
Chairperson
UJS

We, at One Family UK, are honoured and delighted to have been asked to support this most important project marking 60 years since the creation of the State of Israel.

Following the huge success of the 60 Years book commemorating 60 years since the ending of the Holocaust, we feel this project to be of huge importance. It remembers those who have lost their lives defending our homeland, a country of which we should all feel exceptionally proud.

The State of Israel has seen enormous changes since its inception. Unfortunately, one constant prevails – the call for Israel's destruction and the continuing attempt by its enemies to perpetrate murderous terrorist atrocities against its citizens.

One Family was set up in response, to meet the needs of Israel's victims of terror and to deal with the human aftermath. From 3 regional centres and with over 400 volunteers, One Family is presently helping more than 3,000 families who have been devastated by a death or serious injury. One Family is constantly there for them, providing financial and emotional support, psychological and physical therapy, as well as material assistance that many families so desperately need.

One Family also provides the framework for world Jewry to express their natural desire to care and assist by providing direct contact and interaction between survivors and communities around the world. Hundreds of us in the UK, who have welcomed and hosted victims – offering them a needy respite to the trauma of their daily lives – have experienced first-hand the appreciation felt by those less fortunate than ourselves. We care for them as if they were a close family member, and this gives them enormous strength and hope for the future.

We urge you to help us in our efforts by offering a hand of friendship to those whose lives have been shattered by the tragedy of terror.

This book serves to highlight the bravery of every citizen who has died defending our homeland and serves as a testament to their legacy. May their sacrifices bring the lasting peace we all so desire. At One Family, are proud to be associated with this special initiative.

Naomi Nevies and **Clive Rosenfeld**
Co-Chairmen
One Family UK

JNF is proud to have supported Israel since the State was formed. In fact, we started working on the dream 47 years before it became a reality. JNF was established in 1901 at the Fifth Zionist Congress in Basel, and from that moment we raised money to buy land and create the necessary infrastructure to rebuild the Jewish homeland.

Now, we raise funds for the building blocks of everyday life in Israel such as reservoirs, irrigation systems, desalination plants, forest planting, recycling schemes, roads, housing and healthcare centres. We provide shelter for families made homeless by terrorist attacks and acts of aggression from Israel's neighbours. And we help rebuild the infrastructure of their communities.

We are delighted with this inspiring collection of essays put together by Tribe in celebration of Israel's 60th anniversary. This book will serve as an important memento to commemorate this milestone in the development of the State. *60 Days for 60 Years: Israel* will provide Jews all over the world with an educational and historical memorial to all those who have fought for Israel over the decades – and an opportunity to learn in their memory.

The 60th birthday of the State of Israel is a magnificent occasion for all Jews to reflect with pride on the tremendous achievements of the Jewish State.

Gail Seal
President JNF UK

Simon Winters
Chief Executive JNF UK

Commemoration and Celebration

Divesting From Morality: An Academic Hijacking

Alan Dershowitz

Israel has a better human rights record than many other countries in the world. So why is the Jewish state being singled out?

The campaign for academic boycotts of and divestiture from Israel currently being waged on college and university campuses throughout the world is fuelled by ignorance, bigotry and cynicism.

These campaigns seek to delegitimise and isolate Israel as a pariah state and to convey to students the false notion that Israel is among the worst human rights violators in the world, guilty of genocide, torture, racism, ethnic cleansing and Nazi tactics, whereas the Palestinians and their Arab supporters are victims of Israeli aggression.

As an advocate, teacher and student of human rights for almost 40 years, I feel confident in asserting that Israel's record on human rights is among the best in the world, especially among nations that have confronted comparable threats. Israel has the only independent judiciary in the entire Middle East and one of the most highly regarded supreme courts in the world. It is the only court in the Middle East from which an Arab or a Muslim can expect justice, as many have in winning dozens of victories against the Israeli government, the Israeli military and Israeli citizens. There is no more important component in the protection of human rights and civil liberties than an independent judiciary willing to stand up to its own government. I challenge the proponents of boycotts to name a court in any other Arab or Muslim country that is comparable to the Israeli Supreme Court.

Israel is the only true democracy in the Middle East and the only country that has virtually unlimited freedom of speech. Its media are generally very critical of government. Any person in Israel, whether Jewish, Muslim or Christian, can criticise the Israeli government and its leaders. No citizen of any other Mid Eastern or Muslim state can do the same without fear of imprisonment or death. Nor can Palestinians openly criticise their leaders without fear of reprisal.

Israel is the only country in the world that has openly confronted the difficult issue of the civil liberties of the ticking-bomb terrorist, ruling that despite the potential benefits of employing physical pressure, such pressure is now illegal. Brutal torture, including lethal torture is commonplace in every other Mid-Eastern and Muslim country.

To be sure Israel is far from perfect. I have been critical of some of its policies, but there are mechanisms within Israel for improving its civil liberties and human rights record. These mechanisms do not exist in other Mid-Eastern and Muslim nations.

Even when judged against other European countries, Israel's human rights record does very well. It is far better than that of France on virtually any criterion, even if one forgets about the Algerian War, in which the French tortured and murdered thousands of people. It is at least as good as the British record in dealing with terrorism in Northern Ireland and the US record of dealing with al-Qaeda terrorism. The Israeli legal system is far superior to those of Italy, Spain and many other countries, and at least as good as the system in the United States.

There are, of course, difficult issues to be resolved between Israel and the Palestinians. These include the settlements, the establishment of Palestinian self-governance, and the prevention of terrorism. These issues will require compromise on all sides. Anyone should certainly feel free to criticise Israel, as well as any other country in the world whose record on human rights is not perfect. But to single out the Jewish state of Israel as if it were the worst human rights offender, is bigotry pure and simple; the orchestrators of, and adherents to Israeli boycotts should be ashamed of themselves and shamed by others.

It is therefore not surprising that these boycott petitions have garnered so little support among more respectable and experienced human rights advocates, since there is no intellectually or morally defensible case for singling out Israel. And any moral person who is aware of the true facts would not sign petitions or support these activities.

The problem is that these boycott activists couldn't care less about academic freedom, or any other kind of freedom for that matter. Nor do they care much about the plight of the Palestinians. If they did, they would be supporting the Palestinian Authority in its efforts to make peace with Israel based on mutual compromise, rather than Hamas in its futile efforts to destroy Israel as well as the Palestinian Authority. What they care about – all they seem to care about – is Israel which they despise, without regard to what the Jewish state actually does or fails to do. They know that Israel, without oil or other natural resources, lives by its universities, research centres and other academic institutions. After the US, Israeli scientists hold more patents than any other nation in the world, have more start-up companies listed on NASDAQ, and export more life-saving medical technologies.

Israelis have received more Nobel and other international science prizes than all the Arab and Muslim nations combined. Cutting Israel's academics off from collaboration with other academics would deal a deathblow to the Israeli high-tech economy, but it would also set back research and academic collaboration throughout the world. The real losers from such a boycott would be doctors, patients and citizens in every country.

Moreover, many Israeli academics, precisely those who would be boycotted, are at the forefront in advocating peace efforts. They, perhaps more than others, understand the "peace dividend" the world would reap if Israeli military expenses could be cut and the money devoted to life-saving scientific research. If Israel is boycotted, we all end up as losers.

The Jewish Homeland

Sir Martin Gilbert

The establishment of the State of Israel 60 years ago reads easily now as just another fact of history. But in 1948 it was one of the great improbabilities of history.

The Jewish people had just suffered the terrible killings of the Holocaust. Six million were killed – one third of the Jewish people. Vast swathes of Jewish culture and achievement, including the vibrant, creative language of Yiddish, were all but wiped out. Yet the surviving two-thirds did not give up their faith. They did not give up their ethical imperatives. They did not despair of renewal.

In British Mandate Palestine, the Jewish community looked with anger as British warships intercepted the refugee boats and deported those on board – survivors of the Holocaust – to camps in Cyprus, and even back to Germany. British guns and barbed wire prevented these survivors from entering the Jewish homeland. This was the very land that in 1917 Britain had promised as a "Jewish National Home".

In February 1947 the British announced that they would hand over the Mandate to the United Nations. In November 1947, the United Nations voted to set up a Jewish and an Arab State side by side there – in the 90-mile wide strip between the Mediterranean Sea and the Jordan River. The United Nations also decided to exclude Jerusalem from either the Jewish or Arab State.

It was difficult for the Jewish leaders at that time, headed by David Ben-Gurion, to accept such a truncated and emasculated region. Giving up Jerusalem was like cutting off a limb. However, they accepted it knowing that another chance of statehood might not come again in many years, if at all.

What the Jewish leadership did not anticipate was the utter refusal of the Arab States of the region to agree to the United

Nations offer of statehood for the Palestinian Arabs. No element of Jewish statehood, however small, was acceptable to the Arabs. It was total rejection, just as after the 1967 war there was total Arab rejection at the Khartoum Conference of any negotiations or peacemaking with an Israel that was willing at that time to give up the conquered territories.

Following the United Nations vote for a Jewish and an Arab State in a partitioned Palestine an unprecedented assault erupted against the Jewish community. Arab gunmen shot down Jews in the streets and on the roads. The killing of Jews between November 1947 and May 1948 was continuous throughout the land. Jerusalem was besieged. The United States announced that, given the violence, partition was no longer possible and that Palestine should be put under the control of the United Nations. The prospect of a Jewish State was receding.

In May 1948, as the formal date for the ending of the British Mandate approached, the United Nations began to discuss the establishment of a separate, United Nations controlled, Jerusalem. First Guatemala and then Australia put forward resolutions to this effect. When news reached Ben-Gurion that the United States was about to put forward a third such resolution, denying Jerusalem to the Jews, he decided to delay no further in declaring statehood. He did so, at five in the afternoon of Friday, May 14, in the main hall of the Tel Aviv museum.

Israel was born. Within hours, five Arab armies attacked, determined to destroy the new nation in its hour of birth. Egyptian aircraft bombed Tel Aviv, and more than 100 Jews were killed. Iraqi troops drove into the centre of the country. Egyptian troops reached the southern suburbs of Jerusalem.

The Israeli army chiefs doubted that the Arab armies could be defeated. But the desperate danger called forth from them extraordinary courage and defiance. The survival of Israel was the result of these qualities. The nation that possessed them knew that the only alternative was destruction – being driven into the sea.

This fate, of being driven into the sea, was militarily possible – even likely – had the Arab armies been fighting for something other than a destructive cause. Israel's existence was the idealistic dream of Jews throughout the world century after century. Israel's destruction was a perversion of those followers of Mohammed who had long held the Jews to be second-class, inferior, demonised people.

The Jewish people's triumph over adversity in 1948 related to deep longings, prolonged historic struggles and setbacks. It came from a realisation that the Jewish fate was in the hands of Jews not strangers, and faith in the biblical promises that were a part of prayer and study for two thousand years, since the Roman destruction of the Temple.

President Ahmedinajad should read the story of Israel's survival in 1948, and realise that more is at stake here than a piece of land: it is the survival of a people and its cherished ideals – ideals that are as cherished today as they were 60 years ago.

The 60th anniversary edition of Martin Gilbert's book *Israel a History* is published by Doubleday. The most recent edition of his *Atlas of the Arab-Israel Conflict* is published by Routledge, as is his *Atlas of Jewish History*.

The Rebirth of Jewish Life

Lady Jakobovits

The *haggadah* which we read on Pesach talks of our transformation, "from misery to joy, from mourning to a holiday, from deep darkness to great light."

Our generation has experienced the 'accordionisation' of history like none other. In no period of Jewish or general history have opposite poles been compressed into so short a period. We have seen the pendulum swing across the rise and fall of Communism, the mushrooming of science in general and of medicine in particular and most recently, the explosive growth of Islamic fundamentalism. Even in the natural world, the rapid increase in global warming far exceeds the speed of change which prevailed over the last millennia.

Similarly, the smaller world of Jewish society has also seen changes compressed into but a few years. The unparalleled disasters in the first half of the twentieth century, followed by the equally unparalleled rise of Jewish self governance over the second half, occurred within a time span which in a previous era would have taken several generations to evolve. Similarly, while there was a calamitous loss of Jewish identity in the post-war years, it was followed by the current vigorous expansion of people learning about, and practising, Judaism.

However, of all miracles marking the changes in Jewish life perhaps the most remarkable has been the rise of the State of Israel out of the ashes of World War Two. Arguably, the former created a necessity for the latter. The intensity of the Jewish will, coupled with the contrite attitude of a largely silent, if not guilty, non-Jewish world, allowed the geopolitical variables to line up in just the right way. This allowed for the creation of the state and for it to take root in a previously hostile soil of the international community of nations.

My dear late husband frequently stressed the notion that whenever the term *yizkor* (to remember) is found in its original form in the *Torah*, it is always forward looking. For example, after the most universal of all holocausts, the flood of Noah, it says, "*Vayizkor Elokim es Noach*" (God remembered Noah and his family). This yizkor was not dedicated to the flood's innumerable victims. Rather, it focused attention on the survivors. The most meaningful and durable memorial to our losses are the efforts dedicated to building a new generation, the generation of survivors.

More than any museum or monument, Israel is a living yizkor – a living memorial to the Holocaust. The remarkable rebirth of Jewish life, physical and spiritual, confounded the diabolical plans for a final solution. Her spiritual and religious achievements have also confounded the predictions of imminent demise by many of our own. The phenomenal growth of her religious and social institutions has led to a larger concentration of Jewish life to also flourish in the Diaspora. Israel's ascent has had a beneficial effect on these centres too.

True, as the years have gone on, aspects of Israel's mission and message have changed. The identification of Israel as the victim in the Arab-Israeli struggle has long metamorphosed in the eyes of many. The notion that through Israel and its social sensitivities and programmes we should be seen as a light unto the Nations has been eclipsed at times by the realities, no matter how necessary, of forcibly ruling over millions of Arabs within our borders.

On the other hand, the growth of Torah learning and of its supremacy in the lives of many, could have developed only in the fertile land of Jews managed by Jews. Taken as a whole, the Israel experience was built on optimism and confidence in our future. That hope continues to assure us that ultimately our people and its message will be universally respected so that, as the prophet Isaiah says, "the earth will be as filled with knowledge of Hashem as water covering the sea bed." (Isaiah 11:9)

Photo gallery: Israel's many faces

1. An elderly woman taking care of three little children – 26 May 1944. They are walking to the gas chambers.

2. Child leaving a displaced persons camp - 11 July 1945. The eight year old Yisrael Meir Lau, survivor of Buchenwald and future Chief Rabbi of Israel beginning a new life.

3. The Land of Israel.

4. Masada - 2,000 years ago at the heart of the Jewish nation's struggle to fight off the Romans.

5. *The arid landscape - a desert land awaited the return of its people.*

6. *Water filled valley - a precious resource, the importance of water in Israel continues to this day.*

7. New arrivals - European refugees arrive in Eretz Yisrael.

8. Declaration of Independence - 14 May 1948: The land becomes a State.

9. Election time – democracy in action in the Middle East.

10. Jerusalem – the holy capital of Israel.

11. *Jerusalem is united – June 7 1967: This historic photograph captures the spirit of a reunified Jerusalem.*

12. *Yom Yerushalalyim.*

13. The return of the Entebbe hostages in July 1976 - Israel is no stranger to troubles both within and beyond its borders.

14. Partners for peace in September 1978 – Menachem Begin and Anwar Sadat agree a historic land for peace deal.

15. Machane Yehuda market - while the statesmen are at work, life goes on.

16. Jerusalem's Central Bus Station - a special place for a people used to journeying.

17. *The ancient streets of Israel.*

18. *A more modern street scene – although this photo probably pre-dates the advent of Israel's ubiquitous mobile phone!*

19. (Left) Rabbi Shlomo Zalman Auerbach (see essay 30) with the Sanz-Klausenberger Rebbe (see essay 42).

20. Purim in the streets.

21. *After the Sbarro bombing.*

22. *Comforting a victim.*

23. Israel's new generation.

Photo Credits:
1 & 2: Yad Vashem archives
3: NASA, Visible Earth www.veimages.gsfc.nasa.gov
4 & 13: Moshe Milner, State of Israel National Photo Collection
5, 6, 17 & 20: Jack Hazut
7: Zoltan Kluger
8: State of Israel National Photo Collection
9, 12 & 21: Avi Ohayon, State of Israel National Photo Collection
10: Boris Katsman, iStockphoto.com
11: David Rubinger, State of Israel National Photo Collection
14, 15, 16 & 22: Yaacov Saar, State of Israel National Photo Collection
18 & 23: Used with permission of copyright holder, Davka Corporation
19: Mattis Goldberg

60 Days
for 60Years:
Israel

In loving memory of Suzi Bradfield a"h.

1 The Miracle of Israel

Chief Rabbi Sir Jonathan Sacks

Israel has been at the heart of Jewish life since the first recorded syllables of Jewish time, God's call to Abraham to "Leave your land, your birthplace and your father's land and go to the land I will show you."[1] Seven times God promised the land to Abraham, and He repeated that promise to Isaac and Jacob. In a sense, the whole of Jewish history has been a journey to the land.

It was repeated in the days of Moses, and again after the Babylonian exile. Throughout the long centuries of their dispersion, whenever Jews could return, they did. *Judah Halevi* did so in the 12th century. So did *Maimonides* and his family, though they were unable to stay there. *Nachmanides* went there in 1265 and rebuilt the Jewish community in Jerusalem after the ravages of the Crusades.

There was a large Jewish presence there in the 16th century. In the 18th and 19th centuries, long before the birth of Zionism, the disciples of both the *Vilna Gaon* and the *Baal Shem Tov* went there. My own great-grandfather, Rabbi Aryeh Lev Frumkin, made *aliyah* in 1871. His father had done so some 20 years earlier.

Jews never left the land voluntarily, and there are places, especially in the Galil, where they never left at all. The nation states of Europe are relatively recent inventions: France in the 18th century, Germany and Italy in the 19th. The connection between the Jews and Israel is longer and stronger than that of any other Western nation and its land.

Yet there is still something miraculous about the birth of the modern state of Israel in 1948. A mere three years earlier, the Jewish people had been eyeball-to-eyeball with the angel of death in Auschwitz, Treblinka and the other places of destruction. It would have been understandable had the Jewish people been paralysed by trauma and grief. But they weren't. Israel's Declaration of Independence 60 years ago was the most momentous collective affirmation of life in two thousand years of Jewish history. The Jewish people in effect said, *"Lo amut ki echyeh,"* "I will not die but live." Israel is the triumph of life over death.

Yet it almost did not live. The day it was born, it was attacked on all fronts by the armies of five nations: Egypt, Syria, Jordan, Lebanon and Iraq. They were so confident of victory that they advised the Palestinians to leave on the assumption that they would soon return as masters of the land, the Jews having been driven "into the sea."

The Jewish population of Israel at the time was a mere 600,000. Many of them were young. Others were Holocaust survivors. At the start of the War of Independence they had little weaponry or military supplies. Yet somehow they survived and triumphed.

Israel is a miracle of hope over despair; life over the forces of death. And just as it showed courage in war, so it showed courage and persistence in pursuit of peace. In the 1930s, various proposals were made for partition – what today we call a 'two-state solution'. Jews accepted them all; the Arabs rejected them all. In 1947 the United Nations voted in favour of partition. Again, the Jews said yes, the Arabs no.

The offer of peace was renewed after the Six Day War, and again in 1969 when Golda Meir became prime minister. Again it was rejected. On the 1st September 1967, the Arab League issued its famous three no's to Israel: No to peace. No to recognition. No to negotiations. For seven years during the Oslo peace process, culminating in Camp David and Taba, Israel offered the creation of a Palestinian state. Again the offer was rejected.

Egypt could have created a Palestinian state when it ruled Gaza between 1949 and 1967, but it did not. Jordan could have created a Palestinian state when it ruled the West Bank during those years, but it did not. The only country to have offered the Palestinians a state is Israel. There are two words for strength in Hebrew: *koach* and *gevurah*, and they mean different things. *Koach* is the strength needed to wage war. *Gevurah* is the strength needed to make peace. Israel has consistently shown both kinds of strength.

That is why we should look back at the past 60 years in thanksgiving: to God, who brought us back to our land, and to the men and women who had the courage – following in the footsteps of Abraham and Sarah four thousand years ago – to leave their land, birthplace and parents' house and travel "to the land I will show you."

If there were justice in the world of public opinion Israel would be seen as a sign of hope, not just to Jews but to humanity as a whole. For it has shown that it is possible to transform a barren and desolate land into a place of forests, farms and fields; that it is possible to forge a nation out of immigrants and asylum seekers from more than a hundred countries; that it is possible to turn a land with almost no natural resources into one of the great economies of the world; and that it is possible, despite the constant threat of violence from its neighbours, to build a free and democratic society in a part of the world that had never known one.

Israel is the place where, after the worst crime of man against man in history, the Jewish people was reborn, the Hebrew language was reborn, hope itself was reborn. Peace still eludes it. Yet that too will come in time. The prophets of ancient Israel – Isaiah and his younger contemporary Micah – were the first people in history to see peace as an ideal, and what a people prays for, century after century, eventually comes to pass.

In the meanwhile let us give thanks that we have lived to see the fulfilment of the prophetic dream:

I will bring back my exiled people Israel;
they will rebuild the ruined cities and live in them.
They will plant vineyards and drink their wine;
they will make gardens and eat their fruit.
I will plant Israel in their own land,
never again to be uprooted
from the land I have given them,
says the Lord your God.[2]

Notes:
1 Genesis 12:1
2 Amos 9:14-15

ISRAEL IN 1948

- The State of Israel is established and the invading forces of surrounding Arab countries are repelled in the War of Independence
- Israel's first population census is carried out, recording approximately 600,000 citizens from the age of 15 and up
- ElAl airlines is incorporated and becomes Israel's official carrier
- The sweet 'Jaffa' orange becomes one of the top exports of Israel and a word synonymous with this new state

Dedicated in memory of Sheila Rosenthal, Shifra Bat
Shlomo, by Karen and Jeremy Jacobs.

2 Tiberias: A Tale of Romans, Rabbis and Renewal

Dr Raphael Zarum

Tiveriah (Tiberias) is a town on the western shore of Lake
Kinneret (the Sea of Galilee) in northern Israel. It was
established in 18CE by the vassal king of Judea, Herod Antipas,
son of Herod the Great, in order to honour the Roman
Emperor Tiberius. Tiveriah was built on the ruins of what is
thought to be the ancient biblical site of Raqqat.[1]

Initially, Jews refused to settle in Tiveriah because it was built
on cemeteries which rendered it *tumah* (ritually unclean).
However, Antipas forcibly re-settled people there from rural
Galilee and invited distinguished foreigners to come too.
According to Josephus, he was, "so eager to settle the city that
he even welcomed poor people from everywhere, including
[Greek] freed slaves. He granted them significant privileges,
heaping wealth upon certain of them, granting land to others
and houses to others still to keep them in this un-alluring city."[2]

With its natural hot springs and mild, below sea-level
climate, it became one of the most elegant winter resorts in
this part of the ancient world. Classical writers described this
capital of the Galilee as a city adorned with colonnaded
streets, impressive Roman baths and temples made of
imported white marble, and broad marble steps leading down
into the waters of the lake.

With the destruction of the second Temple in 70CE, the *Sanhedrin*, the Supreme Court that legislated on all aspects of Jewish religious and political life, was evicted from the Temple Mount and re-established in Yavneh. But following the *Bar Kochba* revolt in 135CE, Jews were expelled from both Jerusalem and Judea and were forced to move north. So Tiveriah became the new capital of the Jewish community and the Sanhedrin eventually resettled there. In 2004, excavators from the Hebrew University uncovered a basilica that they believe housed the Sanhedrin in Tiveriah.

Tiveriah grew over the next three centuries and became the centre of Jewish scholarship. It is likely that the *Mishnah* was completed here around 190CE, under the supervision of Rabbi Yehuda Ha-Nasi (Judah the Prince). It was also home to great Rabbinic sages including Rabbi Meir, Rabbi Yochanan, Rabbi Ami and Rabbi Assi, and it was here that the commentaries, teachings and sayings of these and other sages were eventually compiled into the Jerusalem *Talmud* in the fourth century.

Though the name Tiberias is Latin, the Babylonian Talmud finds meaning in Tiveriah, its Hebrew name. "Rabbi Yirmiyahu said: Why is it called Tiveriah? Because it is situated in the belly button [*taboor*] of the land of Israel."[3] By this play on words, they were highlighting the centrality of Tiveriah to Judaism. Learning is the lifeblood of our nation, it is the root of our survival. Without a Temple, we found closeness to God in the words of Torah and we have never tired of uncovering ever deeper layers of its meaning.

The Rabbis also knew the place as Raqqat, the name that predates Tiveriah. And why Raqqat? "Because even the emptiest [*rek*] of its inhabitants are full of *mitzvot* like a pomegranate."[4] The abundance of segments in a pomegranate serves as a metaphor for the deeply religious lives of Tiveriah's inhabitants. It must have been quite an inspiring place to live! Read James A Michener's *The Source* and you will find a fascinating chapter dedicated to Tiveriah and 'The Law'. It really brings the place to life. Both the town and the towering scholarship suffered from the fifth century on, due to the many wars fought here by the Persians, Arabs, Crusaders, and Turks. Nevertheless, in the eighth to tenth centuries, the *'Niqqud'* – the standard rules for vowel and punctuation grammar – were introduced into the Hebrew language, by the town's masoretic scholars. To this day, "Tiberian Hebrew" is the most widely used system we have.

In the 12th century, after the Crusades and Turkish reprisals, the original site of the city was abandoned and settlement shifted north to the present location. In 1558, Doña Gracia, a former *Marrano* Jew, rented the site from Suleiman the Magnificent. She restored the city walls, built a *yeshiva* and encouraged *Sephardi* Jews fleeing the Inquisition to settle there. Tiveriah flourished again for a century. It was devastated again, and again resettled by *Chasidic* Jews. In the 18th and 19th centuries it received an influx of rabbis who re-established the city as a centre for Jewish learning. During this time it became known as one of the four holy cities, along with Jerusalem, Hebron, and Tzfat.

Tiveriah today is a honky-tonk kind of town with 30,000 inhabitants. There are only a few kosher restaurants, but you can bathe in the hot springs, hire bikes and cycle round the Kinneret, visit ancient archaeological sites, and pay your respects at the graves of some of the greatest Rabbis in our history.

The brilliant 12th century *halachist* and philosopher Rabbi Moshe ben Maimon, the Rambam, is buried there. On his tomb is written the famous epitaph, "From Moshe to Moshe, none arose like Moshe." Then there is the tomb of Rabbi Akiva on the mountainside overlooking Tiveriah. Rabbi Akiva backed the second century rebel leader Bar Kochba and was put to death by the Romans with the *Shema* the last words to pass his lips. According to tradition, his body was miraculously transported to Tiveriah for burial.

Tiveriah is a crucial strand in the tapestry of Jewish history. Though Roman in origin, it was home to generations of Jewish scholars who committed themselves to the constant renewal of Jewish life. The preservation of the Oral Law, the seat of religious authority, and the key to Hebrew pronunciation are all strongly identified with this little town by a lake. Tiveriah is also a testimony to Jewish survival. We have lived there more or less continuously for almost two millennia. Remember that on your next visit.

Notes:
1 Joshua 19:35
2 History of the Jews 18,3
3 Megillah 6a
4 Ibid

ISRAEL IN 1949

- First elections are held and David Ben-Gurion forms the Government with Chaim Weizmann elected as the President
- Israel is accepted as a UN member. 37 countries voted for, 12 against and 9 abstained
- The first shipment of 3,000 US cows arrive in Israel as special emergency aid aimed at improving the quality of milk

3 Tehillim: The Ultimate Connectivity

Mordechai Ginsbury

Tehillim for health, tehillim for wealth; tehillim petitioning for success and guidance, tehillim for thanksgiving; tehillim for help at difficult moments.[1] Around the world in rallies for peace in Israel tehillim have set the tone.

The ubiquitous nature of Tehillim, the Book of Psalms, is such that we might almost consider it to be the spiritual equivalent of a doctor's broad-spectrum antibiotic. In reality, it is far more than a symptom-relieving and soothing balm. The book of Tehillim is an ever-relevant facility through which we can fully connect with God at all times and in all places if we sincerely attempt to do so.

Compiled and, in the main, written by Kind David, it also contains a number of psalms authored by ten 'notables' including such giants of the spirit as Adam, Abraham and Moses.[2] Perhaps its most remarkable single feature is its timelessness, because as Maimonides explains, "the King of Israel's heart is the heart of all Israel."[3] David, the King of Israel, can thus be said to have included not only his own yearnings, aspirations, concerns and petitions in Tehillim but those of all Jewish people throughout the ages.

Indeed, although David was a king, he made every effort to avoid becoming remote and detached from the world of the ordinary individual. David was linked to his fellow beings; all were considered to be his friend on the simple and equitable basis of their sharing his spiritual sense of aspiration and yearning[4]. In a similar vein, he was able to retain his sense of values and perspective in the presence of other rulers, "And I will speak of Your statutes in front of kings and not be ashamed."[5]

Whilst such ideals are noble and worthy ones, it is reasonable to consider the extent to which the experiences of a king can really be said to match those of his humble subjects. Yet studies of both David's life and the contents of Tehillim reveal that his royal status did not shield him from exposure to the most extreme emotions and events. From the pain of a father rendered a fugitive by his own son: "A psalm of David when he fled from his son Absalom,"[6] to the anguish of a man who trusts in God but feels abandoned by Him: "My God, my God, why have You forsaken me? Why do You stand so far from saving me."[7] David's exposure to harrowing emotional trauma is real, powerful and intense. And surely the frustration, expressed at the end of Psalm 120, resonates all too accurately in the ears of our people today – just as when King David first expressed it nearly 30 centuries ago, "Long have I lived among men who hate peace. I am for peace; but whenever I speak of it, they are for war."[8]

Incredibly, first-hand knowledge of the darkest moments a human being can experience still does not force King David's hand. Despite suffering the ultimate perfidy of "even my best friend in whom I trusted… has raised his heel to trample me,"[9] the psalmist's faith remains. "Princes persecute me without cause, yet my heart fears only for Your word. I rejoice over Your word like one who finds abundant spoils."[10] It is this expression of faith, coming from a very real human being who manages to rise above his pain, hurt and betrayal to grow through his experiences of adversity, that has given Tehillim its central position as the book for those in need of faith or solace.

The book of Tehillim acknowledges human limitation with humility. "Incline Your ear Hashem and answer me, for I am poor and needy"[11] and speaks with certainty of God's restorative powers. It is also a book of instruction and opens with the perceptive advice to avoid the company of scoffers, as their outlook will eventually influence ours.

Several of the tehillim are so central to our relationship with God, that they were incorporated into our prayers. Most famously there is the chapter of *Ashrei* which we recite three times daily. This assures us of both God's omnipotence as a provider and His response to genuine petition. [12] Many other tehillim play a similar role, most notably the psalm for the day. Although bereft of the Temple, we nevertheless connect to it through this daily recitation. This recitation reminds us of Temple times when the Levites would accompany the service through song and the recital of tehillim.

Ultimately though, the book of Tehillim – *tehilla* literally meaning praise – is suffused with an optimistic and positive spirit, "I will sing to Hashem as long as I live; I will sing praises to my God all my life." [13] It is a book of yearning and a work which encompasses the individual and collective aspirations of the Jewish people, to ultimately experience redemption. "I rejoiced when people said to me 'Let us go up to the house of Hashem'. Our feet now stand within your gates, O Jerusalem." [14]

Tehillim constantly remind us that to connect with God, no mediator or enabling factor is required, just heartfelt petition. And it is through the honest relating of one's deepest and innermost emotions to one's Maker, that one can genuinely await His most complete blessing in response, "May Hashem bless you from Zion, may you behold the well-being of Jerusalem all the days of your life; and may you see children's children, Peace be on Israel!" [15]

(At the bottom of each page of this book are suggested tehillim for you to say in memory of those who have passed away in Israel in times of war and terror.)

Notes:
1 See fourth edition of the Singer's Siddur p.924
2 See Talmud Bavli, Bava Batra 14b

3 Hilchot M'lachim 3:6
4 Psalm 119:63
5 Psalm 119:46
6 Psalm 3:1
7 Psalm 22:2-3
8 Psalm 120:6-7
9 Psalm 41:10
10 Psalm 119, 161 – 2
11 Psalm 86:1
12 Psalm 145
13 Psalm 104:33
14 Psalm 122:1-3
15 Psalm 128:5-6

ISRAEL IN 1950

- The third Maccabiah Games opens, originally scheduled for 1938, it was delayed until this year due to the outbreak of World War II
- Israel enacts the Law of Return, guaranteeing citizenship to all Jews
- The Israeli national soccer team wins a surprising 5-1 victory against Turkey
- IBM Israel begins operating in Tel Aviv
- Jerusalem is declared as Israel's capital city

In memory of my father, Asher Loftus zt"l.

4 From Rosh Hashanah to Yom Kippur: Actualising Your Potential

Sara Yoheved Rigler

After crying intermittently for 36 hours, ever since the eerie wail of ambulance sirens carrying the dead and wounded from the terror attack at the Hillel Cafe woke me up last Tuesday night, I thought I had no more tears to shed. Then I saw the picture of the wedding dress.

It appeared in an Israeli newspaper - a photo of a long, white, taffeta and chiffon gown, hanging forlornly on the door of the bride's bedroom closet, because the 20-year-old bride, Nava Applebaum, is clothed in a shroud instead. Nava was buried together with her father, Dr. David Applebaum, on the day that was supposed to be her wedding day.

The photo next to it shows Nava's fiancé, Chanan Sand, beside Nava's open grave, holding the wedding ring he had intended to place on her finger. He placed it instead on her lifeless body as it was lowered into the grave.

There are other pictures in that day's newspaper: A picture of the handsome, smiling 39-year-old Yaakov Ben Shabbat, who was killed in Tuesday's terrorist attack outside the Tzrifin army base. He had left work early in order to purchase a cake for his eight-year-old daughter's birthday.

There's a photo of a bereft, crying 12-year-old, Sapir Moshe, being supported by relatives at the funeral of his mother, killed while sipping coffee with her friend at Cafe Hillel.

There's a picture of two smiling young soldiers: Yonathan Peleg and Efrat Schwartzman, killed together in the Tzrifin attack. Yonathan was killed instantly; Efrat succumbed to her wounds the next morning. "She surely didn't want him to go alone," cried Yonathan's father.

There's a picture of the weeping, anguished parents of 22-year-old Alon Mizrachi, the guard at the Hillel Cafe, who fell on the terrorist, struggled with him, and was blown up with him.

In my newspaper, however, the page with the most tearstains is the photo of the wedding dress. The tragedy of Nava Applebaum is the most wrenching of all of Tuesday's 15 victims because it represents all that could have been - that came so close to being - but was not. The joy of the two sets of parents, the jubilation of the young couple, the union they had planned and waited for, and the rejoicing of the 500 guests who were invited to the wedding and attended the bride's funeral instead.

Tears on the Days of Awe

Jews are supposed to cry on *Rosh Hashanah* and *Yom Kippur*. Rabbi Avigdor Nebanzahl wrote that if the Jewish people would cry tears of repentance on Rosh Hashanah, when all the occurrences of the subsequent year are determined, we would not have to cry tears of grief throughout the year.

But it's hard to summon tears of repentance. What we did throughout the year - in terms of others, God and ourselves, may not have been exemplary, but was it really so bad? I feel a twinge of guilt when I remember speaking harshly to someone, but should I shed tears over that little misdemeanour? I regret my impatience with my husband and children, but, after all, I'm only human.

The Sages say that ever since the destruction of the Second Temple, the "gate of prayer" is closed, but the "gate of tears" is always open. What is the secret to accessing the well of tears?

The answer is *teshuva*. Usually translated as repentance,

teshuva means returning. We are supposed to return to God and to some improved version of ourselves. But how are we to return to a place most of us have never even visited?

Teshuva means not a sudden change of lifestyle, but a determined change of direction; making a concrete plan to actualise change in small but steady increments. The prospect of teshuva frightens many of us, because repentance implies that I am a sinner, sullied by my actions, like a vagrant in need of a bath.

However, Rebbetzin Tzipora Heller points out that the true Jewish attitude toward teshuva is not, "How wicked I am because I did that," but rather, "How could someone like me have done something like *that?*" Teshuva is an affirmation, not a rejection, of who we are on the highest level. Rather than being characterised by our lowly actions, we repudiate our lowly actions as being unworthy of the holy souls we inherently are.

We cry on Rosh Hashanah when we reflect on what we could have been, when we compare our majestic potential to our shabby reality. Every one of us has the potential to be spiritually great, to meet our challenges. On the High Holydays, we reflect on the perfected vision of ourselves, and cry over the mediocrity we permitted in its place.

We could have been magnanimous. Instead we were petty. We could have buoyed up others with kind words. Instead we wounded them with deprecations. We could have esteemed our parents for their ongoing contribution to our lives. Instead we made them feel useless and outdated.

My friend Sarah taught me to visualise what she calls "my full potential self." This is the perfected image of myself in all its details.

One of the words for sin in Hebrew is *chait*, which means missing the mark. The disparity between our full potential and our present reality fuels our heartfelt teshuva.

Too late
The culprit which keeps us from crying over our failures is the sense that we have all the time in the world to fix them.

Unfortunately, patience - a sterling trait when applied to others - can degenerate into complacency when applied to ourselves. The Jewish calendar gives us a deadline for teshuva: Rosh Hashanah.

Rosh Hashanah forces us to confront the truth that we do not have all the time in the world, for two reasons. Firstly, the relationships that we need to mend can be mended only as long as the other person is alive. The other illusion that makes us procrastinate in doing teshuva is our failure to face our own mortality.

Our friends Michael and Miriam live in the town of Efrat. During the first year of the second Intifada, the "tunnels road" to Efrat was an intermittent target of terrorist gunfire. Several people were killed on that road. One evening Michael was driving home while talking to Miriam on his mobile phone. They started to argue about something. Suddenly Michael noticed he was on the "tunnels road." He abruptly ended the argument saying, "I'm driving on the tunnels road now. How would we feel if the last conversation we ever had was an argument?"

Ultimately, we are all driving on the "tunnels road". What a tragedy it would be if our last encounter in this world ends up being an argument, a nasty complaint, a sarcastic joke, a petty criticism.

Two millennia ago the sage Hillel taught, "If not now, when?" If I don't actualise my potential now, who knows if I will have another chance? If I don't fix my bad traits now, in this world, which the *Kabbalists* called, "the world of fixing," I might very well be buried with my shortcomings.

Death is the final, unbridgeable chasm between what could have been and what is. The ultimate agony is the remorse each of us will feel when we find ourselves in the other world, totally unable to fix any of our flaws or failures. This is the Jewish definition of hell.

The Kittel

Yom Kippur is a miraculous gift God gives us every year. God's offer is too good to refuse. If we do teshuva, He will give us *kapara*, atonement. Of course, we are free post Yom Kippur to lapse into old patterns of behaviour, to pick up where we left off, to change directions back again. But on Yom Kippur itself, if we have done teshuva, God picks us up and moves us over the chasm between who we are and who we truly want to be.

According to Jewish tradition, one's wedding day is like Yom Kippur. The bride and groom fast, pray the prayers of Yom Kippur, and all their sins are forgiven. When they stand under the wedding canopy, they are in a state of pristine perfection.

According to Jewish tradition, grooms wear a long-sleeved, knee-length white garment called a *kittel*. The kittel is worn for the first time at the wedding, then on every Yom Kippur, and finally as a burial shroud.

It is possible to be spiritually great. Dr. David Applebaum, who, with selfless dedication, single-handedly changed the face of emergency medicine in Jerusalem, did it. Nava Applebaum, who lovingly cared for juvenile cancer patients, did it. For such individuals who viewed life as an opportunity to perfect themselves and the world, the shroud and the wedding garment can be one.

(This essay originally appeared on Aish.com. It also appears in Lights from Jerusalem, *Sara Rigler's latest book.)*

ISRAEL IN 1951

- Israel demands compensation for Nazi crimes from West Germany
- A new town named Ashkelon is established in the South, populated mainly by North African immigrants
- The national lottery is set up with the intention of collecting funds for educational institutions, the first lucky winner is from Ramat-Gan

- Israel's first nature protection movement forms during the draining of the Hula Lake and its surrounding swamps in order to combat malaria and reclaim the land for agriculture

Dedicated by Pat and Alfie Frei in memory of our son,
Danny Frei zt"l.

5   A Journey Through Israel

Simon Goulden

Israel - the Land and its People - is indelibly marked on the hearts of every Jew in many ways. One short essay can never do justice to the rich variety of sites, locations and features packed into our small, precious homeland. Such is the wealth of locations, that each of us will likely have a different list.

This is hardly surprising. Just before the Jews crossed the Jordan, to enter the Land of Israel for the first time, God apportioned a different part of the land to each tribe, because each contained its own blessing and unique spiritual potential.

Wherever we visit in Israel, we form a connection with our nation's past. We walk in the footsteps of prophets and kings, living in cities with Biblical names and narratives, continuing traditions and practices of old. With a sense of pride, we are able to point to a national history and geography almost 4,000 years old and become one of the links in that glorious chain that is the Jewish People and their Heritage.

Let me take you to just a few of my favourite sites, ones which I feel have helped to create the Israel of today.

Close to the northern border of Israel lies **Tel Chai**, a monument to one of the pioneer heroes of modern Jewish settlement in our land and a reminder of the ways of international politics. The Sykes - Picot agreement of 1919/20 carved up the Turkish Empire, the French claiming Lebanon,

Syria and this part of the country, the British taking the rest. Emir Feisal, the future King of Iraq, having fought alongside the British, laid claim to Syria and this part of the Galilee too, which already contained several Jewish settlements, such as Metulla, Kfar Giladi and Tel Chai. The Jews in the area found themselves unwilling political pawns and victims of Arab terrorist attacks.

The heaviest of these many attacks came on 11th Adar 1920. Joseph Trumpledor, a former Russian officer and colleague of Jabotinsky, sent to reconcile squabbling Zionist political factions, had been recently appointed to command the outpost. Overwhelmed, Trumpledor and his brave fighters could not hold out and, mortally wounded, he died with the now famous words "it is good to die for our country." Eight men and women died there, explaining the name of the major settlement just south of Tel Chai: *Kiryat Shemona* (town of eight).

Perhaps some of the most innovative examples of making the best of limited rainfall can be found when visiting **Avdat**, an ancient settlement built by the Nabataeans, a people with a mysterious origin, who lived in the area in the Mishnaic and Byzantine periods. The Nabataeans, who specialised in transporting spices from the Arabian Sea to the Mediterranean, utilised their intimate knowledge of the desert, harnessing winter floods to grow crops in a significant portion of the Negev. They built dams in their fields to halt the treacherous flash floods, allowing the retained moisture to seep slowly through the soil. Expert farmers, the meticulous stone clearing of their fields encouraged more efficient moisture penetration. You can still see the heaps of stones which they created and which some believe also served to support vines. Dew, forming overnight in the cold air, would trickle through the heaps and water the vines without rapid evaporation. Nearly two thousand years later, Ben Gurion had a dream that the Negev would once again flourish. The Nabateans' ideas are now being developed by the Institute for Desert Research, making Israel one of the world's leading exporters of techniques for making the desert bloom.

In 1945, the *Haganah* decided to establish a secret plant to manufacture the bullets which would win or lose the coming War of Independence. Built in just three weeks, the underground factory, code named the **Ayalon Institute**, was set up just north of Rehovot.

Above ground, a huge ten-ton baking oven (there was a working bakery here) and a large washing machine (from the commercial laundry) revolved on bearings, hiding the noise and fumes coming from the factory, eight metres below.

Between 1946 and 1948, well over 2 million 9mm bullets were manufactured here for the Sten sub-machine gun, the primary personal weapon during the war. At the height of operations, 40,000 bullets a day were made at the Ayalon Institute, the only supply that was not in shortage during the war.

Independence Hall in Tel Aviv, was formerly the house of Zinna and Meir Dizengoff, Tel Aviv's founding father and first mayor, who bequeathed his home to the city as an Art Exhibition.

But more than this, here in this hall, the members of the National Council, representatives of the Jewish settlements and the Zionist movement, gathered on Friday, 5th of Iyar 5708, 14th of May 1948 in the afternoon just before *Shabbat*, to sign the Scroll of Independence.

Two days before the declaration, the situation for the National Council looked very complex. The Jerusalem - Tel Aviv Road was blockaded by Arab bands, and two members of the National Council were unable to arrive in Tel Aviv for the historical decision. After appraisal of the dangers during days of meetings, the Jewish National Council finally decided on the 12th of May, to take advantage of the opportunity provided by the termination of the Mandate to establish the State of Israel. From now on, Israel could set its own foreign policy and import weapons to defend its independence as a sovereign state.

No borders of the state were mentioned in the declaration. When questioned on this point, Ben Gurion replied, "When the United States declared independence, did it define its borders?"

When you visit the hall, left exactly as it was 60 years ago, you may wonder why the chairs do not match? Simply, they could not muster sufficient furniture of their own, so Tel Aviv's restaurants and cafes were scoured for assistance, each offering their own colour and design. And so it was on borrowed chairs, in a commandeered art gallery, 60 years ago, that the State of Israel was born.

ISRAEL IN 1952

- President Chaim Weizmann dies and, despite suggestions that Albert Einstein may replace him, Itzhak Ben-Zvi is sworn in
- Due to a gasoline shortage a decision is made that all vehicles must be stationary for 2 days a week
- The Bulgarian Government commissions 30,000 pairs of the best quality shoes from Israeli factories, paying for them with onions rather than cash
- Israel participates in the Olympic Games (in Helsinki) for the first time

In loving memory of all those who guided us and taught us how to become who we are, and in memory of Rosalia Singer one of the six million who will not be forgotten. Dedicated by David and Nicki Marks.

6   Our Holy Language: The DNA of Creation

Yehudah Silver

Hebrew, *Lashon HaKodesh*, the Holy Language, is the language of creation, the language of the 24 books of the *Tanach* and the language of our Sages. In the creation narrative of the *Torah* we are shown how all that exists came into being through speech. Hence, "And God said, 'Let there be light,'"[1] "And God said, 'Let the land give forth vegetation.'"[2] The process of creation was through speech and the Hebrew language.

Bearing this in mind, we can understand that Hebrew is unlike any other language. All languages are a collection of arbitrary sounds which are merely symbols for concepts, ideas and things. There is, for instance, no particular reason why the five letters K-N-I-F-E inherently denote an implement to cut. It could equally have been S-P-O-O-N. Hebrew however, is different in that the word itself *is* the item.

The word defines the reality of the object, because it was through the Creator's word that the object came into being. Everything that exists has purpose and meaning and that purpose is not merely the external perception of size, colour, weight and its utilitarian use. Rather, it has a spiritual essence and it is that essence which is contained within the word. Therefore, by understanding the word we understand how we, as well as every "thing" that we encounter, are intended to function. It is therefore not surprising that in Hebrew the word for an object and the word for 'word' are the same. **דְּבָרִים** (devarim) means objects, and **דְּבָרִים** also means words.

Hebrew is also unique in that it is based on a root system of three letters and, in rare exceptions, four letters. In actuality, the three letter root is made up of two letters which form the basics of a concept and a third letter which gives the word/object its uniqueness. Therefore, words which are constructed with the same letters not only have a linguistic relationship, they also must have a conceptual one.

In English, for example, there is no conceptual relationship between words comprised of the same consonants. So the words Pear, Pour, Pier, and Pare, while they share the same letters P and R, have absolutely no relationship. Furthermore, the words Confirm, Truth, Educate, Art, Craftsmanship certainly have no linguistic relationship and it is difficult to find any conceptual relationship either.

However, when we look at the word **אָמֵן** (amen) in Hebrew we see a totally different picture. When we analyse this word in depth, it reveals something amazing to us. The term **אָמֵן**, which is said after one hears a blessing, means to validate or confirm that which was just said. At the same time, the word **אָמֵן** also means truth, as Joseph said to his brothers, "Bring your youngest brother to me *so that your words will be true*, "**וְיֵאָמְנוּ דִבְרֵיכֶם**".[3] However, the word **אָמֵן** also means to educate, as we find in *Megillat Esther* where it says, " **וַיְהִי אוֹמֵן אֶת הֲדַסָּה** ", " And he [Mordechai] educated **הֲדַסָּה** " [Esther].[4]

By combining these two meanings we get a deeper understanding of the true process of education.[5] It is not merely the amassing of information and knowledge, rather, it is the communication of the truth which will guide the individual to a purposeful existence.

This is why **אָמָּנוּת** (amanut) means art and **אֻמָּנוּת** (umanot) means craftsmanship. Both the artist and one who applies his craft take raw materials and shape or mold them into a piece of art or into something which can be used efficiently. Isn't this exactly the process of education? To educate means to take the most precious raw material in the world, that which has the greatest potential – a person – and mould him, shape him and guide him into that most magnificent example of true art, the human being.

The Hebrew language system is actually even more intricate and striking. In all other languages, the letter itself is merely an arbitrary symbol, with no meaning. When this symbol/sound is joined together with others, they form a word, which again is an arbitrary symbol of an object or a concept. However, in Hebrew, each letter has meaning because even the letter itself is a word.

For example, the letter א (אָלֶף – Alef) is a word which means to teach, or champion as in " וַאֲאַלֶּפְךָ חָכְמָה ", (vea'alefecha) "Be silent and I will teach you wisdom" [6] or " אַלּוּף נְעֻרַי אָתָּה "(aluf) "You are the champion of my youth" [7]. The letter ב (בֵּית – beit) means a house. The letter ג (גִּמֶל – gimmel) means to give or nourish, as we say in the first blessing of the *Amidah* prayer, " גּוֹמֵל חֲסָדִים טוֹבִים ", "He bestows beneficial kindnesses." Since each letter has meaning, when letters are put together, a complex idea emerges which becomes the word. So if we learn the 22 letters of Hebrew and their meaning, we are able to understand the true message behind each word.

The *Zohar* teaches us, "God looked into the Torah and created the world." [8] In effect, this statement describes the Torah as the blueprint of creation. Everything found in creation has its place in the plan, the Torah. As with any blueprint, one must know the meaning of each symbol in order to properly understand what it represents and what the final and practical outcome will be. God has given us the key to understanding His blueprint of creation, through the wonder of Hebrew. Each letter represents one of the building blocks which make up our universe, and as such, the letters truly form the DNA of creation.

Notes:
1 Genesis 1:3
2 Genesis 1:11
3 Genesis 42:20
4 Esther 2:7
5 See Rabbi Samson Raphael Hirsch zt"l on Genesis 15:6
6 Job 33:33
7 Jeremiah 3:4
8 Zohar II, 161b

ISRAEL IN 1953

- The Academy of the Hebrew Language is established, responsible for creating new Hebrew words and having the final say concerning spelling and grammar
- The Tel Aviv Stock Exchange is formed
- Israel Aerospace Industries is founded on the sand dunes of Lod Airport
- Yad Vashem Holocaust memorial museum opens in Jerusalem

7   Touching Every Human Need

Shalom Verrilli

As they showed me around the sprawling headquarters of
Hazon Yeshaya, on Rashi Street in Jerusalem, I kept thinking
of the verse: "*Mekimi me'afar dal*" "He raises the poor from the
dust."[1]

Walking into the main entrance of the Hazon Yeshaya
Humanitarian Network, the kitchen greets you with its long,
stainless steel tables, staffed by volunteers from soldiers to
visiting youth groups. Even the UK Chief Rabbi, Sir Jonathan
Sacks, visited the premises and didn't leave before chopping a
few vegetables in the kitchen. It is still first and foremost a
soup kitchen, but the centre does so much more. Rabbi
Abraham Israel, its founder and director, works from the
ground up to provide shoes, cooked meals, dental care,
vocational courses, education for boys and girls, and a *kollel*
for the needy.

The ultimate *chesed*, says Rabbi Israel, is to give a hungry
person a cooked meal. He knows what it's like to be
dependent on a soup kitchen for daily sustenance. In 1958, as
a nine-year-old boy, he fled the persecutions of Gamal Abdel
Nasser in Egypt, together with his parents, his sister and
brother. They reached Paris with only the clothes on their
backs, thankful to have survived the journey. For three and a
half years, young Abraham wore the same set of clothes, his

ankles sprouting beneath his trouser cuffs.

"It's not the end of the world if you have holes in your clothes. But food; you need to eat every day. We survived due to the graciousness of the Jews operating the one kosher soup kitchen in Paris. We ate at that soup kitchen seven days a week, until eventually we received a visa to enter the USA as refugees. This is my way of paying back for the kindness I received during those three and a half years."

Young Abraham received a sound *yeshiva* education at Mir and Ner Israel in the USA, and then a degree in accounting and business administration. All aspects of Rabbi Israel's education have served him well in the chesed enterprise he runs today, for which he takes no salary.

The Hazon Yeshaya network has spread out in all directions from Jerusalem, where it began ten years ago, when Rabbi Abraham Israel ran into a woman in her early twenties, who was leaning on a cane as she waited to cross a busy street.

Noticing her plight, Rabbi Israel stopped the traffic and guided her to the other side. Ronit, it turned out, was suffering from multiple sclerosis. She said she wasn't feeling well, and asked Rabbi Israel if he wouldn't mind helping her get home. When he saw the squalid room she called 'home,' he was shocked. No electricity, a broken windowpane replaced with a piece of cardboard and a broken sink with a pail underneath to catch the runoff. There was not a scrap of food in sight. What was she going to eat, Rabbi Israel wanted to know. Ronit said she hoped to get hold of a yoghurt some time that day. A yoghurt? That was all? And didn't she get any government assistance? Yes, she received a 1,200 shekel monthly allowance (about £150), but most of it went towards medication, she said. Her prescriptions were very expensive. Were there other people living in conditions as bad as these? Yes, said Ronit, citing her neighbours as an example.

Rabbi Israel wasted no time. He promptly found a storefront for rent on Rashi Street, where Ronit lived, and hired a woman to cook a hot lunch for three local destitute families. Word spread, and the appeals came pouring in.

Today, Hazon Yeshaya has four soup kitchens which produce over 400,000 hot meals a month at 58 distribution points throughout Israel. The majority of these meals are served in schools to needy children, many of who would be going without any lunch if not for the centre's free meals. Some are delivered to the homes of the house-bound or bedridden. Who else is saved from hunger by these meals? Gush Katif refugees; people put out of work by the second Lebanon War; unemployed single mothers and their children; Holocaust survivors and terror victims.

Up until now, most of the centre's vocational courses have been for women, with preference being given to single mothers. Mrs. Limor Levy at the centre tells me that her work goes beyond the walls of Hazon Yeshaya.

"Sometimes they call me up at home to talk things over. A divorced woman can feel like an outcast. These are women without much education who aren't familiar with the working life. Being part of these courses does more than just provide them with a trade; it gives them a sense of belonging."

Upstairs are the Talmud Torah and kindergarten classes. "The children come and go through a separate entrance," says principal Rabbi Meir Asulin.

"Their meals are delivered to the classrooms from the kitchen downstairs, but we don't want them to feel they go to school in a soup kitchen. They don't even see the soup kitchen. We take children from very needy homes and it's our job to make them feel like normal kids, so that they won't remain in a needy state as they grow up."

I notice the rooms aren't crowded, and Rabbi Asulin explains that each class has a maximum of 24 pupils. "Every child needs personal attention, especially these children." But he isn't quite ready to let me leave yet. "You haven't seen the kollel?" he says. And indeed, the kollel that crowns this building is the glory of Hazon Yeshaya. The *shtenders*, over two hundred of them, are fully occupied. Again, I meet bright eyes and intelligent faces. Students commit themselves to a seven-year learning programme here, after which they will serve the spiritual needs of our Jewish nation, becoming *poskim* or community rabbis.

The atmosphere at Hazon Yeshaya goes beyond just giving handouts. It touches the spirits of the recipients, giving them a sense of hope and dignity. "Frankly," says Rabbi Israel, "I never dreamt it would get this big."

Notes:
1 Psalms 113:6

ISRAEL IN 1954

- The Bank of Israel is founded; the bank issues notes, controls banking supervision and foreign exchange
- Heavy rain falls on Tel Aviv causing serious flooding and the fire brigade, with its four trucks is called out 28 times during the night to pump water from houses
- WEIZAC, one of the world's first computers, is designed and built at the Weizmann Institute

In loving memory of Joe Wise.

8 The Holiness of the Land of Israel

Mordechai Becher

3,750 years ago God instructed the first Jews, Abraham and Sarah, to go and live in the Land of Israel (then known as Canaan) and promised them that although their children would go into exile, ultimately He would bring their descendants back.

Following Joshua's conquest of Israel, the Jews lived there independently for 800 years. King David conquered Jerusalem as our capital city, and his son Solomon, built the First Temple, which stood for 410 years. After a 70-year exile, the Jews returned to build the Second Temple, which stood until 70 CE, when the Jews were dispersed around the world. Subsequently, the land was invaded by Arabs, Crusaders, Ottomans and the British, but through it all, Jews not only remained there, but produced monumental works of learning and liturgy including the *Mishnah, Jerusalem Talmud,* Code of Jewish Law, the song *Lechah Dodi,* and the *Kabbalah* of the *Arizal.*

The *Gaon of Vilna* sent many students to settle in Israel, as did the early *Chasidim*, and in the late 19th century, the Zionist movement brought thousands of Jews to establish agricultural settlements and industry there. The attachment of the Jews to their land throughout over 1,900 years of exile culminated in the establishment of the State of Israel in 1948, now home to over five million Jews. Jews of the 21st century take for granted the presence of Jewish communities in Israel. From a historical point of view, however, the return of a people to their land after 1,900 years of exile, the establishment of an independent Jewish state, and the ingathering of Jews from virtually every country in the world are miraculous and unprecedented events in history.

Land of the Spirit

Aliyah has been the cherished dream of Jews throughout the ages. In fact, the very word aliyah means "to go up" because the Jewish people have always regarded moving to the land that was given to them as an inheritance, as an ascent, an act of spiritual elevation. Furthermore, of the 613 commandments of the Bible, 343 are directly dependent on the Land – that is, 55% of Jewish law. As such, the land is not only distinguished by its history, but also by its spiritual qualities. Most prophets either lived in Israel or prophesied about it. Based on the principle that the nature of the physical world reflects the underlying spiritual nature of reality, we readily understand the pre-occupation of the *Torah* with the agriculture of Israel.

Agricultural Ethics

The Land of Israel and its agricultural products are considered holy, therefore there are special laws that apply to them. The most well known is the obligation to separate a percentage of the crop and give it to the *Cohanim*, the *Levites* and the poor.

The obvious lesson for the farmer is that God, not the human being, is the ultimate landowner. However, the other, more pragmatic, purpose was to support the Levites and Cohanim who were not given any land of their own, and who were designated as the teachers of Torah to the Jewish people and workers in the Temple. These laws also inculcate in the Jewish people the positive character traits of compassion and justice.

Nowadays, with no Temple, tithes are not distributed and the obligation is therefore to separate them and dispose of them in a respectful fashion. Jewish practice has extended the idea of tithing to one's income as well – even outside of the Land – giving 10% of our earnings to charity.

Sabbath of the Land

Every seventh year of the agricultural cycle is *shemittah*, the Sabbatical year, in Israel. No new crops are planted and only maintenance work is done on crops and trees. Additionally, shemittah produce has to be handled in a special manner that demonstrates its inherent holiness. The current Jewish year, 5768, is a shemittah year.

Maimonides and other commentators agree that the primary purpose of shemittah is to allow everyone equal access to the land, and to allow landowners to feel like tenants once in a while. This helps them to understand that "the earth is the Lord's" and that the main purpose of life is not the accumulation of possessions. The Sabbatical year also provides an opportunity for hard-working farmers to devote more time to Torah study. The observance of shemittah fell into disuse during the long Jewish exile from the Land. Today, with the return of Jews to their homeland and the increase in Jewish observance among Israeli farmers, there are farms and kibbutzim that once again strictly observe the shemittah laws.

There is however, an obvious connection between the weekly sequence of six days of work, which are followed by *Shabbat*, a day of rest, and the six years of toil, which are followed by the shemittah year. The Torah employs the identical phraseology in regard to Shabbat day and shemittah, "The seventh day shall be a Shabbat to God." They both parallel the six days of creation and the seventh day of Shabbat. This further corresponds to the six millennia of human history, followed by the seventh millennium of the final Shabbat - the World to Come.

The six years of a human being's labour represent the three-dimensional physical world (which stretches in six directions). But Judaism teaches that the working human being must be perpetually focused on the end-goal, the realm of purpose and achievement – the spiritual realm of *Olam Haba*, the world to come.

In contrast to any other land, Israel in its deepest essence is a piece of the world to come, of endpoint. Shemittah is therefore the symbol of Jewish destiny and represents the existence of Olam Haba, which is the climax and destination of all man's effort. It signifies a Jew's true attachment to God and to the sanctity of the Land and the acknowledgement that, since everything ultimately belongs to God, we may only use it for purposes that are in keeping with His plan for the world.

Jews have the custom to sing Psalm 126 – A Song of Ascents – before reciting the Grace after Meals. The psalm predicts that, "When God will return the captives of Zion, we will be like dreamers… those who tearfully sow will reap in glad song." The haunting, yet joyous words of the psalm describe our exile and return as well as our attachment to a Land which is as much spiritual as physical. These messages are so significant, that some of the founders of the State of Israel wanted to choose this psalm as their national anthem.

(The expanded version of this essay can be read in Rabbi Becher's book Gateway to Judaism *published by Artscoll Mesorah/Shaar Press: pp 259-277)*

ISRAEL IN 1955

- The town of Dimona is established in the Negev
- The Dead Sea scrolls are brought to Israel
- Oil is found in the Negev but this turns out to be the first and (to date) last commercial oil field in the country
- Professor Natan Goldblum from Hebrew University develops the country's first polio vaccine. Israel is the second country in the world to vaccinate against polio; the first time Goldblum's vaccine is used, it stops an epidemic

In loving memory of David and Hetty Collins zt"l.
Dedicated by their grandchildren.

9   **Jewish Medical Ethics**

Dr Kenneth Collins

Jewish tradition, supported by principles clearly laid down in the Torah and the Talmud, has always set great value on human welfare. It has given us all an obligation to preserve life and health as well as giving physicians a divine mandate to heal. Breakthroughs in medical science have often created ethical dilemmas. These issues have been addressed by Jewish scholars around the world, nowhere more so than in Israel where there are numerous institutes dedicated to medical research and *halachah*. Jews have also been closely associated with medicine from the earliest days of its professional development and issues of health and hygiene are closely bound up with Jewish practice.

There has been a consistent system of *halachic* decision making on health related matters dating back through the Middle Ages to *Talmudic* times. Indeed, the medical *halachah* from the mediaeval period, usually based on Talmudic principles, may serve as a crucial precedent for present day issues. Changes in medical practice demand new responses from doctors, laymen and rabbis. Halachah provides a continuing dynamic interpretive framework within which contemporary decisions are made. Israeli law, though part of a secular legal system, is also deeply influenced by halachah and this relationship is especially strong in biomedicine including such areas as coercive treatment and care of the terminally ill.

The term Jewish medical ethics was only coined by Chief Rabbi Lord Jakobovits in his pioneering work on the subject about 50 years ago. Lord Jakobovits was concerned that the quest for scientific advance should be "effectively controlled by the overriding claims of human life and dignity." He clearly delineated the history of Jewish rabbinic decision making on health issues through the ages covering the right of the physician to heal, the duty to save life and the duty of care to the sick. Significantly, he also identified those areas, such as birth-control, abortion and euthanasia which were of crucial importance to patients, rabbis and society.

In the years since then new areas of concern have arisen. Medical ethics has become a major concern for doctor, patient and society as a whole and answers to such questions as organ transplantation, the time of death, surrogate motherhood, genetic manipulation and cloning are required. Rabbis and doctors have debated these issues trying to gain an understanding of all the ethical and clinical dimensions which these topics produce. Given the nature of many of the issues it is not surprising that different approaches to many of the most contentious topics have emerged even in such areas as brain death and abortion for foetal defects.

Because of the complexity of many of these issues and the sensitivity with which rabbis face these problems it is often not possible to give a blanket ruling on particular subjects and patients and family are usually advised to ask a competent religious authority to answer their particular query. In many communities there are rabbis, skilled in the Jewish ethical implications of illness and its management, attached to hospitals who will seek to obtain the appropriate halachic solution to particular difficulties.

Lord Jakobovits was also concerned about training physicians who would be imbued with Jewish observance and understanding and who would embody in their practice the ideals of practice both as Jews and as doctors. Indeed, in the Middle Ages the combination of a rabbinic and medical career was a popular option for many great Jewish scholars. This was exemplified by the remarkable medical and rabbinic career of

Rabbi Moses ben Maimon, (1135-1204) also known as the Rambam, or Maimonides.

A voluminous literature has emerged providing guidelines for patients relating to observance of *Shabbat* and Festivals, the *kashrut* of medication, carrying out circumcisions, visiting the sick and many other *mitzvot*. At the end of life a delicate balance has to be struck between supporting the needs of the patients in life while not prolonging the process of dying. This does not mean that patients are to be coerced into futile and burdensome treatment but rather that such questions are part of the legitimate discussions with doctor and rabbi. As Jewish medical ethical writings have become more widely available there has been a greater acceptance of the need for religious answers to these difficult medical questions provided on a case-by-case basis.

The work of recent rabbinic decision makers (*poskim*) such as Rabbis Moshe Feinstein, Shlomo Zalman Auerbach and Eliezer Waldenberg, has been crucial in producing traditional solutions to contemporary problems. The study of Jewish medical law ethics, as well as the medical writings of Maimonides, has been popularised by Dr Fred Rosner in his insightful writings in English and translations from Hebrew. Dr Rosner has commented on the incontrovertible damage to health posed by cigarette smoking and has urged poskim to make a clear decision against this harmful practice.

In the secular field ethical issues are underpinned by such key concepts as autonomy and beneficence, the underlying assumption being that patients are free to make independent choices regarding their health and that doctors will strive to act in patients' best interests. Living wills, sometimes called advance directives, have become popular in wider society as a means of ensuring autonomy at a time when the patient may be unable to make independent health care choices. Jewish law considers that the human body is held on trust and sees the concept of autonomy as subservient to the demands of halachah. Thus living wills, where required, should be written within a halachic framework nominating as health proxy someone who can be relied upon to make decisions in accordance with Jewish medical law.

Jews today live, in the main, in secular and pluralistic societies. It is important that Jewish ethical values in health care are understood and respected both within the Jewish community as well as in wider society to ensure general acceptance of Jewish traditional practices in medical issues.

ISRAEL IN 1956
- The IDF conquers the Sinai – 171 soldiers killed in action
- Agrexco, Israel's largest exporter of agricultural produce and flowers, is founded – marketing products worldwide under the name 'Carmel'
- Elite establishes the first Instant coffee factory in Safed
- The Knesset Menorah is given to Israel by the British Parliament
- Tel Aviv University is established

In memory of Sydney and Miriam Kett zt"l.

10 Rabbi Kook: Chief Rabbi of Israel

Joel Zeff

Enter the office of any Religious Zionist institution in Israel and you will find the face of Rabbi Abraham Isaac Kook looking directly into your eyes and, seemingly, into your soul. This is visual testimony to the central role accorded to this rabbinic leader in the development of the ideology and institutions of Religious Zionism. Rabbi Kook's life and philosophy are exceedingly rich and complex, but we can gain a glimpse of this giant of a man through several brief vignettes.

Born in 1865, he was the product of an unusual marriage for the period. His father hailed from the world of Lithuanian *Talmudic* scholarship and had studied in the Volozhin *Yeshiva*, the "Oxford" of the yeshiva world. His mother came from *Chasidic* stock. These two approaches didn't usually mix well, the former exalting the intellectual endeavour of *Torah* scholarship; the latter extolling the ecstatic worship of God especially through prayer. Yet these two disparate worlds seemed to blend harmoniously in the young Abraham Isaac. At an early age he demonstrated a prodigal aptitude for Talmud study. Yet he also possessed a remarkably soulful spirituality.

Upon returning from yeshiva for a break he showed his father the first fruits of his literary efforts. His father, a Talmud scholar, expected a clever analysis of some issue in Jewish law. Much to his consternation, the senior Rabbi Kook beheld a love poem for God. Abraham Isaac realized his father's disappointment and upon his return home for the *Chanukah* vacation attempted to make amends with another original composition. Another poem, but this time all the laws of Chanukah in rhymed verse! Just as Abraham Isaac Kook bridged the different religious worlds of his parents, so too, he attempted throughout the rest of his life of Jewish leadership to span the chasm separating the different ideological groupings within Israel.

In 1904, after 17 successful years as the rabbi of several communities in Lithuania, Rabbi Kook was invited to move to Ottoman Palestine to become the rabbi of the city of Jaffa, the urban centre, of the largely secular Zionist movement. As the Rabbi of Jaffa he also took responsibility for the nascent agricultural settlements founded by the Zionist pioneers.

In *Eretz Yisrael* Rabbi Kook encountered two Jewish communities at great odds. The late 18th and early 19th centuries witnessed a heightened interest among Orthodox Jews in establishing the Jewish presence in the Holy Land. Both the Chasidic and the Orthodox non-Chasidic world sponsored migration to Eretz Yisrael. In contrast, the new secular Zionist movement, in the late 19th and early 20th centuries, produced its own waves of immigration creating agricultural communities that were the forerunners of the *kibbutzim*. This community saw itself as forging a revolution in Jewish life, whereby traditional ideas were largely replaced by nationalistic and socialistic concepts. Rabbi Kook devoted much of his rabbinic leadership to serving as a bridge between these two worlds.

In this spirit, Rabbi Kook invited the leading rabbis of Jerusalem to join him on a visit to the agricultural settlements of the Zionist pioneers. Rabbi Kook's motive was to help the other rabbis appreciate the self-sacrificing idealism of the young Zionists and to inspire the pioneers with the nobility of the message of the Torah.

One of the communities visited was Poriya, known particularly for its disregard for Jewish tradition. For reasons of *kashrut*, the rabbinic delegation could not join the pioneers for dinner. When the rabbis heard the pioneers begin to sing, Rabbi Kook convinced his colleagues to join the young men and women of the settlement. Upon entering, Rabbi Kook passionately implored:

"The time has come to end the state of estrangement between us. Dear brothers and sisters, come close. The time has come for the uniting of the hearts of the Old Settlement with those of the New Settlement. We have come to you, but please take a step towards us by the observance of the basics of Judaism, Shabbat and Kashrut, which have preserved our people till this day…"

At this point Rabbi Kook urged all present to join a dance, a dance of *teshuva*. As the pioneers and the rabbis began to dance together in circles Rabbi Kook left the room. He approached the guard of the settlement and exchanged clothes with him. As the enthusiastic dancing was continuing, Rabbi Kook returned, dressed as a pioneer guard, complete with *kafiye* Arab headdress and rifle in hand. Upon noticing Rabbi Kook's entrance, the dancing and singing ceased in curious amazement at the strange sight. Rabbi Kook addressed the crowd with words emerging from the depths of his heart:

"The Chasidim teach that the greatness of dancing lies in the necessity to jump a little off the floor. We then can view the world from a different angle, from a fresh perspective. Let us join in dance. Let us see a renewed world. A world without 'old' and 'new,' without hostility, a world where rabbis can wear the clothes of pioneering guards and where pioneer guards are capable of wearing the clothes of rabbis."

The dancing of the rabbis and Zionist pioneers continued till dawn when Rabbi Kook collapsed muttering, "Blessed be God who has brought me to this moment…"

In 1914, Rabbi Kook embarked on a voyage to Europe to attend the world convention of Agudath Israel to implore his rabbinic colleagues to make *Aliyah* a priority for world Jewry. The outbreak of the First World War caused the cancellation of the convention and also prevented his return to Jaffa. For the next two years, Rabbi Kook was hosted in Switzerland, and then moved to London where he became the spiritual leader of the Machzikei HaDat Synagogue. Ironically, it was during this period of exile that Rabbi Kook wrote some of his most important essays. These essays articulated the uniqueness of the historical moment and his profound philosophical grappling with the significance of the Zionist settlement of Palestine, which he regarded as an expression of Divine redemption, in spite of its irreligious nature. These thoughts were edited and published under the title *Orot,* which became a great classic of his writing.

In 1919, Rabbi Kook returned to Palestine, but this time to Jerusalem where he assumed the Office of Chief Rabbi of Palestine, a position created under the British Mandate. In addition to his public involvement in the great issues of the British mandatory period, Rabbi Kook was a prolific writer whose works cover the entire gamut of issues of Jewish interest. Though dozens of volumes have appeared in print, much of his writing remains in manuscript form.

Rabbi Kook's popularity is due to the rare combination of saintliness, vast erudition, and complete devotion to unifying the disparate groupings within the Jewish people. 60 years after the establishment of the State of Israel we would do well to gaze upon Rabbi Kook's photograph and heed his message of Jewish unity.

ISRAEL IN 1957

- Israel withdraws from Sinai, only two months after the IDF first reached the Suez Canal
- 'Heichal Hatarbut', the largest concert hall in Israel and home to the Philharmonic Orchestra, is inaugurated
- The Israeli Wine Institute is founded to improve the quality of the country's wines and further their export

In memory of Zev and Esther Zlotnik zt"l, who together helped forge the State of Israel whilst remaining true to Torah values throughout their lives.
Sponsored by George and Corinne White.

11 Living Peacefully: A Simple Guide to Life

Dr Abraham Twerski

Our Sages tell us that there is no attribute that contains within it as much blessing as the trait of peace. On a national level our desire for peace is always present, but on a personal level we have a need for peace as well. Consequently, we end many of our prayers with a request for peace: Grace After Meals, the Silent Prayer and the Priestly Blessings. But how simple is it to achieve peace?

The theory contains four simple steps, although the practice is somewhat harder.

1) Don't kid yourself

If I were to choose a single character defect that causes people more misery than any other, it would be the inability to admit a mistake.

When you want to do something badly enough any excuse will do. Strangely, an excuse that appears patently absurd to everyone else will appear perfectly sensible to the person who needs it. For example, if you ask an alcoholic what made him start drinking after he had stopped for a while, he will give you reasons that may be hilarious but that he sincerely believes were adequate reasons to drive him to drink. It is never good to be deceptive, but if you succeed at cleverly deceiving yourself, what have you gained? You have become the victim of your own cunning.

Sometimes we are overcome by temptation and do something we should not have done. That is understandably human. It is even human to make stupid mistakes and if we recognise we did something wrong, we can take proper precautions to avoid a recurrence. However, if we deceive ourselves into thinking that what we did was right, we will never correct ourselves.

If you have ever been involved in an automobile accident, you know what rationalization is. The driver who made a turn without signaling or pulled away from the curb without checking for oncoming traffic accuses the other guy of driving too fast and being the cause of the accident.

So many times we become defensive when we are obviously at fault. Instead of admitting a mistake we try to blame things on others. Refusal to admit that one did wrong brings us back to the pathologic sense of omnipotence, whereas admitting that one was wrong is accepting human fallibility.

Actually, the need to feel that one is beyond blame and to escape responsibility is often indicative of low self-esteem. A person who is very insecure, will cover up this feeling with an attitude of superiority and infallibility, whereas people who truly think well of themselves are able to accept that they may have been at fault.

2) Be willing to ask for forgiveness

No one likes to remember having wronged another person, and it certainly takes a great deal of fortitude to ask another person's forgiveness. But in fact, the first step is not to make amends, rather that we be *willing* to make amends. What is often overlooked is that our psychological systems are programmed like our physiological systems to take on a defensive posture in order to avoid pain. When a thought or idea is painful, our psychological systems put in gear the mechanisms that will deny the very existence of the painful thought, or strip it of its painful character, by justifying it.

Thus, if I harmed someone I might justify it by saying,

"They had it coming." Such defensive thinking is destructive. Firstly, all un-truth is ultimately destructive, and secondly, defensive thinking precludes any possibility of restoring a friendly relationship. If I maintain an attitude of belligerence the severance of the relationship cannot be remedied.

One of the features that distinguish adulthood from childhood is the acceptance of responsibility. Being willing to make amends is an acceptance of responsibility. Furthermore, becoming willing to make amends means that we are willing to ask for forgiveness, and if we can grasp the concept of forgiveness, we also become ready to forgive others for what they might have done to us.

3) Beware Passive negligence

When we think of people we may have harmed, we generally think of acts of commission, something we did that offended or injured them. We may not realise that acts of omission can be just as serious. While silence is indeed golden, there are times when it can be devastating. Failure to appreciate or acknowledge a favour, failure to come to someone's aid when it was within our means to do so, or failure to speak up in someone's defense are examples of such acts of omission. However passive injuries are less likely to be remembered by the perpetrator and require greater sensitivity to redress.

4) Be honest

Finally, we have to understand that making amends should be a result of the realisation that a wrong needs to be righted. If one apologises or otherwise compensates for harm done because of an ulterior motive, that is not making amends – it is simply furthering one's selfish interests.

Prayer

When all is said and done, asking for help from Above, is always advisable. Why is it though, that although we sometimes pray for help in overcoming our shortcomings, our prayers seem to go unanswered? After all, if we do make the effort to improve ourselves, don't we deserve help?

The answer is that our prayers sometimes lack the requisite sincerity. We are, at best, ambivalent about giving up our shortcomings. Too often we have been getting some gratification from them and do not wish to give them up. There is only one successful approach. Decide that you wish to rid yourself of your shortcomings and stick by your decision. It is then that prayer is most effective.

ISRAEL IN 1958

- The cornerstone is laid for the new Knesset building
- Israel's Foreign Ministry creates the Centre for International Cooperation, known as MASHAV, which goes onto develop a legendary reputation throughout the developing world
- Kol Yisrael begins Russian-language broadcasts directed mainly at the Jewish community behind the Soviet curtain and is influential during the struggle of Soviet Jewry to make aliyah
- The Liber company, which later merged with Elite, starts distributing 'Bazooka' chewing gum in Israel

Dedicated by Radlett United Synagogue to the people of Shlomi, our twin town in Northern Israel. In particular, to those who have been injured, maimed or lost their lives for the sake of their country and of the Jewish People.

12 Living in Israel

Binyamin Tabory

As I sit in my house in Alon Shevut, between Jerusalem and Hebron, it seems somewhat unnecessary to extol the accomplishments and virtues of the State of Israel. My children and grandchildren often jest that I repeat the following observations at every family *simcha*.

When the prophet Jeremiah recommended investing in real estate in the land of Israel,[1] even as the prophecy about the destruction of the Temple was unfolding and the painful exile was acutely felt, one can only imagine the reaction of the people. It is quite possible that they felt "the man of spirit is insane."[2] Did anyone believe that some day we would return to Israel and that land would be so valuable! Imagine the value of a property deed to dunams of land in Jerusalem or Netanya, which dates back to the days of *Tanach*.

As the joy of weddings and other celebrations was stilled, Jeremiah exhorted the people that someday we will again hear, as in the times of Yehuda and on the outskirts of Jerusalem, "the sound of joy, the sound of gladness, the sound of groom and the sound of bride." Today, as we sing this verse, *"Od yishamah... b'arei Yehuda uvechutzot Yerushalayim... kol sasson v'kol simcha kol chatan v'kol kallah,"* how can one not be thrilled by the experience of seeing that prophecy come true![3]

The prophet Zechariah said that someday there will be elderly people in Jerusalem and the streets of the city will be filled with children playing.[4] Come and see with your own eyes how this prophecy too is realised.

I never had the privilege or pleasure of meeting my paternal grandmother. However, my father *zt"l* used to describe her piety. Quite often he used to relate how she sang lullabies about the city of Jerusalem and the *Kotel,* in those dark years before the Jews returned to their land. Would she have believed that her grandson would build a house in a community on the outskirts of Jerusalem?!

In the prayer which is recited in many congregations around the world, *Leshalom Ha Medinah,* a prayer for the welfare of the State, there is a phrase which has engendered much debate. Those who have studied the history of this prayer write that the Nobel Laureate Samuel Agnon and the former Chief Rabbi Herzog participated in the wording of the standard text. The phrase under debate is "the beginning of the process of our redemption." Rabbinic opinion is divided. Some feel that it is premature to declare this era as the harbinger of the redemption process. Others feel that not only are we beginning, but we are actually in the process. A *Gemara* in Sanhedrin 98a is used to support the latter opinion. The Gemara quotes the prophet Ezekiel who declared that the mountains of Israel will bear fruit. *Rashi* comments that when the land of Israel bears fruit in an abundant manner this is a clear sign that the redemption is near.

One can obviously comment on the great strides that have been made in medicine, science and technology, but it can be argued that these accomplishments and even the prodigious amount of *Torah* scholarship and proliferation of *Talmudic* academies could have been developed outside of Israel as well. However, the image of the Talmudic scholar who also serves as a soldier is reminiscent of the situation in Biblical times. We live in the land Jews have prayed and yearned for since time immemorial.

Unfortunately, for the fulfilment of our dreams we have paid a heavy price. We have lost many young men and women of the Israeli Defence Forces, as well as many victims of terror.

I would like to mention two terror victims, both medical doctors, with whom I was quite close.

Dr. Shmuel Gills was a brilliant doctor whose speciality was enabling women with haematological problems to give birth, and many children, both Jewish and Muslim owe their lives to him. His wife Ruthi told her children that she pities Shmuel's patients for their loss. To them, he represented hope. In treating his patients, he made no distinction regardless of religion or status. He also treated patients suffering from leukaemia from as far afield as Jordan and Egypt. He was shot while driving to his home in Karmi Tzur, Gush Etzion, after a long day in Hadassah Hospital, leaving behind five children aged 3-13. Ironically, many Arabs were among those who mourned his loss. His modesty and retiring manner did not hide the awareness that he was a rising star in the world of medicine.

Dr. David Appelbaum was another faithful doctor who met his tragic end in the violence in Israel. David was a doctor of emergency medicine who was a fixture in Jerusalem's medical scene, having treated hundreds of terror victims as the Head of the Emergency Department in Shaarei Zedek Hospital. In a short time, he made great progress in revamping the entire system of the emergency room treatment. Here too, Arabs and Israelis were cared for and he saved many of their lives. He was also the founder of *Terem*, Jerusalem's 24-hour private emergency medical clinic, as well as being an outstanding Talmudic scholar and student of Rabbi Ahron Soloveichik. As is well known, he was killed together with his daughter Nava the night before her wedding.

Both these victims were doers of good deeds, and lovers of the Land of Israel. Their commitment to heal without discrimination defines the finest part of us, contradicting every negative stereotype our enemies have hurled at us.

The struggle is great, the pain is deep but we yearn to see even the greater fulfilment of the Torah. "They will beat their swords into ploughshares and their spears into pruning hooks; nation will not lift sword against nation and war will no longer be learned."[5] May we all be privileged to see that day.

Notes:
1 Jeremiah 29:5
2 Hoshea 9:7
3 Jeremiah 33:10
4 Zechariah 7:4–5
5 Isaiah 2:4

ISRAEL IN 1959

- Professor Lev Fishelson develops a hybrid tilapia fish suited to Israel's desert fishponds leading to total worldwide production today of approximately 1.5 million tons
- It is revealed that the Israeli Ambassador to the US, Abba Eban, does not have Israeli citizenship!
- Eleanor Roosevelt visits Israel, and in a trip to the Bedouin market buys a camel for 140 Israeli Lira, which is sent by ship to her granddaughter in the USA for her personal zoo
- Israel's first navy submarine, the 'Tannin', docks in Haifa

Dedicated in celebration of the 50th anniversary of the
rededication of the Central Synagogue on 23rd March
1958, after its destruction by a Nazi bomb on 10 May 1941.

13   The Essence of Purim

Zev Leff

The name of a festival usually describes the motif of the day and
its significance. In this light, the name *Purim* seems awkward. For
as the *Megillah* points out, Purim is based on the word *Pur*
meaning 'a lottery', referring to the lots that Haman cast to
determine on which random day the Jewish people should be
annihilated. It refers thus to an apparently insignificant detail of
the story, rather than the dramatic Divine rescue of the Jewish
Nation. The name does not seem to capture the essence of the
day. Another difficulty is the Megillah translating the word Pur,
to inform us *"pur, hu hagoral"* "Pur is the word lottery." If *pur* is
an archaic version of the word *goral*, why not use the better
known word in the first place.

In order to understand the true message of Purim we must
understand Haman's ancestor Amalek. The nation of Amalek
were the first to attack the Jewish people. They did so, shortly
after the Exodus, while the Jews were on their way to Mount
Sinai. The *Torah* describes them as having 'chanced' upon us on
the way. Amalek view all events as mere chance. Amalek are
further described as not fearing *Elokim* – the Divine name of
God used to describe His interaction with nature. They
refused to recognise God's connection to the world and the
events that occur within it. As atheists, they even deny the
intervention of *Elohim acherim* - other secondary forces. Even
idol worship is foreign to them.

The significance of the description is that one who believes
in the Divine force that created the world and guides it,

believes that the world has a purpose and goal. Hence, the world has a path that has been designed for it. An atheist must believe in random chance and will deny occurrences being part of some master plan. Hence, Amalek attacks us on our path to receive the Torah, challenging the concept of a path that signifies order and meaning in the world.

This also explains another word used in conjunction with Amalek, *machar* meaning tomorrow. Moshe joins Joshua to fight Amalek tomorrow. Similarly in *Megillah Esther*, Esther tells the king she will inform him tomorrow concerning Haman. We who believe in God, Who has a master plan for the world, have a tomorrow. Amalek have no tomorrow, only the present, a chance accident that may or may not continue.

Amalek's adamant denial of God's connection to world events weakens belief by introducing uncertainties. As long as such uncertainties exist, recognition of God is only partial and all appears a coincidence, or purely the result of economic and political causes.

Historically, those who opposed us out of jealousy and intimidation indirectly strengthened our own self-esteem. By prompting our recognition of our innate worth, their enmity was not totally negative. However, Amalek sought to rob us of our self-esteem and recognition of our true worth by proclaiming emphatically our utter worthlessness. This enmity resulted in a weakening of our own self-appraisal. They are the manifestation of both doubt and self-doubt. Hence, only the total negation of Amalek can allow us to be able to appreciate and express our true worth.

Weakened by their lack of recognition of God's direction of the world, the Jewish people were vulnerable to the designs of Amalek's descendant: Haman. He desired to destroy the Jewish people in a manner which would emphasise the random nature of world events, so as to emphasise the total negation of design in history. Casting lots was the underpinning of his philosophy; namely that the Jewish People will have their fate determined by chance. *Pur, hu Hagoral* is a *slogan* not a translation.

Mordechai counters this by recognising his self-esteem as a Jew, and refusing to bow down to Haman. Similarly Esther, saw her true honour coming not from being the Queen of Persia but from remaining closely connected to that which is truly worthwhile, and it is she who advises how to save the Jewish people - repentance to regain a closeness with God. Hence, the miracle of the salvation of Purim lies in appreciating the value of the Jewish people and God.

The Megillah is unique in being the only one of the 24 books of the Biblical canon, in which God's name is never mentioned, because the message of the megillah is to express that history itself testifies to God's guidance of events. Behind the myriad of causes and effects, one can discern the hand of God directing all towards his goals.

The joy of Purim is the joy of knowing that this world has purpose and design and is not left to blind chance - resolving the doubts caused by Amalek. This realisation gives us direction, as well as a feeling of intense self-worth. The Jew is now of great importance in God's plan, given that he has undertaken the responsibility to carry out the script that God has written for the world. Even the physical body is seen to have value in God's eyes, for it was only the physical safety of the Jew that was endangered on Purim, not his spiritual eternity. As such, our festival emphasises the physical; we eat, drink and give *Mishloach Manos*, food presents to others.

Similarly, we give *Matanot L'evyonim*, gifts to the poor, signifying that our importance is not determined by our wealth or power but is rather intrinsic to our being God's special people. This attribute is shared by even the Jew who is destitute and hence we give him a present, not charity, to emphasise our recognition of his and our true importance and worth.

Purim also represents unity, by the fact that we share our food, money and table with others. It is a reflection of unity of purpose. However, it is noteworthy that as a holiday of unity, it is the only holiday that all Jews do not celebrate on the same day. There is Purim on the 14th of Adar and a separate Purim for walled cities (Shushan Purim) on the 15th. The lesson being that true unity is not necessarily everyone doing exactly the same thing, nor only uniting with those exactly like ourselves in every way. Rather true unity comes when those celebrating Purim on the 14th look upon their neighbours celebrating on the 15th with respect and vice versa, since both are actually following the same script and operating within the same framework. Their differences lie only in expression and not in purpose or goal. True unity is appreciating our own strengths as well as those of others; of neither being assailed by our own doubts nor by those implanted in us by others, thereby allowing us to see the picture of the real world – a world which exists for the purpose of bringing God and design into focus.

PURIM IN ISRAEL

The first sign that Purim is on the way in Israel is when shops start selling 'Hamantaschen', those triangle shaped pastries named for our arch enemy Haman. The second sign is the advertisements for Purim costumes that appear in all the newspapers. Purim falls of the 14th of the Hebrew month of Adar, but in Jerusalem it is held one day later and people often travel from one city to the other so they can celebrate for two days. In 2008, Jerusalem will celebrate a special 3-day Purim over Friday, Shabbat and Sunday.

ISRAEL IN 1960

- 'Susita', the first Israeli Car is manufactured with a Ford engine and a fibreglass body (a myth ran in Israel saying that camels found the fiberglass appetizing and would gnaw away parts of the car but no one has ever proven that to be true!)
- Paul Newman visits Israel to film Exodus, based on Leon Uris's bestseller, telling the heroic tale of the illegal immigration to Palestine and the founding of the State of Israel
- The National Commission for Space Research is founded
- The Arab Israel Bank is established to serve the unique needs of Israel's Arabic-speaking population

Dedicated to Rabbi Andrew Shaw for his unique
leadership and inspiration.

14 When Breaking The Law Was Breaking My Word

Sarah Shapiro

Jaywalking is in my blood, as my mother would say. One morning in Los Angeles when she was about 80, Mommy got a ticket for jaywalking on Ventura Boulevard. This in itself was nothing unusual, but hurrying out of the post office a half hour later, she was still so mad at herself about the $35, that she crossed against the light and got another ticket. "On the same corner," said mommy.

"The same policeman?" I asked.

"Oh yes. He's such a nice boy."

For years, I upheld my mother's legacy. The underlying rationale goes something like this, "If no cars are coming, why should I wait here like a dummy just because everyone else is? Don't these people know I'm in a hurry! It's not my problem if they have nothing better to do than stand around like statues because a little man in the red light is telling them, 'Don't walk'."

Which brings us to a sunny morning in Jerusalem when, standing on the corner of Rechov Schatz and King George, I looked to the left and looked to the right, saw that no cars were coming, and kept walking.

"What do you think you're doing?"

An angry-faced policeman, in blue uniform and badge, was

coming right at me. He was jabbing his finger at something overhead and my eyes followed: A traffic light!

He instructed me to halt right there and made his way to my side of the street. All my smug fellow pedestrians - having been well behaved - were flaunting their freedom as they strolled on by.

The policeman took out a pad and started writing something.

"Officer! You're not going to give me a ticket!"
He kept intently jotting things down, glancing ostentatiously up at the sky to check the street sign, and flicking out one wrist to get the exact time.

"Officer, please! Are you giving me a ticket?"
He condescended to give one tight little nod of his official head without lifting his eyes.

"Oh, Officer, please! How much is it?"
Briefly holding the pad out under my nose, he pointed with one index finger. My reading glasses were in my purse so the numbers were fuzzy, but there were definitely three of them, much too much money. And I knew already what would happen. I wouldn't find a stamp and it would take me a while to get over to the post office. The deadline would pass and they'd increase the fine.

"Officer, please don't give me a ticket."
Into each of my eyes sprang one pure tear. It was then that I said those fateful words: "I won't do it again, I promise."

He paused.

Quickly! I told myself, *say bli neder!* This phrase, meaning "without a promise," is added to virtually every verbal commitment, because, according to Judaism, making a promise is an extremely serious matter.

But I knew that if I said *bli neder,* the policeman wouldn't believe me.

He stood there for a long moment, looking me straight in the eye. "All right." He wagged his finger. "Never do it again." Then he tore up the ticket.

I kept my word. What choice did I have? Lights would turn

red and green and yellow and there I'd stand like an automated dummy, at one corner after another, waiting for the go-ahead from the little green man.

Months went by. It was on a trip to America that inwardly I began to weaken. Maybe the *neder* didn't apply in the United States? Perhaps there was a rabbi somewhere who would let me off the hook? But I knew the real answer.

Then one morning back in Jerusalem, I was rushing at 9:05 to a 9:00 class. Everywhere you look on Rechov Keren Hayesod there's another traffic light. I dashed to the curb and glanced down the street. The little man was saying, "Don't walk," but there were no cars coming and I was missing the class! I thought of the *neder* but a soft inner whisper confided, "It doesn't matter," so out I darted.

I don't have the words to describe what happened next. How to convey the tremendous velocity of the bombshell that exploded around me, a great missile the size of a bus…roaring to a screeching halt, stopping a hairsbreadth away from my very soul.

It turned out that the municipality had created additional two-way inner bus lanes, each with their own set of traffic lights, to better accommodate the heavy traffic on Keren Hayesod. Looking to the left, I hadn't noticed that there was a bus hurtling towards me from the right, catapulting at top speed along the unobstructed lane.

The whole world came to a halt. Frozen in time in the middle of the street, I stood in silence, struck dumb with shock, and awe. The massive bus was before me – its great, round headlights like two staring glass eyes – and the furious face of the driver was scowling at me through the dark windshield as he gestured in that Israeli way. "Are you crazy?!" whilst drivers, passengers and passers-by stared blithely, in irritation or scorn.

He was right. I had come so close to death that I sensed its warm, breathing presence… the way it suddenly reared up its head, a vast shadow that mercifully retreated into the darkness from whence it came… If the driver had glanced to one side at that moment, or yawned, or sneezed...If he hadn't braked in that fraction of a second...

Thankfulness came later. For now, a fool trembling uncontrollably, I was a vessel filled with shame. I'd tossed my life thoughtlessly into the arms of death *because I was in a hurry.*

I felt the voice of mommy in my heart, though she'd long ago departed from this world. "Stop jaywalking!"

And God was saying, "My dear daughter, do not break your word."

ISRAEL IN 1961

• The Brazilian football star Pele visits Israel
• Hebrew University introduces specialised medical courses for students from developing countries
• The Shavit II, an experimental meteorological satellite, is launched

---

Dedicated in loving memory of Harold Pearl,
Ruth Harman and Booba Sarah Harman.

---

15 The Mystical city of Tzfat

Ari Kahn

High up in the mountains of the Galilee lies a majestic city: A city of dreams. A city of visions. A city halfway to heaven which has been devastated by earthquakes and elevated by scholars. Its holy citizens of the 16th century are among the most significant scholars who ever lived. The city is called Tzfat, and the following story both encapsulates and characterises the unique personality of that place and time.

The song all modern Jews most associate with the coming of *Shabbat*, *Lecha Dodi*, was written in Tzfat and it is from here that the words ring out and reverberate all over the world every Friday night. All who greet the lovely Shabbat bride are enchanted by this spiritual love song. Today in many synagogues around the world as the words *"bo'i kalla"* (welcome [Shabbat] bride) are said, the congregation turns around to face the back or the door of the synagogue, as if to physically welcome the holy Sabbath Queen.

In Tzfat the ritual was somewhat more elaborate: The author of *Lecha Dodi*, Rabbi Shlomo Halevi Alkabetz, together with a group of mystics led by the incomparable Rabbi Yitzchak Luria known as the *Ari* (Lion) didn't merely turn around. They danced their way out of the synagogue and climbed one of the majestic mountains on the outskirts of Tzfat, and from that lofty vantage-point watched the sun go into hiding, the incontrovertible sign that the holy Shabbat had arrived.

On one particularly glorious Friday eve, the energy was palpable, the air crackled with excitement: Shabbat was coming and soon redemption from the week and all its travails would arrive. Shabbat, the age-old island of spiritual tranquillity, would soon begin. Just as when you put a seashell to your ear you can still hear the sea, when we keep the Shabbat we can still hear the echoes of the six days of creation and the glorious *Kiddush* that God made on that first Friday night.

Their master, the Holy Ari, truly looked like a lion, a spiritual glow surrounding him like a mane of gold, radiating more than the setting sun. As each psalm of the *Kabbalat Shabbat* was recited, they continued their ascent. They could feel the holiness of the celestial world. Then the Holy Ari, eyes blazing turned to his followers and said, "Come, let us go to Jerusalem and celebrate Shabbat in Jerusalem." The students, who only moments before had tuned into their Master's holiness, hesitated. They allowed pragmatism to intrude, and stain the world of spirit. They responded, "Let us first go and tell our wives." Logic told them that Jerusalem was far away and Shabbat was about to begin. Confused, the students retreated to calculations of distance and thoughts of the physical world.

The Ari was crushed, for the moment was lost. The special holiness had vanished. The Jerusalem which is fully built in heaven, and had momentarily been within reach, had now retreated. Disappointed, he cried out "Woe to us! Had you all seized the opportunity and responded together 'let us proceed to Jerusalem', had you really believed, had you really felt the joy and happiness of the moment, the Redemption would have come." But the window of opportunity had been shut; the Messiah must wait. More painful chapters would yet unfold in a world still seeking redemption.

Alongside Jerusalem, Hebron and Tiberias, Tzfat is one of the 4 holy cities of Israel. Even today it retains a uniquely Jewish flavour with over 95% of its inhabitants being Jews.

In the 16th century it enjoyed a golden era, and the teachings of two of its personalities underpin much of today's *torah* learning – one in the field of *Halacha*, the other in *Kabbalah*.

Rabbi Yosef Karo was exiled from Spain in 1492, at the age of four. After wandering through Portugal, Greece, Turkey and Bulgaria, he moved to Tzfat in 1536. Such was his stature in a city of spiritual giants, that soon after his arrival he was asked to serve as the Chief Rabbi and head of the Beth Din, which he continued to do until his death in 1575. He is the author of the most famous Jewish text in the last 800 years: the *Shulchan Aruch* – Code of Jewish Law, which is the reference guide to Jewish practice.

The second personality, Rabbi Yitzchak Luria (1534-1572), gave detailed expression to the ancient texts of kabbalah and for the next two centuries, the greatest part of *kabbalistic* literature devoted itself to his works. The basic elements of his teachings – which are second only to the *Zohar* in influence - are the applications of the ten *sefirot* and the five levels of the soul and the interaction of the four spiritual universes.[1] He also taught the doctrine of the necessity for the spiritual redemption of each part of creation known as *Sod Hatikun* (the secret of rectification).

However, it's not only the people of Tzfat and their writings that speak of the mystical, but even the buildings. The Ashkenazi Ari Synagogue was built in the 16th century and founded by Spanish exiles. Its congregation were Kabbalists, who were joined in 1570 by Rabbi Yitzchak Luria, and it was from here that he would proceed with his disciples to the nearby fields to welcome the Shabbat. More recently, during the 1948 War, shrapnel tore through the synagogue while it was packed with people seeking shelter, yet miraculously no one was hurt.

Meanwhile, the Jewish soldiers defending the town found themselves poorly armed. They did however, possess a small canon called the Davidka. When fired, it made far more noise than damage, but the Arabs fled the city in great panic nevertheless. It was later discovered that they were told the

Jews had an atomic bomb, which would be easily recognised, as it would make a colossal noise and shortly afterwards it would start to rain heavily. And this is exactly what happened when the Davidka was fired. A permanent monument of the Davidka is on display in Tzfat.

As a city, Tzfat has always represented a place of vision, of epiphany. Those with keen eyes can still see those mystics on the mountaintops, those with keen ears can still hear the tunes – and those with pure souls can still sense the impending Redemption. May we all live to see it and join that epic dance from Tzfat to Jerusalem and greet the Messiah!

Notes:
1 He also identified a fifth part (Adam Kadmon). See further Aryeh Kaplan: Meditation and Kabbalah pp210-213

ISRAEL IN 1962
- Adolf Eichmann is hanged, to this day the only death sentence on Israeli soil
- Israel fails in its bid to join the European Common Market
- Meyer Lansky, an international Jewish mobster arrives in Israel and applies for citizenship - the police decide not to arrest him, but wait for his three-month tourist visa to expire, at which point he is deported
- Marc Chagall's stainglass windows for the synagogue of Hadassah hospital are dedicated

---

Dedicated in loving memory of Joshua,
Golda and Anne Myers.

---

16   Some Thoughts About Jewish Memory

Professor Dovid Gottlieb

Memory is selective – we don't remember everything that we experience. But some events are so outstanding that we expect not to forget them. Let's see how this applies to the Jewish nation's experience of God's revelation at Mount Sinai.

Personal Memory
Suppose I tell you that yesterday I saw you borrow a pen from a colleague at work, but you don't remember this at all. Could you accept what I say as true? You'd probably think: "Since this isn't such an important event, yes, I could easily have forgotten it. It may well have happened."

Now suppose instead that I tell you, that yesterday I saw you win £10,000 from a lottery ticket, but you don't remember this at all. Could you still accept what I say as true? Presumably you'd respond: "This event is really quite uncommon. It would have a significant impact on my activities. So, even though you are usually truthful and accurate, you must be mistaken."

Perhaps I could explain that you don't remember the event because last night you received a head injury or suffered a traumatic experience. Maybe then you'd accept my story even though you don't remember it. However my explanation for your loss of memory would in itself have to be likely or provable.

Family Memory

What happens if we try this over a longer period of time? Suppose I tell you that your great grandfather was once injured in a Russian pogrom yet your family has no memory or record of this. Could you accept what I say as true? Quite likely.

Now suppose instead that I tell you that your great grandfather was made supreme commander of the Hungarian Army, and again your family has no memory or record of this event. Could you still accept what I say as true? Very unlikely.

The difference is that the latter event is rare and important; it is pretty unforgettable. Surely the story would be told from generation to generation or there would be records. Therefore unless I can explain how this important memory could have been lost, you would not believe my story.

National Memory

Let's go further back into history. Suppose I tell an Englishman that in 13th century England there was a two-year nationwide craze for French wine, - an event which is absent from all the history books, and which no one remembers.

In contrast, suppose that I'd said that in the thirteenth century, 70% of the population of England made a national pilgrimage to Rome, even though the event is absent from all the history books and no one remembers it.

Which of the two accounts will the Englishman find believable? Only the former (and even then he will want to know how come I alone am in possession of this information). As before, the response to the second story will be: "A past event that is so important in the history of a nation would surely be recorded. If we have no memory or record of it, we won't believe it happened." Such important events can be considered 'National Unforgettables.'

If someone wants to mislead us concerning our memory, (whether personal, family or national), they must choose a forgettable memory. If they try to mislead us by inventing an _un_forgettable memory - something really momentous – then

Day 16. Psalms 47 - 48

even if the event is supposed to have occurred far in the past, we simply won't believe them.

Obviously if they can plausibly explain *why* the memory was lost we may be able to accept the story. But in a case of National Memory, it is very hard to imagine conditions that would wipe out the memory of an entire nation. Perhaps a very systematic, long-term government effort to falsify historical records, or a very drastic and extended war, but this in itself would need to be proven. Just *saying* that a national memory was somehow lost, will clearly be inadequate. Which means that if someone wants to persuade me that a National Unforgettable was in fact forgotten they'll need to show me that their explanation for this is conceivable and historically likely.

In summary:
If someone invents a story about an event, which would be considered a 'National Unforgettable' and tries to convince us that it happened, but we don't remember the event nor have any record of it, then (unless he can give a convincing explanation as to why the event would not be remembered) we will not believe the story.

The Revelation
Let us apply this to the revelation at Mount Sinai 3,320 years ago.

What if there had never been such a revelation? Suppose someone came 2,000 years ago and told the Jews the following: "Hundreds of years ago all your ancestors stood at a mountain and witnessed a national revelation in which they all saw a fire on top of the mountain, felt the ground trembling under their feet and then heard a voice that they understood was from God, commanding them to live according to certain rules. This revelation was the beginning of a new religion. It radically changed the life of the whole nation: its values, attitudes, national organization and priorities. Daily life was profoundly transformed with many new obligations and challenges – some of great difficulty."

Such an account clearly seems to describe a 'National

Unforgettable'. But if it had never happened, what would the Jews have said 2,000 years ago to such an account? If they had no memory and no national record of such events they would have been fairly robust in their response: "You expect us to believe that?! Don't you think we'd remember something that rare and important in the history of our nation – even from centuries ago! If all our ancestors really witnessed an event like that, our whole national life would show it. We'd have holidays to celebrate the event and a history of national decisions implementing the new rules. Our whole nation is just not going to forget that sort of thing! We've got no memory of it, and you can't explain how it could be forgotten, so there is no way are we going to believe that what you say really happened."

Getting a nation to adopt such an *invented* 'National Unforgettable' is unimaginable. And yet the belief in a national revelation at Sinai has been held by the Jewish nation for thousands of years. Where could that belief have come from? Were we duped? Did someone somehow come and persuade us to believe in fabricated events on a scale that has never happened to anyone else, anywhere? No other nation even claims that its religion started with a public revelation; it is unique in all human history.

So where *did* the belief come from? Herein lies the challenge: Either we find a reasonable explanation for a wide-held belief in a nationally unforgettable event that actually did not happen, or we must accept the event as real. The Jewish nation believes that its ancestors experienced a national revelation. Since such a story cannot be invented *we have good reason to accept the story as true.* For, if it were not true, it would not be believed!

[A fuller treatment of this argument, including the reply to the question that the belief may have evolved gradually, can be found at http://www.dovidgottlieb.com/publications.htm and http://www.dovidgottlieb.com/comments/q-a-on-kuzari-principle.htm]

ISRAEL IN 1963

- Yitzchak Rabin is appointed Chief of Staff – in four years time he will lead Israel to victory in the Six Day War
- The Wissotsky Tea Company moves to premises in Tel Aviv (where tea is produced on automated lines) and introduces the teabag string
- The Bamba snack is launched by Osem

Dedicated in honour of Natan Sharansky:
a Jewish hero.

17   Esther Cailingold (1925-1948): A Jewish Heroine

Yehuda Avner

On a dank March morning in 1948, Esther Cailingold rang. She sounded jolly. "I've just interviewed a volunteer who says you can vouch for him. Also, I've got personal news. See you at Café Atara, noon."

"Atara? They've no menu. I'm starving."

"Don't fret. I'll scrape together some leftovers from the Schneller mess."

Esther Cailingold had arrived from London a couple of years before to teach at Jerusalem's Evelina de Rothschild School. Senior to me by a few years, she had signed up as a full-time volunteer with the *Haganah*, and was stationed at Schneller, a disused German Templer orphanage on the fringes of Jerusalem's Geulah Quarter. Vetting volunteers was one of her jobs.

With the British on the verge of quitting the country, Arab violence had become frenzied. Jerusalem was besieged. Arab irregulars laid ambush to Jewish traffic at every twist of the tapered road which snaked through hairpin bends and steep gorges down to Tel Aviv. Fewer and fewer food convoys were getting through, so Esther Cailingold's call that morning with the promise of victuals was a mouth-watering incentive.

As I entered Café Atara on Ben-Yehuda Street a Highlander's voice boomed, "Bonnie laddie! Praise be the Lord!" It was Jock McAdam, an evangelical sheep farmer from the Shetland Islands whom I had bumped into by chance a few weeks before. He was visiting Jerusalem as a pilgrim, and was stranded because of the siege. Wanting to do his bit, he had reported to Esther and she suggested I take him along to join our inglorious volunteer bucket brigade of diggers and hackers, working on trenches on the western edge of the city.

She was dressed for war in a man's battledress two sizes too big for her, her slim figure ridiculously vulnerable in the heavy cloth. The faint light of the café could not totally conceal the fatigue under her eyes which, when turned on you, held a gleam no make-up could improve. They smiled at me now as she bent low to ease a shoebox from a suitcase that stood at her feet, and tipped triangles of cheese, hard-boiled eggs, sprigs of green onion, and black bread onto the table.

"With compliments of the Schneller mess," she beamed.

Tucking in, I glimpsed at her still half-opened suitcase. It was crammed with her personal belongings, so I asked her where she was off to. "That's my news…" she said intriguingly, but before she could share it McAdam threw us a sudden "be careful" look.

Silhouetted in the doorway were two British soldiers, a corporal and a private, their Stenguns slung carelessly over their shoulders. They pushed to a nearby table, their backs toward us. The corporal, a pimply, ginger fellow, rummaged in his haversack and brought out a bottle of Johnny Walker. He knocked back a swig, and wiped his chin with the back of his hand.

Esther, her expression a mixture of defiance and wariness, stared at him as he downed another mouthful. "Discipline's gone to pot" she whispered scathingly. "They'll be gone in a few weeks. Then, we'll declare independence."

The corporal swung around, his face a blotchy red. "Shut your trap, Yid!" he spat.

Jock McAdam rose, flicked a crumb from his kilt, walked over to the soldier, and gazed down at him pensively. "I'm Jock

McAdam from the Shetland Islands," he said gently. "That remark you just made, it was a slip of the tongue, correct?"

The serviceman took a swig of courage, shook a cigarette from its pack, lit it, and rosetting his lips, blew a smoke ring into the Highlander's face.

Jock closed his eyes and said evenly, "I turn the other cheek. Just tell me ye na'er meant it."

"Sorry mister. Too late. Already said it."

"But you can take it back."

"Can't take it back."

"Why?"

"Because Jews are a mouthy lot. Double crossers. Jesus killers."

Jock McAdam smiled down benignly at the slouched corporal and, with the back of his hand, swiped him across the cheek. The boy shot upright, tears in his eyes.

"Skedaddle! Scram!" roared Jock.

Esther and I sat frozen, mouths open, until our attention was grabbed by a radio announcement. An English announcer informed us with the imperturbability of a cricket umpire that downtown Jerusalem was to be sealed off overnight. Esther quickly gathered up her things, saying she was expecting a lift back to Schneller from the nearby Zion Square. So, I carried out her suitcase while Jock toasted her a merry farewell with the last of the Johnny Walker.

As we entered Zion Square there was a sudden clatter of machine-gun fire from the direction of the Old City, setting off a return stutter of rifle shots, followed by a dull explosive thud. Then everything went quiet again.

"My ride should be here soon," she said, and I, avidly curious, asked her where she was being posted to. She looked at me steadily, her hands deep inside her battledress pockets, and calmly told me that she had volunteered for the Jewish Quarter of the Old City.

Nothing in my 18 years had prepared me for this. I sensed an unknown dread. The Jewish Quarter of the Old City was the most perilous place in all of imperilled Jerusalem. It was a place to flee from, not to go to.

A lone car, smeared with crudely applied camouflage paint, swung into Zion Square and screeched to a halt. Esther gave me an affectionate elder sister's squeeze of the hand, dumped her suitcase in the back, and climbed in. The driver, a dusty Haganah fellow, revved the engine, released the break, hugged the wheel, and roared off. There was not even time for a decent good-bye.

Later we learned that Esther went straight into battle. She was mortally wounded on May 25th. Four days later, on the morrow of the Jewish Quarter's surrender, she died. She was 22. She is buried on the slopes of the military cemetery, Mount Herzl, Jerusalem.

The following is her farewell letter to her family in London written in an Old City dugout six days before she died:

"Dear Mummy and Daddy, and Everybody,

If you get this at all, it will be, I suppose, typical of all my hurried, messy letters. I am writing it to beg of you that whatever may have happened to me, you will make the effort to take it in the spirit that I want and to understand that for myself I have no regrets. We have had a bitter fight: I have tasted of *Gehinam* — but it has been worthwhile because I am quite convinced that the end will see a Jewish state and the realisation of our longings.

I shall be only one of many who fell sacrifice, and I was urged to write this because one in particular was killed today who meant a great deal to me. Because of the sorrow I felt, I want you to take it otherwise - to remember that we were soldiers and had the greatest and noblest cause to fight for. God is with us, I know, in His Holy City, and I am proud and ready to pay the price it may cost us to reprieve it.

Don't think I have taken 'unnecessary risks.' That does not pay when manpower is short. I hope you may have a chance of meeting any of my co-fighters who survive if I do not, and that you will be pleased and not sad of how they talk of me. Please, please, do not be sadder than you can help. I have lived my life fully if briefly, and I think this is the best way – short and sweet. Very sweet it has been here in our own land. I hope you shall enjoy from Mimi and Asher the satisfaction you missed in me. Let it be without regrets, and then I too shall be happy. I am thinking of you all, every single one of you in the family, and am full of pleasure at the thought that you will, one day, very soon I hope, come and enjoy the fruits of that for which we are fighting.

Much, much love, be happy and remember me in happiness.

Shalom and Lehitraot,

Your loving Esther"

ISRAEL IN 1964

- Pope Paul VI visits Israel, the first and only visit made by the leading figure in the Christian world until the new Millennium
- The Palestine Liberation Organisation (PLO) is formed
- The National Water Carrier of Israel is completed distributing water from the Kinneret throughout Israel
- Herod's Palace is uncovered during archaeological excavations at Massada

18 Science and Religion: Partners or Adversaries?

Professor Cyril Domb

Science and religion, sworn enemies in the past, seem to be heading for partnership in the 21st century. Look at the titles of some of books published in the last decade: *Can Scientists Believe?* by Nevill Mott, *The Mind of God* by Paul Davies, *The Science of God* by Gerald Schroeder. These are not the works of eccentrics but leading academics.

There have always been scientists who were also deeply religious; Isaac Newton, Michael Faraday, and James Clerk Maxwell are outstanding examples. But these represented a small minority, and until recently most of their colleagues were agnostics.

In the latter half of the 20th century, however, avowed secularists started to put God into their thinking. Fred Hoyle, a distinguished astrophysicist and cosmologist, was a typical example. Hoyle began his scientific career as an atheist. After World War II, while puzzling about the proportions of different elements such as hydrogen, oxygen and carbon in the universe - why some are common and others rare - he had a bright idea. Suppose that they were formed in the vast hot interiors of stars in the early development of the universe; it should then be possible to calculate the proportions of the elements present in the universe today from the structure of nuclei revealed by laboratory experiments of nuclear physics.

Hoyle started on this program and soon encountered a serious obstacle. Carbon is essential to life, but with the data at his disposal it would be unstable and would not survive. The only way out was a daring idea – that there existed a hitherto undiscovered energy level in the tiny carbon nucleus. Experiments were conducted and the level was found exactly as predicted. Hoyle became convinced that this was not a coincidence but evidence of intricate design.

During the following decades, evidence of design came to light elsewhere. The masses of two basic constituents of matter, the electron and the proton, were already known at the beginning of the century. Their ratio is a "constant of nature." No one paid much attention to it, until scientists became aware that its precise value was of vital importance; if it changed even by a minute amount, life as we know it would no longer be possible. The same kind of 'fine-tuning' was found in other constants of nature and in basic aspects of the astronomy of the universe.

Conclusions were therefore drawn in accord with religious thinking. Firstly, that there is design in the universe – as Hoyle put it in his autobiography, "The atheistic view that the universe just happens to be here without purpose and yet with exquisite logical structure appears to me to be obtuse." Secondly, that human beings are an important feature in the design of the universe. Freeman Dyson, a leading theoretical physicist, "I do not feel like an alien in the universe. The more I examine the universe and study the details of its architecture, the more evidence I find that the universe in some sense must have known that we were coming." This contrasts markedly with the conventional evolutionary view that we humans emerged unplanned.

The advantage of forging links between science and religion becomes evident not only in trying to understand the universe at large and how we living creatures come to be here, but also closer to home. I refer to the way science and technology are impacting society.

We are all conscious of the benefits that are conferred by this type of research and development. Every aspect of our daily life has been affected. Houses are comfortable in all weathers, the standard of living has improved greatly, and automation has removed the drudgery from menial jobs and shortened the working week. Modern transport enables us to travel with ease, advances in medicine have greatly increased life expectancy, and the explosion of information has enabled us to obtain precise knowledge on any subject of interest.

But certain undesirable consequences have resulted from science and technology being given free rein. Waterways have become polluted by chemical waste, the use of nuclear reactors has given rise to terrifying accidents like Chernobyl with serious long-term effects, and the discharge of certain gases into the atmosphere may be leading to global warming with unforeseeable consequences. The discovery of insecticides seemed at first to be a gift from heaven to protect and increase our food supplies. But after a few years, the original insects were killed off, and their place was taken by more virulent and resistant strains. Moreover, birds and chickens which ate the insects became poisoned and the insecticides found their way into human bodies and caused cancer. Rainfall also washed the chemicals into the Earth and into water supplies.

The discovery of the structure of the molecule DNA which controls genetics and inheritance in living creatures has opened the door to genetic engineering. It would appear that the genes which control personality, ability, and other hereditary traits, could be changed. How wonderful if hereditary defects which cause haemophilia, sickle-cell anaemia, cystic fibrosis, and other dreaded diseases would be corrected. But how alarming if the power to change human personality were exploited. This made the headlines when scientists succeeded in cloning a sheep. Might this be extended to human beings? A host of questions arise, which science on its own is not equipped to tackle. Why not take religion as a partner?

Albert Einstein, the greatest scientist of the last century, wrote in 1942, "Religion without science is blind, science without religion is lame." Some twenty years earlier another great scientist, William Bragg, had said the following, "Sometimes people ask if religion and science are not opposed to one another. They are in the sense that the thumb and fingers of my hand are opposed to one other. It is an opposition by means of which anything can be grasped." It is significant that when the British government established a committee to report on the ethics of cloning, they chose as chairman John Polkinghorne, a distinguished high-energy physicist, who moved to theology and became an ordained priest. Perhaps this is a herald of the twenty-first century.

ISRAEL IN 1965

- Fatah attempts to carry out its first terrorist attack in Israel
- The Israel Museum, one of the world's ten largest, opens
- Netafim pioneers the concept of drip irrigation, revolutionising irrigation practices in every corner of the world

> Dedicated in loving memory of Henry and Chic
> Soloway a"h, by Sue and Stuart Soloway.

19   The Nobel Prize for Literature (1966)

Samuel Y Agnon

Our Sages, of blessed memory, have said that we must not enjoy any pleasure in this world without reciting a blessing. If we eat any food, or drink any beverage, we must recite a blessing over them. If we breathe the scent of goodly grass, the fragrance of spices, the aroma of good fruits, we pronounce a blessing over the pleasure. The same applies to the pleasures of sight: when we see the trees first blossoming in the spring, or catch a glimpse of any fine, sturdy, and beautiful tree, we say a blessing. And the same applies to the pleasures of the ear. Through you, dear sirs, one of the blessings concerned with hearing has come my way.

It happened when I was brought the news that the Swedish Academy had bestowed the Nobel Prize upon me. Then I recited in full the blessing that one says on hearing good tidings for himself or others.

I will now tell you who am I.

As a result of the catastrophe in which Titus of Rome destroyed Jerusalem and Israel was exiled from its land, I was born in one of the cities of the Exile. But always I regarded myself as one who was born in Jerusalem. In a dream, I saw myself standing among my brother-Levites in the Holy Temple, singing with them the songs of David, King of Israel. Melodies such as no ear has heard since the day our city was destroyed and its people went into exile. I suspect that the angels in charge of the Shrine of Music, fearful lest I sing in wakefulness what I had sung in dream, made me forget by day what I had sung at night; for if my brethren were to hear, they would be unable to bear their grief over the happiness they have lost. To console me for having prevented me from singing with my mouth, they enabled me to compose songs in writing.

I was five years old when I wrote my first song. It happened that my father, of blessed memory, went away on business. I was overcome with longing for him and I made a song. After that I made many songs, but nothing has remained of them all. My father's house, where I left a roomful of writings, was burned down in the First World War and all I had left there was burned with it. The young artisans, tailors, and shoemakers, who used to sing my songs at their work, were killed in the First World War and of those who were not killed in the War, some were buried alive with their sisters in the pits they dug for themselves by order of the enemy, and most were burned in the crematoria of Auschwitz with their sisters.

The fate of the singers who, like my songs, went up in flame was also the fate of the books that I later wrote. All of them went up in flames to Heaven in a fire which broke out one night at my home in Bad Homburg as I lay ill in a hospital.

At the age of nineteen and a half, I went to Israel to till its soil and live by the labour of my hands. As I did not find work, I sought my livelihood elsewhere. I was appointed Secretary of the Lovers of Zion Society and Secretary of the Palestine Council - which was a kind of parliament-in-the-making. I was also the first Secretary of the Voluntary Jewish Magistrate's Court. Through these offices it was my privilege to get to know almost every Jewish person, and those whom I did not come to know through these offices I came to know through love and a desire to know my brethren, the members of my people.

After all my possessions had been burned, God gave me the wisdom to return to Jerusalem. I returned to Jerusalem, and it is by virtue of Jerusalem that I have written all that God has put into my heart and into my pen. I have also written a book about the giving of the *Torah*, and a book on the Days of Awe. During the time I have dwelt in Jerusalem, I have written long stories and short ones.

I have already told how my first songs came out of longing for my father. Who were my mentors in poetry and literature? Some see in my books the influences of authors whose names I have not even heard, while others see the influences of poets whose names I have heard but whose writings I have not read. And what is my opinion? From whom did I receive nurture? Not every man remembers the name of the cow which supplied him with each drop of milk he has drunk. But I will try to clarify from whom I received whatever I have received.

First and foremost, there are the Sacred Scriptures, from which I learned how to combine letters. Then there are the *Mishna* and the *Talmud* and the *Midrashim* and *Rashi's* commentary on the Torah. After these come the *Poskim* – the later explicators of Talmudic Law – and our sacred poets and the medieval sages, led by *Maimonides,* of blessed memory.

When I first began to combine letters other than Hebrew, I read every book in German that came my way, and from these I was certainly influenced.

There is another kind of influence, which I have received from every man, every woman, and every child I have encountered along my way, both Jews and non-Jews. People's talk and the stories they tell have been engraved on my heart, and some of them have flown into my pen. It has been the same way with the spectacles of nature. The Dead Sea, which I used to see every morning at sunrise from the roof of my house, the Arnon Brook in which I used to bathe, the nights I used to spend with devout and pious men beside the Wailing Wall – nights which gave me eyes to see the land of the Holy One, Blessed be He – the Wall which He gave us, and the city in which He established His name.

Before I conclude my remarks, I will say one more thing. If I have praised myself too much, it is for your sake that I have done so, in order to reassure you for having cast your eyes on me. For myself, I am very small indeed in my own eyes. Never in all my life have I forgotten the Psalm in which David said, "Lord, my heart is not haughty, nor mine eyes lofty; neither do I exercise myself in great matters, or in things too high for me."[1] If I am proud of anything, it is that I have been granted the privilege of living in the land which God promised our forefathers to give us.

Notes:
1 Psalm 131:1

ISRAEL IN 1966

- Moving from Frumin House in King George street, the new Knesset building in Jerusalem is inaugurated
- Writer S.Y. Agnon becomes the first Israeli to win a Nobel Prize, with the 1966 prize for literature
- The Harry S. Truman Institute for Peace is established at the Hebrew University

20 Yom Kippur, Repentance and the Land of Israel

Yitzchak Schochet & Chaim Kanterovitz

Yitzchak Schochet

A man came to Rabbi Israel of Ryzhin.

"*Rebbe*, I am a sinner, I would like to return; to do *teshuva*."

"So go ahead and do teshuva," the Rebbe instructed.

"I don't know how," replied the man.

"How did you know to sin?" the Rebbe retorted.

"I acted, and then I realised that I had sinned," came the reply.

"Well," said the Rebbe, "the same applies to teshuva: repent and the rest will follow of itself."

What did the famed Rebbe mean with his apparent simplification of the repentance process? How indeed does teshuva work? And to what degree is the day of *Yom Kippur* responsive to and responsible for teshuva?

Our Sages tell us that the power of teshuva is such that "even the perfectly righteous are surpassed by the one who does teshuva."[1] Every Jew maintains an ultimate attachment to God. Thus the verse calls the soul of man "a lamp of God."[1] While the righteous Jew may draw steadily nearer toward his source in the Divine, the sinner is pulling further away. But like a stretched elastic band, when consciously determining to return, he is propelled forward with such great intensity, as to surpass even the righteous. The journey he takes, is from so much further away, that his return is so much more of an achievement. Teshuva therefore, reveals the infinite Godly spark permanently within our souls and connects us to God at a level above the most sublime levels of Divine service.

Without teshuva, man would despair, crushed by the burden of his errors. While *Torah* and *mitzvot* sustain and nourish the existence and soul of the Jew, teshuva ensures his survival. Its power is awe-inspiring. There is no sin that cannot be remedied by teshuva. The *Talmud* declares: There is nothing which can stand in the way of teshuva.[3] Moreover, sin is time-consuming. It is an evolutionary process. Teshuva on the other hand, even in the worst of cases, is immediate. It is but a momentary decision to tear oneself away from sin. So great is its power, that it even affects Jewish law. When someone betroths a woman on condition that "I am a righteous person without sin," we do not dismiss the betrothal even if he was known to be wicked,[4] because at that moment of proposal he could have had teshuva in mind.

The Talmud lists teshuva as one of the seven things created before the creation of the world.[5] The significance of this is compelling. Jewish mysticism compares the human body to a wick and the soul to the flame above it. The light must have oil to keep it burning which is the Torah and mitzvot. If so, when one sins, one is effectively cutting the fuel supply to the soul, how indeed do we continue to exist? The answer is teshuva. God, in His divine compassion, introduced teshuva before creating the world. It transcends time and as such doesn't merely atone for sins but literally *redefines* one's past so as to eradicate every remnant of the misdeed.

The essence of teshuva is in the mind and in the heart. The single thought, the brief meditation of teshuva, is sufficient to move man from the greatest depths to the greatest heights and restore his relationship with his Maker.

Everything in Creation is categorised in terms of matter and form (body and soul). The act of sin, its external manifestation, is the matter (the body) of sin. The underlying thought, the will or passion that generated the transgression is the form (the soul) of the sin.

To truly rid ourselves of sin, we need to rectify both, which explains both our conduct and our outlook on Yom Kippur. Fasting on Yom Kippur is an act of purification and a means through which man expresses remorse. Its observance is an essential cause of teshuva, yet it does not constitute its essence. Fasting and self-mortification attack the body and purify the 'matter' from the sin. However, they do not hit at the root, the very essence, the 'soul' of the sin. Thus, while the exterior association with sin is no longer, the essence still remains, allowing the sin to re-emerge. Only the elimination of the thought, intent and desire that caused the sin, will eliminate the soul of the sin. When you deprive the soul, when you strike at the roots, the sin ceases to exist in its entirety.

The Torah informs us that, "This mitzvah which I command you this day, is not beyond your reach, nor is it far off."[7] *Nachmanides* interprets this verse to refer specifically to the principle of teshuva. The Torah follows this up by promising, "Even if your outcasts be in the outermost parts of Heaven and you are under the power of the nations, you can yet return unto God."[8] "Teshuva is not beyond reach, nor is it far off…it is exceedingly near to you, in your mouth and in your heart to do it" and it is Yom Kippur that provides us with the opportunity to achieve this goal in its entirety.[9]

"Repent," said the Rebbe. "And the rest will follow of itself."

Chaim Kanterovitz

The Day of Atonement evokes powerful images of purity and sanctity. The serene holiness of the day is intended to transcend the physical. Thus, we are taught that on this day we are akin to celestial beings for it is the only time of the year that we state aloud and in unison the mystical proclamation that follows the first line of the *Shema*, "Blessed be God's name for ever and ever," words we dare not call out in the holy tongue all year long.

Dressed in white, wrapped in our *tallit,* it is a day without physical concern. No telephone, or internet to hinder our meditation. No work or bills to deal with, all is set aside on this day. Instead we turn to our *Machzor* for words to reach deep within our soul.

There seems to be a link in time, one that connects us to the generations before. My father, my teacher, follows the custom passed down to him by his father, of not leaving the synagogue throughout Yom Kippur. Instead, dressed in his starched white robe, the *Kittel,* he remains rooted to his seat all night long immersed in the study of sacred texts, reciting liturgical poems and prayers.

Yet, to leave the synagogue on the day of Yom Kippur, if one is to walk out into the street, one is astounded by the stark reality of the mundane. Cars and buses, people rushing to work, leading their lives as if nothing has happened, as if nothing has changed. Gone are the robes and prayers; gone is the sense of heaven and soaring holiness.

Consider the teaching of our Sages that although all of creation is infused with holiness, the holiest country is *Eretz Yisrael,* the holiest place is the *mikdash* – the Temple mount, the holiest person is the *Kohen Gadol* - high priest and the holiest day of the year is Yom Kippur, the Day of Atonement.

Leaving a synagogue filled with worshipers in modern day Jerusalem, one can most certainly feel that sanctity resonating in the streets. Silence and quiet reign. No hustle or bustle, the holiness of the day has permeated the public domain. It is a holy day in the holy city, kept by a holy people.

On Yom Kippur, 1973 Jews were immersed in worship uttering the prayer *Netane tokef,* "You alone sit in judgment…who writes and seals… who will live and who will die…who will live in harmony and who will be harried…" In the midst of this holy day, Israel's enemies from the north and south coordinated a surprise attack against the Jewish state. Their purpose was to "drive them [the Jews] into the sea." Yet a miracle occurred in this holy state on this holy day. The Master of the Universe, through the brave soldiers of the Israel Defence Forces, foiled this surprise attack. However, the price we paid was a heavy one. Heavy in life and heavy in morale. Gone was the euphoria of the victory of the Six Day War, the sense of invulnerability was no more.

That year there was no serenity. Gone was the quiet; gone was the sense of elevation. My late grandmother, of blessed memory, seeing the tumult in the street but not yet knowing its cause, wept. She saw the cars and buses filled with Jewish men, reserve soldiers making their way to their designated army bases to join their fellow soldiers at the front. "Is there no longer a holy day in our own country," she wailed even as the sirens warning of impending danger were sounded in the streets of Givatayim, her home town.

Many years later, I asked my grandmother, "Did you fear the end? Did you think we would lose the war and we would all be thrown into the sea?" She answered me by relating the following story: When the late Rabbi Herzog *zt"l* visited Washington to plead for Jewish causes in 1942, the German general Erwin Rommel was approaching the borders of the then British mandated Palestine. President Roosevelt advised him not to return to Israel since the situation seemed dire. However, Rabbi Herzog was determined to return, explaining, "The prophets of Israel prophesised of two destructions and not a third." Indeed so it was, went on my grandmother. Rommel was defeated, and a Jewish state was established. "So you see," she said with a smile, "there was nothing to fear."

Indeed, Rav Kook writes, "The entire nation believes that there is no other exile following the redemption that is unfolding before us, and it is this deep faith itself which is the secret of its endurance."[10]

The themes of Yom Kippur, atonement and redemption, are all the more real in our generation. A generation where we have merited to witness the great miracle of the establishment of the State of Israel. A state that has survived despite the odds and is in itself the greatest testimony to God's providence over His people.

Yet it is the internal spiritual composition of our state that will lead to the complete redemption, which we still await. We await the time when we shall experience the celebration following the *avodah* worship of the Kohen Gadol in the Holy Temple: A celebration of relief, hope and security. Relief that we have been forgiven, hope in a brighter, holier future and security in the Divine protection afforded to the Almighty's nation, Israel.

Notes:
1 Berachot 34b; Rambam Hilchot Teshuvah 7:4
2 Proverbs 20:27
3 Yerushalmi, Pe'ah 1:1
4 Kiddushin 49b; Shulchan Aruch, Even Ha'ezer 38:31
5 Pesachim 54a
6 Rambam, Hilchot Teshuvah 2:2-3
7 Deuteronomy 30:11
8 Deuteronomy 30:4
9 Deuteronomy 30:13
10 Orot Pg: 77

ISRAEL IN 1967
• The Six Day War sees Israel capture the Old City and officially unite all of Jerusalem
• 250,000 Jews celebrate Shavout at the Kotel (Western Wall)
• Coca Cola begins operating in Israel

21 The Tzaddik Reb Aryeh (1885-1969)

David Mason

In Psalm 107, we read of those who sit in darkness, shackled in affliction, who cry out to God in their distress, and whom God would rescue. This psalm is a reassurance that God cares.

For nearly 30 years, there was a Jew who emulated God in this way. His name was Rabbi Aryeh Levin, and he will forever be remembered as the *Tzaddik* of Jerusalem. He was the Rabbi of Jerusalem's Jewish prisoners, and one who loved his fellow Jews from of all walks of life, without limits.

Reb Aryeh, as he was affectionately known, was born in 1885 in north-eastern Poland. His love for *Torah* was such that his parents sent him to study in *yeshivot* in Lithuania and Russia when he was only 12. In 1902, he achieved his dream of learning in the internationally renowned Volozhin *Yeshiva* where he thrived. Two years later, the young Aryeh, worried about being drafted into the Russian army during the Sino-Russian war - a likely death sentence for a Jew - decided to realise his ambition of living in Israel. With just enough money to fund the trip, he boarded a ship and arrived in Jaffa in March 1905, where he befriended Chief Rabbi Abraham Kook. He then moved to Jerusalem, where he married and, in1909, he received *semicha* from three of Palestine's greatest rabbinic leaders, including Rav Kook and Rav Shmuel Salant. This was a testimony to his scholarship and dedication to Torah study.

Eight years later, Reb Aryeh, became the *mashgiach* (spiritual mentor) in the junior school of the Etz Chaim Yeshiva, a position he retained for over 50 years. He loved his work there, and cared deeply about the children he taught – addressing both their spiritual and physical needs. In his last will and testament, he asked that his final month's salary be given to the school so that running water could be installed for the children.

In 1931, Jewish political prisoners began arriving at the prison in Jerusalem's Russian Compound, having been arrested by the British Mandate police forces. The British granted the Jewish inmates their own chaplain and Chief Rabbi Kook immediately recommended Reb Aryeh for the post – a job he accepted and carried out for decades, without remuneration.

And so began Reb Aryeh's chaplaincy of love. Every *Shabbat* without fail, through snowstorms, curfews and shelling, he would visit the prisoners, pray with them, counsel them, and cry with them. He learnt to file in his mind a massive amount of information, that he would shuttle between the prisoners and their family or vice-versa, sometimes for as many as 25 inmates at once. Under the Mandate, Jewish political prisoners could be freed if they had someone to take care of them in Palestine. Reb Aryeh met one such Jew from Syria, who told him where an old pupil lived in Geula, a neighbourhood of Jerusalem. As he left the prison, Reb Aryeh realised that he did not have the exact address, so he proceeded to knock on every door in the neighbourhood until he found the prisoner's pupil!

Reb Aryeh was so loved by the Jewish prison population that they would count the days until his next visit. One Jewish policeman who had been arrested wrote that Reb Aryeh was "the only vessel into which the tears of the wronged and oppressed can pour."

Another prisoner, Yaakov Kotok, was sentenced to death by the British, and placed in the isolated cell for condemned men. Reb Aryeh visited him on Shabbat.

"He just came in, took my hand, and said, 'They will not succeed in hanging a Jew in Jerusalem!' After praying with me, he put a Tehillim in my hands. 'Recite this,' he told me; 'say the words constantly, and have absolute faith that you will not go to the gallows.' He spoke quietly, but with so much faith and a sense of relief came over me."

Reb Aryeh would visit the women's prison in Bethlehem as well, and one of the prisoners said, "We couldn't understand his words, since his voice was choked with tears." It was also his practice to pay regular visits to the lepers' hospital in Jerusalem.

His life centred around other Jews and Rabbi Kook would say, "if there were three Jews in our generation like Reb Aryeh, the Messiah would come." So it is hardly surprising that when one of his students, was about to get married, that he came to Reb Aryeh for advice and asked, "How should I behave toward my wife?"

Reb Aryeh looked at him in wonder. "How can you ask a question like that? A wife is like your own self. You treat her as you treat yourself." And indeed, when his own good wife Hannah felt pains, he went with her to Dr Nahum Kook and told him, "My wife's foot is hurting us…"

Rabbi Tz'vi Pesach Frank, the Chief Rabbi of Jerusalem, was Reb Aryeh's brother-in-law. Knowing how good-hearted his relative was, Rabbi Frank forbade him to co-sign as a guarantor on any IOU's, because often Reb Aryeh was exploited by borrowers who did not meet their obligations.

On one occasion, Reb Aryeh was summoned to appear in court, to pay a debt on which he had co-signed. Although he did not remember the loan, he went to court as required. There he had a look at the signature on the document, and saw at once that it had been forged. Right before him stood the poor debtor with his eyes lowered, unable to look Reb Aryeh in the face, since it was he who had forged the signature.

The judge asked Reb Aryeh if he had signed the document? So as not to shame the indigent guilt-laden debtor, Reb Aryeh acknowledged it as his, but asked the judge the favour of allowing him to pay off the debt in monthly instalments (as he could not clear it off all at once). And for several years, Reb Aryeh paid out 28 Israeli pounds a month for an IOU that he never signed.

For his 80th birthday, 1,500 former prisoners gathered at the site of the central prison, to honour him. They ranged from ministers to bank clerks, from rabbis to ranking officers. At the gathering Reb Aryeh told those who attended, "Tell your children: 'There was an old Jew in Jerusalem who loved us so very much.'"

Reb Aryeh was a Jew who lived a frugal life, taking little but giving much. Whilst never compromising his own considerable religious standards or commitments he related to Jews of all backgrounds. He was truly the Tzaddik of Jerusalem.

(We are grateful to Simcha Raz, Author of Aryeh Levin a Tzaddik in Our Time *for allowing us to include stories from his book in this essay.)*

ISRAEL IN 1968

- The first heart transplant in Israel is completed at Beilinson Hospital
- Avshalom Cave, also known as the Stalactites Cave, is discovered accidentally, after the use of explosives during development work
- Israel Television starts regular broadcasts, initially broadcasting three days a week
- The Dakar submarine vanishes without a trace

22 What Does Shema Yisrael Really Mean?

Dr Shlomo Riskin

The Jewish people is unique among all the peoples of the world - it is both a nation and a religion at the same time. Biblically speaking, this duality is reflected in two separate covenants that God entered into with the Israelites.

The first - the covenant of a nation - was with Abraham. God promised Abraham, the first patriarch and founder of our family nation, both progeny as well as boundaries to the Land of Israel.

The second - the covenant of a religion - was with all of the Israelites, after the Exodus from Egypt. God gave us a faith and commandments which would link us together even when we were bereft of a land and were scattered through all four corners of the world.

One might think that the logical moment for the establishment of this second covenant was at that moment at Sinai when more than 600,000 Israelites heard the Divine Voice presenting the fundamental laws of fealty to God, observance of the Sabbath, and the morality which demanded that we not murder, steal or commit adultery.

Is it not then strange, that this covenant is neither presented nor ratified in the *Torah* portion of *Yisro* that catalogues the ten commandments but is rather to be found at the conclusion of the following week's *sedra* portion of *Mishpatim*. "Behold the blood of the covenant which God has established with you on the basis of all these words."[1] Meaning that an entire series of civil laws followed by a description of the future conquest of the Land of Israel intervenes, between the actual giving of the ten commandments and the covenant itself.

Why the long delay?

I believe that the religious covenant was waiting for a single word to be uttered by the Israelites before the Almighty established an eternal agreement with them. A word very familiar to every Jew: *Shema* – hear. In the Biblical portion of *Yisro*, God says to the Israelites, "*You have seen* what I have done to Egypt…but now if you will hear, yes hear, my voice and observe my covenant, you will be for me a unique treasure among all nations."[1] The Jews have *seen*, but apparently they have not yet *heard*.

The Torah portion continues and testifies to the Divine descent on Mount Sinai and lists the ten Divine words or commandments. Words and sounds are generally heard, but in some way the Israelites have not yet heard them. Indeed, the very verse following the commandments reads, "And the entire nation *saw the sounds* and the torches and the *sound of the ram's horn* …. and the nation *saw* and trembled."[3] They are only able to *see* the words and the sounds. At which point God instructs Moses to tell the People, "You have seen that from the heavens I have spoken to you. Do not make with me gods of silver and gods of gold."[4] Since they only see and they have not yet heard, they receive a strong message about not descending into idolatry. After all, if you do not hear, you can even combine belief in God with belief in idols.

It is only after the laws in Mishpatim that we finally find the magic word. "And they said, 'Everything which God says, we shall do and we shall hear (*Nishma*).'"[5] Only then is God ready to establish his covenant with Israel.

What then does this Hebrew verb Shema really mean? Why is it so important? The clarion call of the Jewish faith is well known as, "*Shema Yisrael HaShem Elohenu HaShem Ehad.*" This is usually translated, "Hear O Israel the Lord our God the Lord is One." However, there is a fascinating difference of opinion within the *Mishnah* as to how to explain this word Shema. One sage insists it means that we must express each word of the Shema prayer out loud so that our ears hear what our mouths are uttering; namely that Shema is to *hear* audibly with your *ears*. A second Sage insists that the recital of the Shema must be done in a language that is understood by the individual. Shema therefore meaning to hear in the sense of to understand, to listen with our minds as well as our ears.

The third view insists that neither is sufficient; the words of this call are a commandment to accept the yoke of the Heavenly Kingship, to commit ourselves body and soul to obeying the will of the Divine. Shema is therefore internalisation; to transform our very personalities. The words of God must enter our actual beings, until they remake us into different people.

We can now understand God's insistence on there being more than just *seeing* at Mount Sinai. He is ready to enter into a covenant, but can only do so if we hear, if we understand the life changing ramifications of His words. Listening without internalising does not merit the Divine covenant.

A story is told that Rabbi Yisrael Salanter, the 19th century founder of the Ethicist (Mussar) movement, once found himself stranded in Kovno for *Shabbat*. Everyone wished to invite him, but when he discovered that the local baker had no young mouths to feed at home and so he wouldn't be taking away anyone's portion of food, the great rabbi accepted the baker's invitation. The baker was an observant Jew but was hardly a great Torah scholar or even a polished individual with courtly manners. He entered his house with the revered luminary, and immediately bellowed,

"Yidineh, wife, why are the *challot* not covered? How many times must I remind you?"

The woman, immediately recognising her distinguished guest, had tears in her eyes as she secured the *challah* cover which had already been prepared. The baker, full of self-pride at his punctilious observance, then invited Rabbi Yisrael to sanctify the wine.

"One moment," said the sage, "Can you tell me why we cover the challot?"

"Of course revered Rabbi," responded the baker, "every child knows the answer. When there are many different foods on the table, the first blessing is always made over the bread, after which no other blessing need be made. On Friday night, however, the first blessing has to be made over the wine. So as not to shame the challah who expects the blessing over her, we must cover her over until after the sanctification of the wine."

Rabbi Yisrael looked at the baker incredulously,

"Why do your ears not hear what your mouth is saying? Do you think that our Jewish tradition does not understand that a piece of dough has no feelings and would never become embarrassed? Understand that our laws are trying to sensitise us to the feelings of human beings, our friends, our neighbours and especially our wives."

Only when the Jews were ready to internalise God's messages was He ready to establish His covenant with them. The watchword of our faith enjoins us to understand, to internalise the fact that our God must become the God of a united world, which will happen when it recognises Him as the God of love, morality, truth and peace. Only if that happens, will the Jewish people and humanity survive and prevail.

Notes:

1 Exodus 24:8
2 Exodus 19:4-5
3 Exodus 20:15
4 Exodus 20:19-20
5 Exodus 24:7

ISRAEL IN 1969

- Golda Meir becomes Prime Minister – the world's second elected female leader in modern times
- Maccabi Tel Aviv becomes sponsored by Elite, Israel's largest food company

- The Ben-Gurion University is founded by the government
- 15,000 people attend a rally to protest against USSR's refusal to allow emigration under the banner 'Let My People Go'
- Levi Eshkol, Israel's third Prime Minister, dies

Dedicated by the Muchnis with thanks
to Rabbi Aubrey Hersh for all his shiurim.

23   Luggage Versus Baggage

Aubrey Hersh

Have you ever observed people at airport carousels? Look closely and you'll be able to identify the individual by their luggage. On the one hand the tried and tested travellers, who pack exactly what they need – their luggage reflecting their experience of life. Then there are those who bring along so little you wonder how they'll cope – the lost souls of air travel. Finally, you notice the group who schlepp everything but the kitchen sink. Their cases contain not so much luggage as baggage.

These observations are equally true of us as a nation; we have spent the last two millennia as travelers, and this journeying has impacted on our identity. Whenever we now travel, we do so with thousands of years of history in our suitcase, even if we're just staying overnight. To avoid being overweight therefore, we really need to define what is authentic luggage and what is simply just baggage – what to travel through life with and what to discard. Otherwise, we may end up as Charles Wade did when he bought Snowshill Manor estate in 1919.

Being an avid and eclectic collector, he amassed an enormous inventory of items which included butter stamps, cowbells and suits of Samurai armour. By 1951, he owned over 22,000 pieces, and had filled the entire mansion.[1] Faced with having to part with some of his collection, he decided instead to move out of his country manor into a small cottage at the back of the garden – thus ultimately confusing luggage with baggage!

But where do we get hold of the checklist that advises us what to carry?

The answer lies at the origin of our national history. Here the first recorded instruction to the very first Jew, Abraham, was to travel. To ensure that he did so successfully, God told him what to pack – or more precisely what not to, "*Lech Lecha Me'artzecha, Mi'moladetecha U'mibeit Avicha.*" "Go for yourself from your land, from your birthplace, and from your father's household." [2] All of those things that would weigh him down, that would prevent him from living a life based on eternal values, he was told to leave behind when he left town; packing only that which would endure, that which was worth preserving.

Closer to our times, Naftali Lau embarked upon a journey in October 1942, that was to last three years. He writes of the heartrending parting from his father, the Rabbi of Pietrokov, and his father's instructions as to how to travel.

"When I got home, I found Father sitting in his study. We exchanged glances. Father came over to me and kissed me, his warm tears falling onto my cheek. 'We must act as our Patriarch Jacob did when faced with confrontation,' he said. 'He divided his camp into three, in the hope that at least one would survive.'

The rumble of gunfire was growing louder. We could feel time running out. Mother pulled a few things from Milek's backpack and put them in mine. She admonished me to walk carefully, to avoid being seen by the murderers. She held me tight – a hug that was to last me a lifetime. Only with great effort did I manage to move to the stairwell.

Once outside I found myself face to face with Father. We stood there just the two of us, a sixteen year-old boy heading into the maelstrom alone, and Father, a communal leader, who would not abandon his flock, who valued loyalty and responsibility above his own life. He placed his left hand upon my head and blessed me.

Then speaking about the tragic end of European Jewry he quoted from Jeremiah, 'Both the great and the small shall die in this land; they shall not be buried, neither shall men lament them... neither shall men give them the cup of consolation to drink.'[3]

He spoke of his close relations and of the future of his sons. He named several generations of distinguished rabbis from his and Mother's side, to emphasize the responsibility on any surviving son to continue the heritage of an unbroken chain of thirty-seven generations of rabbis.

'Take special care of Lulek [i.e. Yisrael Lau – the future Chief Rabbi of Israel – then only five years old].'

I was gripped by his words. Not even the sounds of shots, screams and rumbling vehicles could distract me. Father believed that I would come out alive from this inferno and by his parting words was transmitting to me his values and guidelines for the future. His face did not reflect his inner tension, even when he voiced the possibility that this might be our very last meeting. His voice was clear, concise, and articulate.

He did not attempt to counsel me how to behave in the face of unforeseen challenges, but stressed that whatever I do, should be in the firm knowledge that there was an overriding factor, watching over us. Then he read more from Jeremiah, 'And there is hope in thine end, saith the Lord, that thy children shall return to their own border.'

'You are young and must not despair. Jeremiah's prophecy is not just a figure of speech, but a recommendation to those who come out of this. God willing, you will know how to find your home, not here, not on any alien and hostile soil. Your home will be in Eretz Yisrael, even if it has to be acquired at cost of great pain and suffering.'

Had there been a choice, I would have stayed there forever clasping Father's warm hand, but the inexorable ticking of the clock meant the last chance for me to leave the ghetto. There was nothing left to do except one last, strong hug. It was Father who finally pushed me away and led me to the stairs. His brimming eyes looking straight at me, he again put his hand to my head, then sent me on my way."[4]

At the war's end only the two boys had survived. Whilst recuperating in France, Naftali Lau contemplated where to start life anew and how to preserve the family heritage, and recalled his father's advice.

"At times I had visions of Father, particularly of our last conversation. I remembered his trenchant words when we parted on our last night. Now I saw his words as an obligation to follow the road that he and his forefathers had traveled for dozens of generations. Now I also remembered the verse that he had quoted. 'And there is hope in thine end, saith the Lord, that thy children shall return to their own border.'"[5]

Naftali Lau would continue the long journey he had begun in Poland a lifetime ago, bringing with him both the younger brother whom he had protected all those years, and the promise he made to his father. Eventually both they and their genuine luggage - which their ancestors had proudly carried through the many years of a long and bitter exile - would make it home.

Notes:
1 His estate and its collection are now part of the English Heritage Trust.
2 Genesis 12:1
3 Jeremiah 16:6 and 31:17
4 Bala'am's Prophecy pp. 77-79 and personal conversation with Dr. Naftali Lau (19th August 2007)
5 Ibid p.162

ISRAEL IN 1970
- Israel and Egypt negotiate a cease-fire in the Suez Canal, bringing to an end the War of Attrition
- Israeli archaeologists excavate Burnt House - the remains of a house in Jerusalem where a well-off Jewish family had lived before Jerusalem was destroyed by Roman soldiers in 70CE
- The Israeli Philharmonic Orchestra performs in Germany and plays Hatikvah 500 yards from the Reichstag

24 Jerusalem: Peace and Beauty

Shaya Karlinsky

In times of old, all roads led to Jerusalem. It was the site of Temple and the city to which the nation would make its pilgrimage three times a year. It contained both the seat of the monarch and that of the Sanhedrin – the supreme legislature. Indeed, throughout history, many maps featured Jerusalem as the centre of the world. Even today we respond to its call – we build our synagogues facing towards it and reflect on its absent glory at our weddings.

What is the secret behind Jerusalem and wherein lies its centrality to Judaism?

In discussing the origin of the name Jerusalem, *Yerushalaim*, the *Midrash* teaches us: Abraham called it *Yira'ah* meaning awe/fear[1]. Shem called it *Shalem* meaning peace/completeness.[2] "Said God: If I call it *Yira'ah*, as Abraham did, Shem, will object. If I call it *Shalem*, Abraham, will object. Rather, I will call it *Yerushalaim*, as they called it together, *Yira'ah Shalem*."[3]

While this sounds like a parent trying to broker a compromise in an argument between two immature children, this Midrash is in fact revealing to us the fundamental nature of Jerusalem.

In a world of different personalities and elements, differences result from each person striving to fully actualise his or her own unique potential. But these differences can have two very different motivations, one "for the sake of Heaven" and one "not for the sake of Heaven."[4]

A dispute that is "not for the sake of Heaven" is the pursuit of self-actualisation for the sake of the self, with no other goal beyond the desire for personal fulfilment. It is true **self**-actualisation, and one who is motivated by it views all other forces and talents unaligned with their personal agenda as a threat and competition. These conflicts lead to a desire and often an attempt to destroy the competing force.

"A dispute for the sake of Heaven," on the other hand, whilst also reflecting diversity, is for the pursuit of common service. It has as its goals, others, society and that which transcends the individual. Each individual has something unique to contribute, and the focus is on making that contribution to accomplish bigger goals. There is also a realisation by the individual of their personal limitations, and that the greater good is served by additional resources being available. So that others who have different talents and personalities are viewed as allies rather than adversaries.

But it is not a simple matter to create co-operation and alignment when there are differences. Jerusalem, and the secret behind its name, provides the formula.

One of God's attributes is *din* – absolute justice. Everything must conform to exact standards, and any deviation from the ideal is not true *din*. In this system, there is no room for mercy or stays of execution. Actions are inevitably followed by their full consequences. Awe and fear are the product of this attribute, since anyone falling short of the ideal is fearful of the results. In *Kabbalah*, 'fire' is the element associated with *din*. Beyond having a strong characteristic, it is also the force which causes separation, because when something is completely dry, there is no mechanism for it to be attached to anything else. Sand, cement, and metals are just a few of many examples.

In human terms, when a person demands to actualise his potential with no deviation or compromise, i.e. *din*, the result is that everyone else becomes an adversary, creating separation rather than bonding.

For two elements to bond, water is needed. In Kabbalah, water is associated with *chessed,* meaning kindness, which, making no demands is the opposite of *din.* However, kindness has its drawback. The potential of the recipient is never actualised, since they remain passive.

We therefore require the third attribute – that of *Shalom* (harmony).

Jerusalem, both in the Bible and in the Talmud, as well as being the City of Peace, is known as the City of Beauty.[5] These two attributes are identical. Beauty is created by contrast, whether in music, in art or in nature. So too the true beauty of Jerusalem, is the coexistence of many conflicting elements – but living in harmony. A canvas with only one colour cannot depict harmony; similarly peace can only be achieved where there are two sides with different potentials that join together. There is *din*, but it is being used to further the goals of shalom.

In this vein, the *Talmud* quotes the verse, "Jerusalem rebuilt, like a city which has been rejoined together."[6] This also teaches that Jerusalem creates unity among Jews, when they ascend to it. The tribes ascend to Jerusalem, each with its unique personality, each with its discrete mission. But when they are united in their striving to accomplish a common goal, to honour God in the Holy Temple, then that honour is actually *amplified* by having conflicting forces of a diverse nation.

In our times, we too often see Jerusalem as a city of division and strife, because actions start off being *din* as is usual, but they are motivated by the pursuit of "negative din", "my way or the highway", and not by *din* which can lead to *shalom*. The result is destruction and discord, hence our Temple being destroyed as a result of hatred and specifically through the medium of fire.

But when contrasts can be unified, using underlying kindness, and channelling it into accomplishing transcendent goals, it becomes a city of great beauty and harmony.

The true beauty of Jerusalem is its unity through diversity. When God was choosing a name for Jerusalem, he knew that the city which would be home to the Holy Temple, the focus of His glory in the world, needed to blend together many conflicting elements and forces. Therefore, he incorporated both *yirah*, motivating everyone to actualise their own potential to the fullest, and *shaleim*, pursuit of unity creating true peace and harmony.

It is an almost universal custom to end both the Passover Seder and the Yom Kippur prayers with the statement "Next year in Jerusalem." The path to making this dream come true is by creating a Jerusalem that lives up to the standards of its name.

Notes:
1 Genesis 22:14
2 Genesis 14:18
3 Breishith Rabba 56:10
4 Ethics of the fathers 5:16
5 TB Kiddushin 49b
6 Tehillim 122:3

ISRAEL IN 1971
• The Massada cable car opens
• Nathan Tsirolnikov, emigrating from Russia on 11 January, brings the number of Israeli citizens to three million
• Israel's First Drive-In Movie Theatre opens, showing Walt Disney's Jungle Book

Dedicated to Sheila and Harry Lawrence,
who are truly inspirational parents.

25 The Blooming of Israel

Samuel Green

When the early Zionists arrived in pre-state Israel, their experience of *aliyah* was something of an anticlimax. Instead of the land of milk and honey of legend, they were greeted by vast swathes of arid desert or swamp. Disease was rife and living conditions were extremely poor. And yet, despite incredibly difficult conditions and despite being only 60 years old, our people have already brought so much to the rest of the world and achieved the miraculous. This should not really surprise us though; after all Israel is where miracles have always happened. As the *Torah* tells us, it is a country like no other, "the land that God continuously looks out for, from the beginning of the year to year's end."[1]

The early pioneers' battle to build a country, started quite literally, from the ground up. The swamps had to be drained and the deserts made to bloom. Their dedication allowed Israel to establish techniques in desert farming and create a strong agricultural industry that exports around the globe, including 1.5 billion flowers annually. And its wine industry, now nearly 5,000 years old, has won a host of international trophies and medals.

This trend has extended to Israeli businesses, currently at the forefront of advances in technology and, in many cases, the world leaders. Teva Pharmaceuticals is one of the 20 largest pharmaceutical companies in the world. Amdocs and Comverse provide best-in-class telecoms software and may well provide you with your bills and voicemail. ICQ internet messaging was invented in Israel in 1996, as was M2A, a tiny video camera in a disposable swallowable capsule which delivers 50,000 images within eight hours to allow diagnosis of internal disorders without pain or discomfort. These examples of homegrown successes, of which there are many, are indicative of the significant talents of the Israeli workforce, which is also being tapped by non-Israeli global corporations, such as Motorola, Intel and Microsoft. Indeed, it is in the field of technology where much of Israel's modern day pioneering takes place. The fact that Israel has the second largest number of start-up companies, and the second largest venture capital industry in the world is indicative of the spirit of adventure and desire to excel which has permeated its history.

Much of Israel's success in hi-tech, results from the high emphasis that Israelis place on education, which has always been a top Jewish priority. Indeed, Israel has the highest ratio of university degrees to the population in the world. With four Nobel laureates in the fields of economics and chemistry, Israeli academics are often world leaders in their fields.

Israel has also made great strides in developing its arts scene. Israeli writers have long been respected in international circles and in addition to Samuel Y. Agnon's Nobel Prize for Literature in 1966, others who have been awarded international literary prizes include Amos Oz, Aaron Appelfeld and Natan Zach. Israel's classical music scene is also significant, with the Israeli Philharmonic Orchestra rated as one of the top in the world. Itzhak Perlman, one of many Israeli virtuosos, is widely recognised as being one of the century's most distinguished violinists. More contemporary music has featured in mainstream media outlets such as the BBC and *Rolling Stone* and Q magazines. And of course, Israel has won the Eurovision Song Contest on three separate occasions, since 1978. Furthermore, Israeli cinema has now developed to the extent that it is gaining international recognition and over the past few years several films have taken prizes at top international film festivals. Although there have been no Oscars as yet, there have been six nominations.

Many of us will be familiar with the scene in the film *Airplane* where on being asked to suggest something light to read, the stewardess offers the passenger a small piece of paper entitled *Great Jewish Sporting Legends!* Israel is no major player when it comes to international sport but considering its size it has consistently punched above its weight. At the last Olympics, Israel took its first ever gold medal, a feat which can hopefully be equalled or even bettered in 2008. Maccabi Tel-Aviv are one of the top basketball teams in Europe, and have been crowned European champions on five separate occasions. The Israeli national football team has appeared in the World Cup, and come close to qualification on other occasions; extremely impressive given that they are handicapped by having to qualify against the European football powers and not their Middle-Eastern neighbours. Israelis have also risen to prominence in international tennis with Shahar Pe'er, currently ranked number 15 in the world, and the doubles partnership of Andy Ram and Jonathan Erlich, also at number 15.

Considering its age, Israel's achievements are quite incredible. It goes to show what can be accomplished with hard work, drive, a considerable amount of talent and a Helping Hand from above. Most Jews nowadays no longer recall a time when there was no State, in fact we often take both it and its achievements for granted. But we really owe it to ourselves to stop and reflect, to see how high we've climbed. So much has happened so quickly, that we can be justifiably proud of what we've done and be grateful for the blessings which have made it possible.

Although the news we hear from Israel is not always positive, we should take note of its many successes. Even better, we should consider making aliyah, and aim to take an active role in the fantastic narrative of the Jewish people in our homeland.

Notes:
1 Deuteronomy 11:12

ISRAEL IN 1972

- The IDF manages to rescue all 100 passengers and crew of a hijacked Sabena airliner at Lod airport
- 11 Israeli athletes are murdered by Palestinian terrorists at the Munich Olympic games
- Actor Chaim Topol is nominated for Best Actor at the Academy Awards for his role in Fiddler on the Roof

Dedicated by Edinburgh Hebrew Congregation, in memory of Maurice David Katz who died in Israel in the Yom Kippur War 1973, aged 21 years.

26 Love, Relationships and Parenting

Gila Manolson & Danya Ross

Gila Manolson

Love is a Choice – A few years ago, I spoke to a group of teenagers about the Jewish idea of love.

"Someone define love," I said. No response.

"Doesn't anyone want to try?" I asked. Still no response.

"Tell you what: I'll define it, and you raise your hands if you agree. Okay?" Nods.

"Okay. Love is that feeling you get when you meet the right person." Every hand went up. And I thought, "Oy!"

Unfortunately this is how many people approach a relationship. Consciously or unconsciously, they believe love is a sensation (based on physical and emotional attraction) that magically, spontaneously generates when Mr. or Ms. Right appears. And just as easily, it can spontaneously degenerate when the magic "just isn't there" anymore. You fall in love, and you can fall out of it.

The key word is passivity. Erich Fromm, in his famous treatise, "The Art of Loving," noted the sad consequence of this misconception, "There is hardly any activity, any enterprise, which is started with such tremendous hopes and expectations, and yet, which fails so regularly, as love." (That was back in 1956 – chances are he'd be even more pessimistic today.)

So What is Real, Lasting Love? Love is the attachment that results from deeply appreciating another's goodness. The word 'goodness' may surprise you. After all, most love stories don't feature a couple enraptured with each other's ethics. ("I'm captivated by your values!" he told her passionately. "And I've never met a man with such morals!" she cooed.) Judaism says that while, nice looks, an engaging personality, intelligence, and talent (all of which count for something) may attract you, it is goodness that moves you to love.

If love comes from appreciating goodness, you can make it happen. Love is active. You can create it. Just focus on the good in another person (and everyone has some). If you can do this easily, you'll love easily. While most people believe love leads to giving, the truth (as Rabbi Eliyahu Dessler writes in his discourse on loving kindness) is exactly the opposite: Giving leads to love.

Of course this is true in all relationships. If we are genuine and giving, we will create love.

Experience, Don't Conceptualise – A few years ago I came across a schools programme where children were shown the effect that unkind or thoughtless words and actions had, on people they interacted with every day. The programme made me think back on something I had heard only a few days earlier.

A rabbi had told his audience "When you meet a new person, instead of judging and categorizing them, take them in as they are." "Don't conceptualize," the rabbi said. "Experience." Most of us are guilty of relating to people somewhat superficially. We sometimes size up others quickly and too shallowly. The result may not be calling them names or putting them down, but simply assuming that we've "got their number."

When I was subsequently invited to speak at a large social-religious gathering, I decided to try out this experiment. If someone wanted to talk to me after my lecture, I would try to go beyond that superficial impression we all get of people. I would try to see him or her in a more real way, as they truly are.

Indeed, several people came over to speak with me. All

asked intelligent, sensitive questions. At the same time, none of them had the looks or charisma of a Hollywood celebrity. Yet the experiment left me stunned - and in awe. Every one of these individuals, without exception, came through loud and strong as a beautiful human being.

Danya Ross

Rabbi Shlomo Wolbe, one of the 20th century's most prolific Jewish educators, points out that God expresses his trust in us by allowing us to become parents. We are in possession of an exceptionally precious gift, placed in our safekeeping to be guarded, cared for and looked after. It is both a privilege and a responsibility to be a parent.

We all want to be good parents to good children. However, we find that even the greatest of people did not always have the children they would have ideally wanted. Abraham fathered Ishmael, Isaac gave birth to Esau and King David's son Absalom rebelled against him. Nobody is above the law. And, with the presence of so many negative influences in society today, it is unrealistic to assume that we alone will determine our children's future.

So how can we help our children flourish?

Love – The way children grow best is in a loving environment. The more one's children experience love the healthier they will be. However, in order to be able to give them the full experience of love a person needs to love themselves: acknowledging their strengths, accepting their own shortcomings, and using the attributes that they actually possess. A maths professor may excel at presenting a lecture, but will not necessarily be able to play a classical instrument. This need not and does not take away from his greatness. If we are able to accept and love ourselves we will more effectively be able to instil love in our children.

Leading by example – If we look in the *Torah* we see that there is hardly any dialogue between the forefathers. A total of eight words are recorded between Abraham and Isaac! Is the message here that we should not speak to our children? Surely not! Rather that in parenting it is not what we say to our children that counts the most, it's what one does and who we are. We need to lead by example. For children to be polite, we must be polite. For them to be honest, we too must have this quality. A parent is a role model for their children.

Prayer – We have to invest both physically and emotionally in parenting, but ultimately our success depends on Divine blessing. To access this we turn to prayer. At certain times, such as candle lighting before *Shabbat*, there is a potency and power to a parent's prayer which enables them to connect to the Divine. The heartfelt prayer of a loving parent is something very special indeed!

ISRAEL IN 1973
- Israel is invaded on Yom Kippur by Egyptian and Syrian forces
- Ariel Sharon forms the Likud party
- David Ben-Gurion dies aged 87 and Lod airport is renamed after him
- Israel issues a series of 12 stamps – each bearing the name of one of the tribes of Israel
- Danny Kaye, actor and comedian, arrives in Israel to sign up to the IDF forces and perform for troops at the front

Dedicated by Gillian and Eze Silas in loving memory of our parents Rev. Abraham Joshua and Sybil Mozelle Silas, Raphael and Dora Hanstater.

27 An Inspirational Shavuot

Yitzchok Rubin

The old Jew's name was Reb Shlomo. He was elderly but his eyes were alive, on fire, filled with youth. And he came with special credentials: he had been born in Ger, the greatest *Chasidic* centre in Poland. As youngsters, we would often stand around after prayers just to hear his stories, and we never left without some new nugget of gold. This was just a few years after the Holocaust and we were thirsty to learn of the yesterday that had once been.

Of course that Ger was no more, Hitler had come and ripped apart all that was holy. We were living in a world built on the ashes of what was, and these scraps from Reb Shlomo were manna from heaven.

His greatest tale was about *Shavuot* in Ger.

The festival of Shavuot celebrates the giving of the *Torah* on Mount Sinai. However, in Judaism we do not merely commemorate Biblical events, we actually re-experience them. Every year the energy of that wondrous moment when Heaven met Earth can once again be ignited and those who connect with it are imbued with the spiritual uplift that came into the world 3,320 years ago. In hundreds of synagogues and homes, Torah is studied through the night; recreating that point in time that saw our Nation stand at Mount Sinai and proclaim our acceptance of the Torah and its study.

Reb Shlomo would explain to us, that of all the Chasidic groups in Poland, Ger was not only the largest, it was the one with the greatest reputation for intense Torah study. The Rebbe of Ger once said that each spiritual leader brought his followers closer to God in a unique fashion; his was to bring each student closer to Torah knowledge.

But despite being the epicentre of the world's most vibrant Chasidic court, the town itself was very small, and few actually resided there all year long. Rather it was in the hundreds of Ger *shtibels* throughout Poland, that groups gathered to study and pray.

Shavuot though was different. Shavuot saw ten thousand Chasidim converge on that one small *shtetl* of Ger, for the highlight of the year, the moment when Mount Sinai became almost palpable. Shavuot was the time to receive Torah anew in the presence of the Rebbe:

"There was a special train from Warsaw called the Kolleka and it came to Ger filled to the brim with Chasidim", his eyes burned with distant memories, "We would run to the station to greet them, looking for cousins, watching out for the *Rabbonim* and *Gedolim* (Torah Sages). There was no room for everyone to stay; the town just didn't have enough space, so hundreds slept in the *Shul*, or in barns, anywhere and everywhere."

Reb Shlomo's eyes would now be dancing, "Oh that was a *Shavuot*, ten thousand Chasidim, 'a kleinekeit?' (no small thing)." He would tell us this tale over and over, each time some new nuance was added. He would remember yet another Yid, or an insight he heard. After each such recital there would come a moment when his eyes would cloud over and one could detect the weight that this Jew carried within his heart. "It was all there, the Rebbe, the Chasidim, the Rabbonim, everything, such passion for life, for Torah, and then it was crushed." Shlomo had lost his whole family, but we never spoke of it. Like so much more, it was in his eyes. He would sigh an old weary sigh and put his head down for a moment.

Then he would add, "You youngsters will never know, will

never have the merit to see what it was, I feel sorry for you." Reb Shlomo had seen the glory that was.

One Shavuot Reb Shlomo went missing from the Shtibl in Boro Park. It was said he had travelled to Jerusalem, to the Ger *Beit Hamedrash* (Chasidic Prayer house), to the new place of his yesterdays. After some time he returned, and we all saw a wondrous transformation. Reb Shlomo walked tall and there was a new spring to his step.

We all waited until after *davening* and as Reb Shlomo drank a glass of coffee he told us of his trip. "Kinderlach (Children) Ger lives! *Yiden* (Jews) are dancing in Jerusalem to the old songs we heard in Poland! It's a miracle!" He went on to describe a new Ger, with thousands of Chasidim, a new Ger with the old lustre and *bren* (Chasidic fire). He spoke of his friends, the few saved from the ashes, he told of the Rabbonim, of the Rebbe's family. He was alive, Ger was alive, and Torah was alive.

Where else but in Israel, a land of holiness, could such a rebirth happen? Where else but in Jerusalem could such fire be lit? The miracle of a Torah-world rebuilt; tens of thousands of Jews living God's word. Reb Shlomo soon moved to that holy place and lived there to a ripe old age, and on his death bed was still that same fervent chasid.

Today in all corners of our holy land, there is a vibrant renewal of Jewish strength that speaks of our eternal goals. We hope that soon we will be blessed to see the advent of our final redemption, when all communities gather together and find their future in the holiness of our special land.

But until then we can hold on to the message of Shavuot. Gora Kalwaria (Ger) in Poland, may be home to only two Jews today, but around the world, and especially in the Land of Israel, the legacy of Shavuot and the study of Torah, is being carried out by a people rejuvenated.

ISRAEL IN 1974

- American based Intel establishes its first overseas design and development centre in Haifa
- Perach, a mentoring programme for children from disadvantaged socio-economic backgrounds is founded. Today it sees 30,000 Israeli students work with 60,000 children from all parts of Israeli Society
- Israel is accepted as an Associate Member of the International Cricket Conference, now known as the International Cricket Council

> Dedicated in thanks for the wonderful work of
> University Jewish Chaplains.

28 Coincidences: God's Way of Saying Hello

Yitta Halberstam

Traditionally, Miami, Los Angeles, and New York are the three cities in the United States to which most Israelis flock, both as tourists and as immigrants. Pittsburgh, Pennsylvania, on the other hand, has never proven to be a major magnet for the expatriates, and Hebrew is certainly not the lingua franca of the grass-roots natives there. So Eric Blaustein pricked up his ears attentively on *Rosh Hashanah* when he heard an uncommon language - Hebrew - being spoken on the street outside his synagogue in Mount Lebanon, a suburb of Pittsburgh. People often laugh about how much Hebrew is spoken in New York but certainly no one has ever made that claim about Pittsburgh. Nostalgic to hear the language that he once knew well, Eric Blaustein listened appreciatively, and then, unable to suppress his curiosity, approached the Hebrew-speaking group. Who were they, he wanted to know, and what were they doing in - of all places - Pittsburgh?

"My company just transferred me," a young man in the group explained, "and of course my family has relocated with me" he said, introducing his wife and children. He then gestured toward an older man and woman at his side. "These are my parents. They don't live here, but they came to visit us for the High Holidays."

Eric felt drawn to the father, a man close to his age, and began a halting conversation with him in his own rusty Hebrew. The older man was visibly impressed, even though Eric wasn't very fluent.

"Where'd you learn to speak Hebrew?" the Israeli asked, pleasantly surprised.

"I'm a survivor of the concentration camps," the German-born Blaustein replied. "I went to Israel after the war, and in 1948 I fought as a volunteer soldier during Israel's War of Independence. I served with the Twelfth Brigade, Seventh Regiment."

The Israeli looked at Blaustein with quickened interest. "I know this is a long shot, but were you by any chance in the second company?"

Indeed, Blaustein said, he was.

A variety of emotions, which Eric couldn't quite decipher danced across the Israeli's face. "You weren't in the third platoon, were you?"

Right again.

Then the Israeli asked a startling question: "Were you a second lieutenant?"

"Yes, as a matter of fact," Blaustein answered in amazement, "I *was* a second lieutenant."

"And your unit had only one second lieutenant, right?" the Israeli pressed on.

"Now, how would you know that?" Blaustein demanded, flustered by where the line of questioning was leading. "How could you *possibly* know that?"

"Because I've been looking for you for 52 years!" the Israeli shouted, grabbing Eric's hand and pumping it vigorously. "Remember the French Commandos? You *saved my life!*"

It had happened 52 years ago, but the memory was as vivid as if it had been yesterday. In a flashback, Eric Blaustein remembered it all: The Negev... the Israeli advance unit made up of French volunteers under enemy attack by the Egyptians and almost out of ammunition ... his own platoon being called on to rescue the stranded soldiers caught in the line of fire.

Eric's unit had broken through enemy lines to pick up the dead and injured and bring them back to safety. And then there had been the one wounded soldier whom Eric had carried on his back... all the way to the field dressing station. Eric had made sure the soldier was tended to, and had then left, never learning the man's name nor his fate. But Eric was not easily forgotten by the man, who had been conscious throughout the ordeal and had stared at Eric's second lieutenant shoulder insignia, burning them into his memory.

All his life he had wanted to meet the man who had rescued him, so he could thank him.

"To think I had to come to Pittsburgh to meet you again!" the Israeli exclaimed, and went on to say that this was his first time here.

Eric Blaustein stared at him, incredulous. "But I wasn't even supposed to be here tonight," he told the man. "Every Rosh Hashanah my wife and I travel to Chicago to be with our daughter, whose husband is a rabbi and who obviously can't leave his pulpit at this time. It's practically a tradition – we've done it for several years straight."

But this year he and his wife had suddenly decided to stay home in Mount Lebanon, for the first time since their daughter had moved to Chicago.

Eric told the *Pittsburgh Post,* "The Israeli wound up coming to Pittsburgh for the first time, and I wound up staying for the first time...and we both wound up in the same synagogue together."

Both men felt that they had been touched by a miracle. The Israeli was thrilled that he was finally able to thank his benefactor, and Blaustein was touched to witness the miracle of life he had given this man, his son, and his grandchildren. Three generations stood before him now, testifying to the impact of his one action 52 years before.

It was a great way to start the New Year.

Coincidences are God's way of saying hello – they are the miracles that happen in our daily lives, and show us we're not alone.

ISRAEL IN 1975

- The United Nations General Assembly passes Resolution 3379, defining Zionism as a form of racism and ethnic cleansing, often used as an example of UN discrimination against the state of Israel
- Israel becomes an associate member of the European Union free trade area, significantly increasing trade
- Aviva Lombard develops HIPPY, a home instruction programme for parents of pre-schoolers, now used by more than 23,000 families worldwide
- Hadassah Hospital re-opens on Mount Scopus after a 27 year gap

In memory of Nina and Alfred Meyer.

29 A Diaspora Yearning

Harvey Belovski

In the spring of 1990, a few months after my wife and I were married, we moved to the northern-English town of Gateshead. We lived there for more than seven years, during which time I had the tremendous privilege of studying full-time at the institution affectionately known as 'Gateshead *Yeshiva*'. It was a transformative experience in every way. I studied *Talmud*, Jewish law and *Torah* thought under the tutelage of outstanding scholars, while we thrived on the heady brew of intense prayer and unswerving religious ambition that pervaded every facet of the yeshiva society. And, perhaps most importantly, we took up the challenge of constantly reviewing and refining our aspirations for ourselves and our family. We were, and remain, truly blessed by an incredible seven years, which gave us not only a meaningful career, but quite literally, recreated us as people.

Yet we never expected to go to Gateshead at all! Having spent a magnificent summer in 1987 studying Torah in Israel, I had decided that on completing my university studies I would return to Jerusalem to learn in yeshiva there: where but the centre of the Jewish universe would one want to study God's Torah?

But, as they say, "Man plans and God laughs." By the time I finished Oxford in 1989, I was about to get married, sponsorship for yeshiva study had all but dried up, and the mass Russian *aliyah* had hiked the property prices in Jerusalem. In short, we couldn't afford to go to Israel. Our rabbinical advisers suggested that we consider Gateshead instead. It wasn't Israel, but in the circumstances it would be an excellent second-best. After two years of study, despite the fact that we loved it in Gateshead, we made another attempt to move to Israel. Once again, funding eluded us, so we stayed in the frozen north for the duration of my studies.

It was curious that we kept feeling drawn to Israel, particularly as my learning was so successful in Gateshead. Looking back, I believe we wanted to be part of one of the most astonishing miracles of the modern Jewish world: the explosion of Torah study in Israel. Yet it was more than simply wanting to "get a piece of the action."

I remember my late teacher, Rabbi Mordechai Miller, *zt"l*, talking about the arrival of his *rebbe*, Rabbi E.E. Dessler, zt"l, to take up a senior yeshiva position in Israel in the late 1940s. Rabbi Dessler reached his lodgings after dark, unpacked a few things, went to *Ma'ariv* and then returned to his room. Some of the students asked him jokingly, "How do you like *Eretz Yisrael*?" To their astonishment, he replied, "It's wonderful here. I've already resolved some Torah conundrums that have been bothering me for years!" Rabbi Dessler was referring to the Talmudic notion that the very air of Eretz Yisrael makes one wise.[1] He assumed that the sudden clarity of thought that he had gained in the few hours since his arrival in Israel was attributable to the innate spiritual excellence of the land.

Living in Israel endows one's life with a unique quality. This was expressed by the ecstatic behaviour of certain Talmudic sages: Rebbi Ami kissed the stones of Acre; Rebbi Hiyya bar Gamda rolled in the dust (of Israel).[2] It is also explains why throughout Jewish history, Jews of all types yearned profoundly to live in the land. Sadly, for most of our ancestors, it was never to be. In stark and blessed contrast, we have the freedom to visit Israel whenever we wish and can make aliyah with relative ease.

At a more esoteric level, Torah, the life-blood of the Jewish people, is deeply entwined with Israel. The Torah itself refers to Israel as the land upon which "God's eyes rest from the start of the year to its end."[3] Rabbi A.Y. Kook, zt"l, the first chief rabbi of Palestine, explains that holiness is the natural condition of Eretz Yisrael; elsewhere, spirituality is locked in mortal combat with other forces, and can thus never be fully manifest[4]. He asserts that "in Eretz Yisrael one's imagination is lucid and patent, refined, purified and attuned to the emergence of Divine truth."[5] This is the inner meaning of the special quality of the "air of Israel", a rarefied spiritual ambience conducive to the attainment of clear understanding and profound communion with God. Indeed, the Rabbis tell us that Torah scholars living outside Israel are "out of place."[6]

So while my wife and I thrived in Gateshead, and may even have succeeded in ways that would not have been possible had we actually made it to Israel, we were always acutely aware that there remained a clarity of Torah experience that eluded us. The Talmudic promise that "in the future, synagogues and yeshivot in Babylon (outside Israel) will be established in Eretz Yisrael"[7] would have to suffice.

I am fortunate to visit Israel frequently, and when I do, I hear the Torah of Eretz Yisrael, something extremely similar to, but not synonymous with my own learning experience. Strolling through a religious district, where I can sense the vibrancy of the Torah study, I think of my Gateshead years with great fondness. Yet I try to remember Rabbi Yosi bar Halafta's question to his father Rabbi Yishmael: "Do you want to see the Divine presence in this world?" His answer? "If yes, study Torah in Eretz Yisrael."[8]

Notes:
1 Bava Batra 158b
2 Ketubot 112b–113a
3 Deuteronomy 11:12
4 Orot HaTehiyah 28
5 Orot Eretz Yisrael 5
6 Shabbat 145b

7 Megillah 29a
8 Midrash Tehillim 105

ISRAEL IN 1976

- The IDF succeeds in a spectacular military operation to save Israeli hostages that had been on a hijacked flight diverted to Entebbe, Uganda
- Vineyards are established in the Golan Heights
- Yad Sarah, Israel's largest voluntary organisation, is founded by Uri Lupoliansky, helping one in two families and saving the economy about $300 million per year

In memory of HaGaon Rabbi Shlomo Zalman
Auerbach, who always made himself available for
others. Dedicated by a grateful JLE.

30 Rabbi Shlomo Zalman Auerbach (1910-1995): Torah Leader of the Modern Age

Jason Kleiman

Rabbi Shlomo Zalman Auerbach was one of the leading religious authorities of the twentieth century, yet when he died, President Ezer Weizman - who came to comfort the family – admitted very frankly, "It never dawned on me that so remarkable a figure lived only a few hundred metres from my home."

Who was this sage, whose sphere of influence reached all areas of the Jewish world, and whose thousands of students continue to influence the Jewish world today, yet who was born, lived and died in *Eretz Yisrael* – never leaving its borders once, despite many invitations to do so?

What was the secret to his greatness, that brought over 300,000 Jews of all walks of life to his funeral – more than the numbers for any Israeli Prime Minister or President, and the largest ever in the country for over two thousand years - yet who had no official title, shunned the limelight and lived in an apartment with almost no furnishings?

His maternal great grandfather, Rabbi Naftali Zvi Porush,

was amongst the pioneers of 'the old *yishuv*' – the term used to refer to those devout Jews who made *aliyah* to the Land of Israel some two hundred years ago. The family settled in the Old City of Jerusalem, braving many material difficulties including a scarcity of food and water. His son became the founder of the Sha'arei Chessed neighbourhood and established its Free Loan Fund, whilst Rabbi Shlomo Zalman's father founded Sha'ar Ha-Shamayim, a *yeshiva* for *Kabbalistic* studies, which still flourishes today in Jerusalem.

It was into this religious environment of self-sacrifice, compassion and care that Rabbi Shlomo Zalman Auerbach was born, in 1910. Their family's financial situation was so dire that on days when their meal consisted of more than plain bread, a single egg would be divided amongst the entire family.

None of this deterred him from his study, and as a youth he entered the prestigious Eitz Chaim Yeshiva in Jerusalem. His desire for learning was such, that despite being the top student in his class, he asked to repeat a year and sit with children a year younger than him, so that he could continue to be inspired by a particular teacher.

By the age of 11, he was fluent in an entire tractate of Talmud, (*Kiddushin*), the precursor of his love affair with the Talmud, which he would complete in its entirety more than one hundred times during his lifetime!

In his early 20s, he published the first *halachic* work ever written on the use of electricity on *Shabbat*, demonstrating both a knowledge of complex Jewish law and of physics. At the age of 40, he was approached to head the Yeshiva of Kol Torah in Bayit Ve'gan. Although initially reluctant to accept such an important post, once he joined, he never regretted his decision to devote himself to teaching, and remained there for over 40 years.[1] This was despite being offered the position of Dayan on the Rabbinical Court by the Chief Rabbi of Israel, Rabbi Yitzhak Herzog, and subsequently the Chief Rabbinate of Jerusalem.

His status and reputation did not stem from his knowledge alone, as was proven from his inaugural lecture at the Yeshiva, which was delivered in front of the entire faculty. One of the older rabbis – Rabbi Marzbach – was present, and interrupted the lecture to pose a difficult question. Rabbi Shlomo Zalman paused for a moment in thought. With all eyes on him, he turned to Rabbi Marzbach and said: "I'm not sure how to answer your question."

Leaving the lecture, he was approached by Rabbi Marzbach. Rabbi Shlomo Zalman said to him, "I had answers to your question, but without proper reflection I couldn't be certain of their validity, so I remained silent."

When he was nevertheless chosen as the Rosh Yeshiva, he expressed surprise that they would elect someone who had proven himself incapable at his first public appearance. The board replied, "Your unwillingness to offer an off-the-cuff answer, only proves your integrity. A person who is honest and straightforward has the most worthy criteria for becoming our *Rosh Yeshiva*."

His clarity of thought and teaching also revealed itself in his halachic rulings, especially those on scientific, technological and medical matters. Hundreds of his answers to contemporary medical questions – including those on organ transplants and on birth control - appeared in writing, most especially in the Halachic Medical Encyclopaedia. He was also responsible for producing a definitive book on the laws of Shabbat as they applied to life on the 20th century, as well as tackling the issues of finance and banking in modern day Israel, and its agricultural laws.

That Rabbi Shlomo Zalman Auerbach was a renowned scholar is clear from his writings, however his true greatness came from something more than this. Inundated as he was with enquiries from across the world, he was nevertheless accessible to anyone for advice or guidance, whether layman or sage. As a result he was both loved and admired by hundreds of his pupils who felt a close bond to their teacher, and by many thousands more besides. The following brief story demonstrates his extraordinary ability to combine his immense learning with integrity, humility and tremendous sensitivity towards others.

Rabbi Shlomo Zalman encountered a young married student of his by a hospital elevator one Saturday night. The student happily shared with his *rebbe* the news that his wife had just given birth to a boy.

They entered the elevator together and Rabbi Shlomo Zalman congratulated him warmly, inquiring at length about the details of the birth - his every effort directed towards sharing the happiness of his student. However, for the Rabbi this was no ordinary Saturday night. Just a few hours earlier, he had suffered the agonising loss of his wife, to whom he had been married for 54 years. He was on his way to deal with the funeral arrangements, and yet he was not prepared to allow his personal mourning to intrude on a student's joy.

This was the man to whom so many came to pay their last respects. He was quite simply the embodiment of Torah.

Notes:
1 One of his students was Rabbi Yisrael Lau, a future Chief Rabbi of Israel, who used to transcribe his teacher's lectures

ISRAEL IN 1977
- Likud win the elections, with ex Irgun leader Menachem Begin becoming Israel's first right-wing leader
- Maccabi Tel Aviv win the European Basketball championship, beating CSKA Moscow in the final
- Vietnamese refugees are rescued at sea by Israeli cargo ships

In loving memory of Yettie Wiseman.

31 Successfully Meeting Life's Challenges

Esther Jungreis

I was born at a turbulent time in history. The Nazi Party had gained ascendancy. Overnight, the world became a hunting ground; we Jews became the hunted and many nations joined the hunters. Much of my family was killed in the gas chambers, but, through the grace of God, my parents and I survived and made our way to the blessed American shores. With the passage of time, life returned to normal, and we, who only yesterday were the hunted, became builders. We were committed to build a better, kinder, more peaceful world. We built schools and communities, and most important, we built lives. The struggle was no longer one of mere survival, but rather, for more meaning and more purpose.

But what is life all about?"

On a national level, Israel's fragile existence has often raised this question. However, at one time or another, all of us wrestle with this challenge. Having no clear answer we tend to dismiss the question and continue our humdrum existence.

Some years ago however, I read a brief news item in The New York Times about an Olympics for Special Children in Seattle, Washington. The story was about disabled children who competed in a race. When the whistle sounded, they started to run. Suddenly, one of the young boys fell, skinned his knee, and began to cry. When the others heard his cry, they stopped in their tracks, turned around, and went to his aid. One little girl, who had Downs Syndrome, bent down, kissed his knee and said, "Here, this will make it feel better." The children helped the boy to his feet, linked hands, and ever so slowly, they all walked as one to the finish line. Could it be that these children know something that we have lost sight of? One must wonder therefore, who is really disabled?

There are some who view life only as a game, and to them, the main thing is to have a good time. They seek one form of entertainment after another; from movies to sports, to the latest in computer games, there are myriad distractions guaranteed to numb and anesthetise hearts and minds. In the not-too-distant past, people took walks to clear their heads, but such introspective moments are relics of the past. Today, when people walk and jog, cell phones and iPods accompany them - all filtering out reality. One cannot help but wonder what would happen if all movie theatres, television stations, sports stadiums, computers and iPods were shut down for one day. For those to whom life is simply a game, distractions become necessities: tools to escape reality.

But the 'high' of acquisition, quickly palls and life becomes purposeless. Long ago, the *Torah* admonished us "not by bread alone does man live."[1] If we do not see that which emanates from God and instead take solace only in artificial stimuli, be it shopping, a pill, a drink or drugs we are robbed of the essence of our lives.

So what is life?

From the Torah we learn that the definitive metaphor for life is a test. God tested the patriarch Abraham on ten different occasions, and he passed each time. Today God continues to test each and every one of us. These tests are custom-made, designed with our unique needs in mind, so that we might discover and fulfil the higher purpose for which He created us.

From the moment we are born, to the day that God finally calls us, we are tested. These tests come in many shapes and forms - the way we relate to God, our parents, teachers, neighbours, co-workers, even to a clerk in a store or a fellow driver on the road. These tests reflect the genuineness of our commitment, the depth of our faith and the measure of our character.

But why test us at all? A physician tests his patients to determine the nature of their illness, and a teacher in order to evaluate progress. But, an all-knowing God Who sees and is familiar with even the most secret machinations of our hearts - why does He have to test us?

Simply, because although our Creator knows us, the problem is that we do not know our own selves, our own potential. We have no understanding of the energy that God planted within our souls, therefore God has to test us to bring forth those treasures that are buried deep within ourselves and make us unique.

In the 'University on High,' even little things count - things that we would normally consider innocuous and insignificant. For instance, when we wake up in the morning and have a mental tug of war over whether we should get up and pray, or linger in bed just a little bit longer. After all, we reason, our little prayer won't make a difference; it won't really matter to God whether we pray or not. In any event, God would certainly want us to take care of ourselves and protect our health. But how much sleep do we really need?

The Yetzer Hara - that little voice inside us that seeks to entice and divert us from passing our test and fulfilling our higher purpose - will cunningly persuade us that we need "just a few minutes more." "A few more hours" we would reject out of hand, but a few minutes more seems reasonable enough, so we succumb. We allow ourselves to be seduced and shut our eyes for those few minutes more, but those few minutes turn into many minutes and sometimes even a lifetime. Because often one failure can lead to another and we don't realise that we are being tested and failing. To be sure, every once in a while, people may sense a void in their lives - something is missing, but they don't quite know what, and with renewed zeal, immerse themselves in metaphors, hoping that they will provide the relief they seek as life passes by.

But the good news is that it's never impossible to overcome that little voice and get off the merry-go-round. Even if we stumble occasionally, we can pass the tests that Life throws our way.

All this applies equally to relationships. They are equally a test and we need to invest in them for them to work and be aware that the same destructive inclination can make itself felt. Desire is a magnificent gift, to enhance love and marriage. But as with all-powerful gifts it must be handled with care. If it is confused with passion, often only after much emotional pain does the couple realise that they have little in common, leaving them with deep scars.

Equally, marriages don't go sour over the things that transpire at the United Nations or in Parliament. But they do become battlefields over little things, which in the end are not so little. To share a relationship, both partners need to be on the same page spiritually and emotionally, which requires an honest evaluation, not least of yourself.

No one can hope to live life without difficulties, but they take on a very different shape when we recognise that overcoming those tests will allow us to grow into greater people. Because the greatness of man is ultimately measured not by knowledge or wealth, but by the tests he passes.

Notes:
1 Deuteronomy 8:3

ISRAEL IN 1978

- Menachem Begin and Anwar Sadat are awarded the Nobel Peace Prize for their efforts in bringing understanding and peace between Israel and Egypt
- Michael Herziano sets up a factory in Arad to increase production of his game Rummikub
- Israel wins the Eurovision song contest with the song 'Abanibi' performed by Izhar Cohen & The Alpha Beta

In memory of Esther and Sonny Levine.

32   A Divine Document

Daniel Rowe

Is our *Torah* an exact verbal record of God's words to Moses 3,320 years ago? Or is it, as theorists argue, an ancient text that has evolved as other ancient documents have? At an academic level, Hebrew University and Bar Ilan University have dedicated substantial research to this field, especially regarding the 'documentary hypothesis'.

This line of thinking (the documentary hypothesis) was formulated by Julius Wellhausen in the 19th century.[1] He stated that since the Torah contains several different names of God, as well as several literary styles, four different authors must have been involved. He argued that these authors wrote at varying times over a period of four centuries (950 BCE to 500 BCE) and were followed a century later by a final editor.

In response to this theory, a number of great Western European orthodox Jewish scholars including Rabbi Samson Raphael Hirsch, Rabbi Dr. Dovid Zvi Hoffmann and the Malbim produced systematic and extensive works which dealt comprehensively with the questions put forward by Wellhausen and earlier critics.[2]

They demonstrated that the issues raised by Welhausen had been fully addressed by the established Jewish commentators throughout the ages. They further argued that the secular critics often failed to understand the crucial role played by the Oral Law in the proper understanding and study of Biblical text, and that any attempt to analyse the written Torah as a completely independent text was certain to lead to flawed conclusions. It would be equivalent to a reading of the shorthand notes of a lecture, without attending the presentation.

Nevertheless, Wellhausen's hypothesis became the dominant view in academic circles for several decades, causing many Jews to doubt the veracity of Judaism and leading many to sever their ties with Judaism altogether.

The dispute over the origin of the text of the Torah was therefore far more than a theoretical question, given that it was this Divine text that made man submissive to God. It would take some time before the Rabbinical refutations became a part of mainstream thinking.

One of the first academic acclaimed works that attacked the documentary hypothesis was that of Umberto Cassuto who felt able to assert:

"I have not [simply] shown that it was possible to solve the problem in a different way from that of the documentary theory. I have shown that one must necessarily solve them otherwise and that it is impossible to solve them according to this [Documentary Hypothesis] system. I did not prove that the pillars are weak, I have proved that they are not pillars at all, that they are non-existent and imaginary."[3]

By the late 20th century, the documentary theory had finally fallen from mainstream acceptance, and though there are dozens of alternative (and often radically contradictory) hypotheses, no one theory has achieved universal acceptance.[4] It is important to examine some of the key reasons for the downfall of the documentary model.

The hypothesis was based on alleged textual inconsistencies, particularly the different names of God used throughout the Biblical text. The inconsistency argument was always subjective in nature and was dealt a strong blow in 1985, when advances in computer research allowed a programme at the Technion Institute to analyse variations in literary style in Genesis and compare them with the variations in style of works of single authors of the same length. The result showed far less variation in the book of Genesis than in the other works!

As for the argument that differing names of God somehow implied differing textual antecedents, the entire argument simply ignored the existence of other Near Eastern documents that are incontrovertibly of single-authorship and that use different names for the same god![5] More importantly, it overlooked Jewish tradition, which has long understood the different names to reflect differing manifestations – much as a single human may variously go by John', 'Mr. Smith', 'Sir', and 'Daddy', depending on the context of their appearance.

When God is manifest as the Infinite Creative Will, who loves, shares, creates and gives, the four letter name (HaShem) is used. When God is more hidden, and is manifest only in justice or in the laws of nature and in the patterns of history – the name Elokim is used.[6] When God is manifest in the totality of relationship, both names are used - both the veil of nature and the loving Source within.[7]

Once examined in this light, the precision and consistency of the Torah text itself ultimately renders unrealistic the notion that these Divine names once represented totally alternative religious traditions that were somehow merged into one.[8]

Wellhausen's theory also involved the existence of an editor. This editor, he argued, arranged passages and altered sentences a century after the last additions in an attempt to prevent detection of the fusion of the four editions. This rather convenient assumption enabled Wellhausen to support his theory irrespective of the verses in question: if a verse pointed towards multiple authorship, he could treat this as proof of the human origins of the Torah, whereas if a verse pointed to single authorship he could treat this as the work of the editor trying to hide the multiple authorship!

Other than the documentary hypothesis, known as 'higher criticism', other forms of criticism ('lower criticism') assume ancient texts such as the Torah to have evolved through copying errors, scribal editing, etc. Many ancient texts clearly have evolved with recent versions strongly diverging from originals.[9] Nevertheless, whilst there are some divergent Torah texts, the majority of those found, throughout antiquity, are virtually identical to our own.[10]

For centuries the Jewish people have spared no effort in order to preserve the absolute integrity of the Torah. When Yemenite Jews arrived in Israel in the 1950s they brought Torah scrolls of their own. They had been in little contact with world Jewry for 2,000 or more years. Yet when their Torah was compared, they found only nine letters differed, out of 304,805. Of these nine letters only one of them altered (slightly) the meaning of a single word!

By comparison, the New Testament which is more recent than Torah, and whose communities have undergone far less persecution than Jews, has thousands of letter differences, and hundreds that are very significant.[11]

Other critics have claimed that various ancient documents appear to resemble Torah law, and so assert that Torah has been copied, directly or indirectly, from them. One example is the Hammurabi Code,[12] which critics claim could be the origin of parts of the book of Exodus.[13] However, closer examination reveals this theory to be equally unfounded. The area of strongest alleged correlation (Exodus 21-23) discusses 38 laws. Of these, 14 are not discussed in the Hammurabi Code, 13 differ totally and only 4 are identical!

But the clearest difference of all is in the underlying philosophical principles upon which the documents are founded. The Hammurabi Code appears to be a vengeance code. By contrast, Torah law forbids taking revenge, or even bearing a grudge. Torah law instead seeks to place the responsibility for rectifying damage upon the aggressor. The difference is highly significant in explaining the differences in law.

There are other ideological differences too. The Hammurabi Code distinguishes the value of a person's life according to which strata of society they belong to, whereas Torah law repeatedly emphasises legal equality. The Torah repeatedly instructs social responsibility - for the poor, the widow, the orphan and the stranger. The Hammurabi Code is devoid of moral instruction.

The Torah's value system is so radically different to anything on offer in the ancient world as to render claims of copying implausible. In a world where ancient societies practiced infanticide, the Torah proclaimed a universal right to life. Where warriors were heroes and conquest a mark of valour, the Torah taught mankind to strive for peace and prescribed universal literacy.

In conclusion, the Torah remains the Divine document that has always served as both the foundation of Judaism, and the essential link between a living people and their homeland. Wellhausen's criticism has been employed by many who seek to undermine the connection of Israel to her eternal homeland.[14]

To the Jew, Torah has always been the love-letter that cemented the relationship between mankind and God. It allows man, from the depths of exile and despair, to reach out to the Above, and to keep alive the dream of a return to a homeland. There we can begin, once again, to live the vision of the people of Israel in the Land of Israel.

Notes:

1 Welhausen published many works, the best known being his *Prolegomena zur Geschichte Israels* of 1883, in which his theory of four original documents and a later redactor is discussed.

2 The original form of the documentary hypothesis can be traced to Jean Astruc 1753.

3 Cassuto's *The Documentary Hypothesis and the Composition of the Pentateuch* rejected both the central idea of the documentary model and Wellhausen's dating.

4 Other theorists include H. H. Schmid, Rolf Rendtorff, Erhard Blum and Thomas L. Thompson. The fact that scholars can look at the same text with radically opposing interpretations must minimally indicate that there is nothing

about the text itself that offers any clear indication of fixed original texts from which ours evolved.

5 For instance in Babylonian mythological literature the sun god 'Shamash' is also 'Babber' whilst 'Aruru' has four names.

6 The very name Elokim shares its Hebrew 'gematria' (numerical value) with the word 'hateva' – the totality of natural law.

7 Thus in the unfolding of creation, only the name Elokim is used: God as is manifest in nature (Gen 1:1-2:3). When man becomes the focus in the second chapter the double name of totality of relationship becomes central (2:4-3:1). When the serpent seeks to prise mankind from God he employs only the name Elokim: God as distant, and man replies in kind, eating from the forbidden fruit and wrenching himself away from the presence of God (3:1-3:7). As God offers to re-engage in relationship, again the double name is used. But man hides, and must be ejected from the Edenic core into the outer layers of creation when he exists as homo-sapiens. (3:8-3:23)
Whenever man reconnects with God the double name is used. Thus at the fullness of revelation at mount Sinai it is the two names that are employed together. But as man again recoils from God at the golden calf, it is only the name of distance that is spoken of. And so the pattern continues throughout Torah.

8 Professor Y. Kaufmann proved that Monotheism did not originate from any surrounding cultures as was supposed by Bible critics, but was solely an original creation of the people of Israel.

9 Significant examples include the New Testament and the Iliad of Homer.

10 Most ancient scrolls that do diverge derive from non-

Rabbinic communities such as Essenes and Samaritans. The Rabbinic / 'Masoretic' version is more or less totally uniform throughout the historical record. Even at Qumran (where the most ancient scrolls have been found) where the sect in control had theological differences to classical Judaism, the majority of scrolls are as ours.

11 For an easy-to-access discussion of 1,500 of these, see http://www-user.uni-bremen.de/~wie/TCG/index.html

12 The Code of Hammurabi is one of the earliest known legal systems, created c. 1760 BCE. The code was engraved on an 8ft stone that today can be found in the Louvre in Paris.

13 See eg Chilperic Edwards, *The World's Earliest Laws*

14 For instance, Dr. Jarir Al-Qidwah, P.A. Television, August 2, 2004, "Solomon's Temple, I believe, was built by the Canaanites... The issue of the temple is a Zionist innovation. No one said that the temple that was built in Jerusalem, neither the Canaanite nor Roman, no one said that it was in the place of the [Islamic] Al Haram."

ISRAEL IN 1979
- Israel and Egypt sign a peace treaty bringing to an end 30 years of hostility
- The town of El-Arish is returned to Egypt after 12 years under Israeli control
- 'Halleluyah' performed by Milk & Honey becomes the second Israeli song to win the Eurovision song contest
- The first PC anti-virus software is manufactured in Israel

In loving memory of Suzi Bradfield a"h.

33 Pride in our Judaism

Chief Rabbi Sir Jonathan Sacks

Once, when I was a child, my family was on holiday in a little coastal town in England. It was *Shabbat* and we had just left the synagogue. Behind us, another member of the congregation came rushing up and pointed to the *yarmulka* I was wearing. He said to my father, "Your son has forgotten to take his yarmulka off." This was in the days when it was not done to wear overt signs of your Jewishness in public. The old dictum, "Be a Jew at home and a man in the street" was still in force. By walking down the road with my head covering I was committing a solecism, and our friend from the synagogue assumed, not unnaturally, that I was unaware of it. He meant it kindly. He was simply trying to save me from embarrassment, much as if my shirttail had been hanging out. For once my father got angry and replied, "No child of mine will ever be ashamed to be Jewish in public." And we continued on our way. It was not a very tactful response, but it taught me - as perhaps no more formal lesson could - never to be ashamed of who I was.

Another incident occurred many years later, when I had finished university and was teaching philosophy. At that time, most of my other colleagues were Marxists. Some were Jewish, most not, but almost all were irreligious or anti-religious. In those days I had no thought of eventually becoming a rabbi, but the lesson of my childhood had stayed with me enough to make me wear my *yarmulka* at all times. One particularly windy day, as I was crossing the playing fields, it blew off and instead of putting it back, I carried it until I reached the lecture room.

The next day the head of the department summoned me. "Is everything all right, Jonathan?" he asked.

"Yes", I replied, puzzled by his question.

"It's just that I saw you yesterday crossing the playing field not wearing your skullcap, and I wondered whether anything had happened."

It was an astonishing moment. I suddenly realised that though he was not Jewish, he was deeply troubled at the thought that I might be losing my faith – whether out of philosophical doubt or the sheer isolation of being the only religious Jew on campus. I don't know if even now I fully understand his reaction, but I think it meant that my being true to my faith was part of the security of his world. He was neither religious nor Jewish, but in some obscure way it helped him to know that there were people who were both, and if I gave up, something larger was giving way.

Since then I have encountered these phenomena so many times, that I am tempted to assert them in the form of two principles which, if not always true, are true more often than not: *Non-Jews respect Jews who respect Judaism, and they are embarrassed by Jews who are embarrassed by Judaism.*

Ambivalence is bad for us, for those who relate to us and above all for our children. And ambivalence has been writ large in the identity of Jews for the last two centuries. An entire literature, Jewish and non-Jewish, testifies to it. Perhaps it was inevitable, given the double bind of emancipation. Jews, embarrassed to be Jews, resolved the tension by keeping the lowest possible profile. As Sidney Morganbesser wittily put it, the Jewish maxim was *Incognito, ergo sum,* "I am invisible, therefore I am."

Ambivalence spells the end of an identity because it cannot be passed on to our children. They will seek, for their own psychic health, to escape from it; and that in effect is what a whole generation is doing by leaving Judaism. It is a tragedy, and not only for ourselves. For as long as Jews are Jews, they contribute something unique to the intellectual, spiritual and moral life of society.

Therefore pride is always a healthier response than shame. Some years ago a rabbi told me of an episode that happened to him in Russia. *Glasnost* was in its early days. For the first time in 70 years Jews were free to practise Judaism openly. He had gone there to help in the revival of Jewish life. He discovered, as many did at that time, that "openness" meant also that antisemitism could be more freely expressed. One day a young woman came to him in distress. All her life, she said, she had hidden the fact that she was a Jew, and she still did. Now, though, for the first time, her neighbours muttered *Zhid* ("Jew") when she passed. What could she do? The rabbi thought, then said this. "If you had not come to me with your story I would have no way of knowing that you are a Jew. But when I walk in the street, people can see I am a Jew. I wear a yarmulka. I look like a rabbi. Yet in all the months I have been here, no one has said to me Zhid. Why do you think that is?" The girl took a minute to reflect, then said, "Because they know that if they call me 'Jew' I will take it as an insult. But if they call you 'Jew' you will take it as a compliment."

There is all the difference in the world between pride and arrogance. Arrogance diminishes others, and therefore diminishes us. Pride values others because we have learned to value ourselves.

I learned this lesson from an old Israeli boatman in Eilat. We had gone there, my wife and I, to find the sun after a cold northern winter. Eilat is hot but bleak, set in the desert among brown and barren hills. There is not much to do there, so one morning we decided to go out in one of the glass bottomed boats, through which you can see the multicoloured fish that swim in Eilat's waters. We were the only passengers on that trip.

The captain overheard us talking and rushed over to us. "*Atem me-Anglia?.*" "Are you from England?"

"Yes," we said. Why did he want to know?

"Ah," he said, "I have just come back from a holiday there."

What did he think of England?

"Wonderful! The grass – so green! The buildings – so old! The people so polite!" And then a vast smile filled his face, and he spread his arms and looked around him at the barren desert hills and said, with an air of infinite delight, "*Aval zeh shelanu*" – "But this is ours."

Then I knew what it is to be a Jew. There are other cultures, other peoples, other faiths. *But this is ours.* This is our faith, our people, and our heritage. By loving them, I learn to love humanity in its diversity. At peace with myself, I find peace with the world.

(This essay is an edited extract from the book Radical Then, Radical Now, *published by Continuum.)*

ISRAEL IN 1980
- Shimon Peres beats Yitzhak Rabin in the race for leadership of the Labour party with 70% of the vote
- A team based at the Hebrew University of Jerusalem creates ExLibris an automated multilingual library system, which today powers the British Library
- The Israeli Lira changes its name to the Shekel

In honour of Rabbi Yisrael Meir Lau for his dedication to the welfare of Jews both in Israel and in the diaspora.

34 A New Look at the Shemoneh Esrei

Emanuel Feldman

Although we can turn to God and pray to Him spontaneously at any time and in any language, there are three times each day when prayer is required. At these times, whether as part of a congregation or praying alone, the Jew stands and, wherever they are in the world, faces towards Jerusalem and whispers a prayer; acknowledging God and petitioning Him for the basic needs of his physical and spiritual life. This is the *Shemoneh Esrei,* the climactic prayer of the morning, afternoon and night-time services.

This prayer is known by several names: the Shemoneh Esrei (the eighteen); the *Amidah* (the standing); and *HaTefillah* (the Prayer). In fact, it embodies all three names. It originally contained 18 blessings – expanded to 19 after the destruction of the Temple, to include a prayer for protection against heretical Jewish sects. It is also the Amidah, because one is required to stand while reciting it; and it is *the* prayer par excellence.

Times
The three Patriarchs established the three times for daily prayer.[1] They also correspond to the daily offerings and service in the Temple.

Abraham best represents morning, the dawning of a new

day. Through him and because of him, the idea of one God began to spread throughout the ancient world. The service he established mirrors his life and begins each new day: *Shacharit* - which takes its name from the Hebrew *shachar* meaning dawn.

Isaac represents the afternoon service - *Minchah*. The bright sun of the morning begins its gradual, imperceptible descent into darkness, and soon the world around us disappears. Ever since the *Akeidah*, his near-sacrifice by his own father at Mount Moriah, Isaac has become an other-worldly figure, unattached to the ordinary physical world. For him, this world has disappeared. He moves from place to place in his own land, while his blindness separates him further from mundane, transient things. He is the bridge between the morning of Abraham and the unending darkness of his own son Jacob. Isaac is *Minchah*, which can be recited from the afternoon until night.

Jacob is *Ma'ariv*, the evening service. He is very much in this world, but his life is one long series of difficulties. Already in his mother's womb he is engaged with his brother Esau in the unending struggle for spiritual dominance. He flees from Esau's murderous wrath, works slavishly for the devious Laban; his daughter Dinah is assaulted by Shechem; his sons do not trust his favourite, Joseph; his beloved Rachel dies in childbirth; and then Joseph vanishes for 22 years. Despite all this, his faith in God never wavers. He is the living fusion of the path established by his grandfather Abraham - spreading the word of God to mankind; and the path of his father Isaac - always attempting to focus on higher truths. Although on the surface Jacob is the wanderer and sufferer of night-time, he represents the continuity and eternity of the people Israel. Hence the Ma'ariv prayer can be recited all through the night until the next dawn. Similarly, Jacob represents the preparation for the new day when God will be recognised by all mankind, and when "He will be One and His name will be One."[2]

Structure

The Shemoneh Esrei is exquisitely structured. Modelled on the magnificent silent prayer of Hannah[3], mother of the prophet Samuel, it begins with words of praise that establish the sovereignty of God, His greatness and power and His mastery over the universe – as is customary when entering the palace of the Monarch. This is followed by petitionary prayers which ask for all our basic needs as individuals – such as wisdom, health, prosperity – and our collective needs as a member of the Jewish people – such as Messianic redemption, ingathering of the exiles, and peace. There is even an all-inclusive paragraph in which we ask God to heed our prayers and in which we may insert any personal supplications.

After making requests, it is fitting for us to express gratitude before departing. Therefore, the Amidah ends with an expression of gratitude to the Creator and acknowledgment of His goodness.

True prayer, of course, is not only petitionary. It is more than making requests of heaven. Prayer establishes a connection between us and our Creator, and creates within us attitudes of humility. It acknowledges that we are imperfect and in need of divine assistance.

Baruch

A word about a certain word: perhaps the best known term in Jewish prayer: *baruch*, as in *baruch atah*. Every blessing, from the blessing for food to the blessing for Shabbat candles, begins with this word. So too in the Amidah, each of the 19 paragraphs contains a brief blessing that begins with the word *baruch*.

If *baruch* is the most widely used term in Hebrew prayer, it is also the most widely mistranslated. The normative translation is: "Blessed art Thou…." But when addressing the Creator, what can that mean? All blessing emanates from Him. Is it not ludicrous for mortals to say to Him, "You are blessed?" Who are we to bless him? With what can we possibly bless him? Clearly, that word *baruch* requires another look.

Two cognate words help clarify its meaning. The Hebrew word for a pool of water is *breichah*. A *breichah* supplies a constant flow of water. It is the source of sustenance for living. When we utter *baruch* to our Creator, we are thus acknowledging that He is the constant source of our lives, the wellspring of our sustenance.

One other word defines *baruch*, and that is the Hebrew word *berech*, which means knee. The bent knee is the symbol of submission, "For to Thee will every knee bend."[4] *Baruch atah* thus means, in effect, that You are the one to whom all creatures submit.

Kavannah

One major element in prayer transcends all else, and that is the need for *kavannah,* which literally means intention or direction - directing our words to God Himself. Prayer without kavannah is like a body without a soul. Kavannah is the very opposite of repeating words by rote, or of mumbling them in a mechanical, perfunctory way. Praying with kavannah means that we concentrate on what we are doing, and remember that we are standing before the Divine Presence. That is what the Torah means when commanding us to serve God with all our heart.

May the Amidah's closing petition be fulfilled in our lives, "Let the words of my mouth and the meditation of my heart find favour before Thee."

Notes:
1 Talmud Bavli, Berachot 26b
2 Zechariah 14:9
3 I Samuel 1:15
4 Isaiah 45:23

ISRAEL IN 1981
- The Israeli Air Force destroys Iraq's fledgling nuclear reactor
- Intel Israel puts itself on the map by creating a cheaper version of Intel's 8086 processor renamed the 8088, IBM chooses the chip to power its first personal computer
- Hebrew University develops a biological agent to control soil-borne plant diseases

In memory of our father and grandfather
R' Elozor ben R' Chaim, who was a positive influence
on so many lives. Dedicated by Family Hersh.

35 Delivering in Dallas

Paysach Krohn

In 1983, Rabbi Aryeh Rodin, a graduate of *Yeshiva* Chofetz Chaim in New York, assumed the spiritual leadership of the newly formed Young Israel of Dallas, Texas. He gave lectures to the community at large, and through his sincerity and warmth was responsible for a number of families becoming more knowledgeable and committed in their Judaism.

Rabbi Rodin was in his office one day, when a gentleman he had never seen before walked in. "Rabbi," he said in a deep Texan drawl, "can I have a word with you?"

"Sure," said Rabbi Rodin. "Please sit down."

"My name is Leonard Fruhman," the man began, extending Rabbi Rodin a very firm handshake. Leonard and the rabbi started talking and after a while Leonard said, "I would like to make a contribution to your synagogue."

Rabbi Rodin was somewhat taken aback. People do not normally walk in off the street and donate money to a synagogue they're not associated with, without being asked, pressured, or honoured. He was even more surprised when Mr. Fruhman told him the check would be for $2,000. "I don't have any checks with me," said Leonard with an easy smile, "but I will be back next week. You can count on that, Rabbi."

Rabbi Rodin returned the smile and wished Leonard well. In his heart though, he was convinced that this was the first and last time he would see Leonard. After all $2,000 was a substantial amount of money for anyone to give, especially for someone with little or no affiliation to Judaism. He assumed that Leonard would rethink his pledge and decide he had been too generous.

Against all odds Leonard did return the next week with a cheque, although it was not for $2,000, it was for $3,000! "I thought about our conversation throughout the week, Rabbi, and I liked what you told me," Leonard said with enthusiasm, "so I increased the amount I am giving."

Rabbi Rodin was speechless. When he regained his composure, he began a serious conversation with Leonard and soon realized that Leonard was very committed to searching for meaning in his life. The two men embarked on a long and warm relationship, which soon encompassed other members of Leonard's family, as well. When the rabbi moved to Far North Dallas to establish Congregation Ohev Shalom, Leonard came along. Tragically, Leonard passed away at the untimely age of 49 and his mother and family committed to rebuilding and renovating the Ohev Sholom Synagogue, in his memory. In a moving eulogy, given at Leonard's *shloshim*, a memorial held 30 days after his passing, Rabbi Rodin told the following remarkable story.

In 1986, Leonard made his first trip ever to Israel. He was determined to see all the sights. One morning he went to the *Kotel*, the holy wall, where Jews the world over, come to pray. Unfamiliar with the conventional text of prayers, Leonard walked up to the massive wall, respectfully put his right hand on the stones and slowly caressed them. Leonard closed his eyes and in silent prayer, expressed to God his innermost yearnings.

After a while Leonard became aware of a religious Jew standing to his right, totally immersed in prayer. Wrapped in his tallit, the fellow was swaying gently to and fro, his eyes glued to the worn pages of his *Tehillim* (Psalms). Every once in a while, the Jew would close his eyes, raise his hands to Heaven and sigh. As Leonard observed him, he noticed the rhapsody on his face, the peaceful bliss of a man connecting with his Maker. Leonard was overcome by a sense of spirituality he had never felt before. He wished he could experience that bond between man and his Creator. If only he could touch it, feel it, or bottle it.

He left the Kotel uplifted and strengthened, but in a sense, empty. Suddenly the Judaism he hadn't been close to meant more to him than ever before. The experience stayed with him for the remainder of his trip in the Holy Land.

When he returned to Dallas, Leonard went into a kosher bakery. He told the owner about his trip to Israel and described his emotional experience at the Kotel. "Tell me," Leonard said earnestly, "What synagogue in town do you think that man at the wall would feel comfortable praying in?"

The reply came promptly, "In Rabbi Rodin's synagogue."

And that is how Leonard's friendship and generosity with the Orthodox community began.

Rabbi Rodin paused and then said with emphasis. "Imagine for a moment the scene, when that religious Jew who was praying at the Kotel, comes to Heaven after his prescribed years in this world are complete. God will inform him that he is about to be rewarded for being instrumental in maintaining and refurbishing a synagogue in Dallas. The fellow might never have heard of Dallas, and if he did, he certainly wouldn't know where to find it. Yet, because he prayed the way he did, where he did, he was instrumental in helping a Jewish community thousands of miles away. And his reward in the World to Come will be immense."

"Consider therefore, the responsibility we have for each of our actions. Could the religious Jew at the Kotel ever imagine that donations to charity would be made only because of him?"

Even if we are unaware of it, we have done a lot more with our lives than we actually realise – both positive and negative – through our influence on other people. What we do and say has an effect on others even if it is sometimes only months or years later and all of us carry around certain memories that stick out in our minds, long after the people involved have forgotten them – which makes us duty-bound to think before we act.

ISRAEL IN 1982

- The first Lebanon War
- Israel's first test-tube baby is born - a 3.78kg baby is born to a 32-year-old woman who has been married for 12 years
- Tel Aviv University research forms the basis for the infectious disease diagnostics company Orgenics, its "HIV system" is used by the World Health Organisation for its global campaign against AIDS

In memory of Esther and Danny Kaplan.

36 Chanukah: Accepting Others

YY Rubinstein

Chanukah celebrates an event which took place over two thousand years ago. Alexander the Great had conquered most of the known world. The Land of Israel became a part of the new Greek empire. Alexander's rule was benign. He was quite happy to allow his subjects to practice whichever religion they choose. His successors were not. The religion of the Empire had to be the Greeks' religion. Everyone was accepted and *acceptable...* as Greeks. Judaism was to be stamped out.

There could have been no position more calculated to provoke Jewish revolt than that. So the Jews rose and defeated the Greeks, liberating the Holy Temple in Jerusalem, which had been turned into a shrine.

All the Jewish symbols as well as the altar had been removed or despoiled. So the Jews set about restoring their holiest site to its original purpose and appearance. The Temple's *menorah*, its golden candelabra, was re-lit but only enough of the consecrated oil could be found to last one day, yet it burned for eight. God saluted the Jew's fight with a miracle.

In Jewish windowsills or porches you see one light burning to be joined the next night by another and another until eight flickering flames recall and strengthen an age old Jewish conviction, a people's right to be themselves.

The notion of creating identity is true today as well. Very often I have come across young Jews from non-religious backgrounds, who have gone on in their own lives, to keep many of the laws and traditions that the Jews of Chanukah fought for. And because of that, both family and friends feel upset and rejected.

The newly religious Jew may well want to maintain their friendships but because they've changed and no longer go to non-kosher restaurants or play sports on the Sabbath, his or her old buddies sometimes end their friendships.

But truthfully it's a peculiar sort of friendship that says you will be my friend as long as you are just like me. As long as you share my views and tastes, then friends we are and friends we will stay. But if you change and I no longer see myself when I look at you, then you can't be my friend.

Obviously most friendships start as a result of people discovering they have things in common. But friendship is enriched when it realises that there is much to be discovered from people who have different views and see the world differently. These people and their different ways of doing things have made positive differences to the way that *we* do things.

One of Judaism's holiest books tells a story of a rabbi who was riding along on horse, when he passed a very ugly looking man. The rabbi was revolted by the fellow's appearance and actually spoke his thoughts aloud, "What an ugly fellow."

The man heard the rabbi's words and shouted after him, "Take your complaint to the One who made me this way."

The rabbi was startled and the man approached him and shouted again, "Go on, take your complaint to the one who made me this way, tell God you don't approve of His design, give Him a real telling off."

The rabbi was thoroughly ashamed. God has made us all different. It's through our differences that we are meant to serve Him.

Yet that doesn't mean that I need to focus on other people to find who I am. As Rabbi Menachem Mendel of Kotzk once said, "If I am I because I am I, and you are you because you are you, then I am I and you are you. But if I am I because you are you, and you are you because I am I, then I am not I and you are not you." God salutes us when we are a friend to, and accepting of, others as long as we are true to ourselves.

So at Chanukah when we say a prayer that thanks God, "*Al ha nisim sh'asisah l'avoseinu bayomim hahem baz'man hazeh*", "for the miracles You did in those days at this time," we light the candles, to symbolise how our identity today is based on those precious ideas of old – our right to be ourselves.

CHANUKAH IN ISRAEL

The Chanukah experience in Israel is unique. Living in Israel we easily identify with the life of Judah Maccabee, the religious warrior hero whose small Jewish army defeated the many.

Most people here light their channukiot outdoors, so that from any balcony you can see hundreds of lights across the city. Occasionally you even see bus drivers waiting for people to finish lighting their candles so they can answer Amen. And of course, it's also the time of year when sufganiyot (doughnuts) make their annual appearance.

ISRAEL IN 1983

- Israel takes part in a prisoner exchange, with the release of 4,765 terrorists in return for six soldiers who were being held in Lebanon
- The Egged bus company, founded in 1933, celebrates its 50th year
- Rehov Sumsum, Israel's version of Sesame Street, airs on the educational television channel with its American Big Bird equivalent as a hedgehog named Kippi Ben-Kippod and its Oscar the Grouch as Moishe Ofnik

In memory of Rabbi Shmuli Kass zt"l, a gifted
and passionate educator.
Dedicated by Tribe and the United Synagogue.

37 King David: Our First and Greatest C.E.O.

Menachem Leibtag

I realise that this title for King David may sound a bit bizarre. After all, he was a man of virtue, a fearless warrior, a righteous poet (the Psalmist), and a great King. So why do I refer to him as a C.E.O. [Chief Executive Officer]?

Allow me to explain by analogy. Take, for example, a modern day hi-tech company. It can have a bold mission statement, hire and train the most skilled employees, and acquire the newest technologies. However, it remains the responsibility of the C.E.O. to tie everything together – to ensure a successful product.

Similarly, the nation of Israel was charged by God with a bold mission statement – to establish a model nation, living by the highest ethical standards and to then bring the Name of God to all mankind. Towards these goals, God redeemed His people from slavery and guided them through the desert, thus training them for their important mission. At Mount Sinai, He charged them with the *Torah* – the newest 'technology' of laws, designed to guide their national and individual behaviour.

However, after the conquest of the Land by Joshua, this goal was still unfulfilled. As the Book of Judges attests, Israel was often at war with its neighbours, its borders constantly shrinking. Plagued with idol worship and suffering from a leadership crisis, God's special nation did not attain any level of international recognition or respect.

Enter King David: our first C.E.O.

Thanks to his brilliant leadership, he turned the nation around. Within several decades the people of Israel were following God's laws properly, reaching their widest borders, and achieving an economic prosperity that earned them the respect of all their neighbours.

What was the key to his success?

The Book of Samuel alludes to a key element of his reign – which later becomes synonymous with the 'House of David'. In its brief summary of these golden years of King David's reign, the prophet Samuel carefully chooses two words to describe this success, "And David reigned over all of Israel, and David executed *justice and righteousness* (*'tzedek u'mishpat'*) among all his people."[1]

The prophet's choice of these specific words is not by chance, for it is these very same two Hebrew words that we find in Genesis, when the Torah explains God's mission statement for which He chose Abraham. "For I have come to know him – that he will command his children, and their children, to follow the way of God – which is to do justice and righteousness (*tzedek u'mishpat*)."[2]

King David is the first leader who enables the nation of Israel to achieve their Biblical goal. A nation, gaining the respect of the international community, known for its national character of performing 'justice and righteousness', and affirming God's Name publicly.

To support this point, note these very same words in the special Psalm that King David wrote for his son Solomon:

"God – endow the king with your *mishpat*
and your *tzedek* to the king's son.
that he may judge Your people rightly...
Let all kings bow to him, and all nations serve him –
for he saves the needy who cry out,
and the lowly who have no helper..."[3]

These aspirations come true, within a decade of King

Solomon's reign, as the Book of Kings records, "The Queen of Sheba heard of the fame of Solomon in the Name of God..."[4] Amazed by what she sees during her royal visit, note the concluding words of her farewell blessing, "The report that I heard about your kingdom is true... Praised be the Lord your God who delighted in you and set you on the throne of Israel... and made you king to do *tzedek u'mishpat* (justice and righteousness).[5]

Israel had become a "light to the nations." Israel's mission statement had been fulfilled.[6]

It is because King David became the first leader to accomplish this goal, that in the eyes of the Rabbis and the Prophets, he is known as the quintessential Messiah.

For example, note how the prophet Jeremiah describes the nature of the messianic era, "A time is coming – declares the Lord – when I will establish a true branch of the House of David. He shall reign as King and shall prosper by doing *tzedek u'mishpat* in the land. In his days Judah shall be redeemed, and Israel shall dwell secure..."[7]

Three thousand years have passed since the time of King David, and during the last two thousand years, the people of Israel have dwelt in Exile. However, with the help of Divine Providence, a Jewish state has once again been established. The Biblical stories about King David can certainly inspire Israel's brave soldiers, its righteous *Yeshiva* students, and its fledgling poets. But more so, the Biblical theme of King David, our first C.E.O., must serve as a guide to Israel's political leaders, to inspire them to help establish a society, as King David did, known to the entire world not only for its prosperity and culture, but more so for its aspirations towards the values of justice and righteousness.

Thus the words of Isaiah, read every year on the *Shabbat* prior to *tisha b'av* as we contemplate the destruction of our Temple: "Zion will be redeemed through *mishpat*, and its repentant ones through *tzedakah*."[8]

Finally, it is also worth noting that in the silent prayer (the *Amidah*) there is a blessing which requests a CEO worthy of leading the Jewish people. This blessing ends with the title of God as the King who loves *tzedakah u'mishpat*.

Notes:
1 II Samuel 8:15
2 Genesis 18:18-19
3 Psalm 72
4 I Kings 10:1
5 I Kings 10:6-9
6 Isaiah 42:5-6
7 Jeremiah 23:5-6
8 Isaiah1:27

ISRAEL IN 1984
- IDF soldiers rescue 25 passengers on board an Egged bus hijacked by terrorists on its way from Tel-Aviv to Ashkelon
- The world's first commercial solar power plant, SEGS I, is installed in California by the Israeli company Luz, and starts producing electric power
- The New Shekel replaces the Shekel at the rate of 1000:1
- The Israeli phone company Bezeq is founded

38   Jewish identity:
Let's make it positive!

James Kennard

Jewish history appears to be punctuated by seemingly countless episodes of victimisation and oppression. The Babylonians, who destroyed the first Temple and thousands of Jews with it, gave way to Persians, Greeks and finally Romans, who crushed the remnants of Jewish independence, destroyed the second temple and left a third of the nation either dead or enslaved.

Subsequent Jewish uprisings were put down with extreme brutality by Roman or Persian emperor. The Crusaders decimated hundreds of Jewish communities throughout Western Europe and in subsequent centuries Jewish life in Eastern Europe was characterised by pogrom, discrimination and expulsion.

The promise of emancipation brought by the modern world proved false as the Nazis and their willing helpers despatched six million Jews into mass graves and crematoria. And even after the Holocaust, the Arab armies and suicide bombers try to drive Jews out of the one place that we can call home. Today, in parts of the world where we presume that we are safe, the Anti-Zionists who single out Israel for boycotts and resolutions remind us that they regard Jews as inherently different from others.

But there are dangers that follow from an over-emphasis on antisemitism and persecution when reviewing Jewish history.

One result is that the story of the Jewish people appears to consist of nothing other than catastrophe and near-destruction, ignoring glories such as the triumph of the reign of King David; the majesty of the Temple era; the vibrancy and intellectual profundity of Jewish life in exile and the miracle of the return to Zion after two millennia.

A deeper problem still is a concentration on the horrors of our past leads to a distorted answer to the question of what do the blood-stained chapters of our history tell us? What obligations and responsibilities does this chronicle of hatred impose on us today?

For many Jews since 1945, the response to antisemitism in general and to the Holocaust in particular is "never forget" and "never again." But such a reaction is not typical of other incidents of near-destruction in our past. The *Talmud* tells how *Rabbi Yochanan ben Zakkai* was given an opportunity by Vespasian, the leader of the Roman army that destroyed the Temple and Jerusalem in the year 70CE, to save one thing from the ruins of his people's independence. His primary concern was not just remembering the past, but building the future. He asked for the city of Yavneh, with its academy and scholars, to be saved, so that Jewish learning could continue.

With the same spirit whenever we remember the loss of Jerusalem and the Temple we also focus on the future, as we cry "Next year in Jerusalem." Despite centuries of antisemitism we insist on being defined positively, by who we are: Jewish, rather than what others attempt to make us - victims. Thus the response to those who wish to end Judaism, or to cause Jewish deaths, is to create, and to live, Jewish lives.

It is with this spirit that the years after the Holocaust saw not only the birth of the State of Israel, but a flourishing of *Torah* learning in day schools, *Yeshivot* and Seminaries; the publishing of books of Jewish knowledge and practice on an unprecedented scale. These responses gave substance to the plea that not only should the Holocaust never occur again, but also that Jewish life must be strengthened and renewed.

Another reaction to this history of antisemitism is to view

Jewish history itself in a special light. Realising how difficult and often tenuous has been our existence makes one realise that the story of our survival is not just long and impressive, it is miraculous! Very few other nomadic tribes that existed more than three millennia ago are identifiable today, and certainly none that have been subjected to so many attempts at extermination or forced assimilation as we have. Yet we still endure, linked directly to our ancestors, not only by genealogy, but by a common culture and philosophy.

Our history is indeed drenched with blood and infused with suffering. But the pain of loss is eclipsed by the joy and wonder that we have survived, and the appreciation that we survived for a purpose: to live as Jews.

ISRAEL IN 1985

- The dramatic operation to airlift thousands of Ethiopian Jews is made public as 'Operation Moses' results in more than 6,000 Jews being brought to Israel
- The Ayalon shopping mall in Ramat Gan opens – 70,000 people visit the mall in one day and 27 children get lost
- A free trade agreement is signed between the Israeli and US governments

39   The Land and its Unique Mitzvot

Dayan Yonason Abraham

The Jewish nation received the *Torah* at Mount Sinai seven weeks after leaving Egypt. This raises an obvious philosophical question: why did that great Divine Revelation, the single most important event in the history of mankind, take place at a nondescript mountain in a nondescript desert rather than in the most obvious location: Jerusalem, the eternal capital of the Promised Land?

Many answers are given. Perhaps the most basic one is to teach us that *Torah* observance isn't limited to, or dependent on, living in *Eretz Yisrael*. It is beyond, and indeed above, borders or geographical limitation of any sort.

There is, however, a deeper message to be drawn. The Torah was given prior to us entering *Eretz Yisrael*, indicating that our entry into and survival within the Promised Land was conditional on it being maintained as the Holy Land. Only by maintaining our standard as the Holy People could and can we maximise the spiritual potential of the Holy Land.

Furthermore, descending from the sublime spiritual state of existence,[1] which we experienced in the desert, to mundane agricultural activities, was fraught with spiritual danger. Would we master the land without becoming its servant? Would we throw ourselves into the wondrous new opportunities of working the soil whilst forgetting to tend to the soul?

God therefore commanded us to observe a series of special *Mitzvot* unique to the Land of Israel itself, the *Mitzvot Hateluyot Ba'aretz* – dependent on the Land. They collectively serve to highlight the fact that we elevate this holy home of ours by connecting the earthly to the eternal, realise its potential by imbuing the very soil with soul and that we can rejuvenate its dormant land by arousing its divine core. The land, the universe and indeed all of Creation is God's. Life itself is our most precious gift from God. Even the lowliest and most basic of physical needs and material requirements can be infused with meaning and eternal value when used in accordance with the Torah's directives.

Broadly speaking the land-dependent mitzvot fall into two categories. Firstly, the mandatory contributions and tithes which are separated prior to using the produce, and secondly restrictions in the agricultural usage and development of the land.[2]

The first category of mitzvot apply Biblically to the primary products of grain wine and oil, whereas other fruit are subject to Talmudic and halachic dispute as to whether their obligation is Biblical or Rabbinic.[3]

In brief outline, *Terumah* is the first contribution which is made after the produce has been gathered and processed. Prior to that time, the crop is referred to as *Tevel* by the Torah and its eating prohibited. Whilst there is no Biblically mandated minimum, the Rabbis instituted that approximately two percent be given to the *Kohen* (who's dual function in Temple times was to carry out the service in the *Beis Hamikdash* as well as to teach *Torah* to the nation). It has hallowed status and may be consumed only by a Kohen in a state of ritual purity.

Maaser Rishon, the first tithe, follows, consisting of a full ten percent being given to the *Levite*, whose function was of similar nature (though on a lower level) to that of a Kohen. From this, the Levite himself has to separate *Terumas Maaser*, a tenth of his received gift which he too has to give to the Kohen. Although *Maaser Rishon* belongs to the Levite, nonetheless it has no sanctity and may be eaten by all.

Next, *Maaser Sheni* – a second ten percent tithe was taken.

This had to be set aside and transported to *Yerushalayim* (either as fruit or redeemed onto coinage and then reconverted into edible produce) to be eaten there by its owner with his family and friends, with certain restrictions reflecting its sanctified status.

These all serve to connect our material success with the source of Torah inspiration, in the form of our Priestly and Levite teachers or indeed, by consumption of *Maaser Sheni* in *Yerushalayim*, which was (and, Baruch Hashem, once again is) the greatest source of spiritual rejuvenation and Torah learning.

In the third and sixth year of the seven year agricultural cycle, the *Maaser Sheni* is replaced with *Maaser Ani* – the poor man's tithe, where ten percent is given to the poor. This contribution to the poor is in addition to the harvest time gifts of *Leket, Shikcha and Peah*, – gleanings, forgotten sheaves, leaving an uncut corner of the field, as well as their vineyard-specific equivalents. These collectively engender the realisation that spirituality is to be found no less by sharing with the less fortunate than by sharing with the privileged, holier members of society.

As to the second category of these *Mitzvot Hateluyot Ba'aretz*, they serve to reinforce our awareness that we are merely tenants on God's earth and that usage of His land is subject to our displaying that attitude. The self-restraint evident in the practice of the following mitzvot is ample testimony to our subjugation before God and our acceptance of His ownership of the "Universe and all that lies therein".

Orlah is the term for the first three years' produce of a fruit tree, which may neither be eaten nor any benefit derived from. The fourth year's produce was taken to *Yerushalayim* and eaten there with the same conditions as *Maaser Sheni*. *Chadash* literally "the new (produce)" refers to the new year's grain harvest, which may not be eaten until the *Omer* offering was brought on the sixteenth of *Nissan* (the second day of *Pesach* from which point the Sefiras Ha'omer count begins). In our times when the offering can't be brought, the day itself permits the new grain

Finally, and perhaps the most challenging and

contemporarily relevant mitzvah of them all: *Shemittah* – the Sabbatical year. This requires us to leave the entire Land of Israel fallow every seventh year with no work on or development of the agricultural land. Additionally, all produce grown during the Shemittah year may not be traded and has to be left *hefker* - abandoned by the owner, and open for any and everyone to take. Produce grown whilst disregarding the Shemittah laws becomes prohibited. The amazing trust in God and courage shown by those champions of the spirit, the farmers in Eretz Yisrael who are observing this vital mitzvah, which the Torah states explicitly is the key to our survival in the Land[4], is a lesson and inspiration to us all. It challenges our own complacency and financial self-assuredness.

There is much to be written about the details, applications and conditions of these mitzvot as well as the *halachic* debate about which apply Biblically nowadays and which only Rabbinically. Furthermore, there is much to discuss regarding the controversial *Hetter Mechira* notional sale of the land in an attempt to bypass the *shemitta* restrictions. These details are clearly beyond the limits of this essay.

What is beyond any doubt is that whilst these are the *Mitzvot Hateluyot Baaretz*, it is also *Aretz Hateluyah Bemitzvot*, a "land dependent on the fulfilment of its mitzvot"! During this shemittah year as we celebrate 60 years since the establishment of the State of Israel and its miraculous survival since, may we speedily merit to see true and everlasting peace in our land with the coming of *Mashiach*.

Notes:

1 Throughout our forty year sojourn in the desert we enjoyed Divine protection by being surrounded with the Clouds of Glory, were guided by pillars of fire and cloud, sustained by the daily provision of "bread from heaven" in the form of manna and water from the Rock, all the while being camped around the *Mishkan* – the Tabernacle.

2 It is instructive to note that the dietary laws regarding Kashrus of meat products prohibit the consumption of certain spiritually contaminating animals and derived products. In contradistinction there are no prohibited fruit vegetables or plants. Rather, agricultural produce must be used to further spiritual qualities and engender positive character traits. By taking the tithes and sharing with both the less fortunate and the more sanctified members of our communities we are acknowledging that our material wealth has been given to us by God as a tool to further spiritual objectives. Only if and when these objectives have been met may the produce be used.

3 This first category also includes *Leket, Shikcha* and *Peah*: produce left in the field for the poor, *Challa:* the tithe separated from dough and given to the Kohen, *Bikkurim*: the first fruits of all the seven species which were taken to the Temple to be eaten by the Kohen with the same hallowed status as *Teruma*. The latter includes the laws of *Yovel:* the additional fallow year, occurring once in fifty years (the Jubilee), but which no longer applies nowadays (to be reinstated in Messianic times) and *Kilayim*: the prohibition of grafting or planting different species together.

4 Leviticus 26:34

ISRAEL IN 1986
- Natan Sharansky arrives in Israel after a prisoner exchange with the Soviet Union
- Ron Arad, possibly the most well known of the Israeli MIAs, is captured after his plane fell in Lebanon (today, over 20 years on, nothing is known of Arad's whereabouts)
- Morderchai Vanunu, the man who revealed Israel's nuclear secrets, is brought to Israel to stand trial
- The first liver transplant in Israel takes place

In loving memory of our wonderful parents and grandparents Pearl and Manny Forman - Malka bas Shaul Halevi and Menachem Mendel ben Chaim - whose love and guidance we continue to cherish. Dedicated by Rosalinde, Eddie, Elliott and Darren Bloom, and Jacqueline, Melvyn, Sara and Sofie Segal.

40 To Listen and To Do

Naftali Schiff

I learnt a new Hebrew word last month – a *bitzuist*. One of those beautiful gems of modern Hebrew slang that so perfectly hits the concept on the head. A doer: one who doesn't talk, talk, talk… rather one who does. My cousin, Major Benji Hillman of blessed memory, was a bitzuist. He was not a talker. He was a doer as the statement in Ethics of the Fathers says, *"Lo hamedrash haikar-ela hama'asse."* "It is not the learning that is the most important, it is carrying it out."

This was Benji. He was shy. He was modest. He didn't talk about what he did – ever. He didn't brag about his achievements – ever. I am not sure if Benji liked to do what he had to do, but I know that he did it. He did it because he knew it had to be done. He loved the Jewish People. He loved Israel. He heard his calling and grew to become what it takes to get the job done.

From the start he did what he did with excellence, which is why he rose so quickly through the ranks. That's why he was a platoon commander in one of Israel's most elite commando units. That's why he led his men from the front in the first IDF foot incursion to attempt to defeat Hizbollah terrorists in Lebanon in July 2006. That's why his men loved him and followed him. That's why his wife of only three weeks, his parents, his siblings and all the Jewish People mourn his so tragic, painful loss.

We need people like Benji.

We need people who look around at the world, see the gaps and get up and do. We need people of principle who don't just do blindly and without thought – people who have standards and who lead from the front. His men, both superiors and charges knew what his convictions were. He didn't need to shout about them. They heard what they needed to hear.

We need Jews who, because they listen, they hear. They understand that *"Shema Yisrael"* (Hear oh Israel) means precisely that: to listen. The most powerful words of *Am Yisrael* start with one simple word – *shema* meaning to listen. Listen to that quiet, determined still small voice inside you. Then listen to the voice of Israel. Ask yourself what are Yisrael, the Jewish People, saying? What are they crying out for? What is the meaning of the almost subliminal Jewish universal mantra that continues the command to listen *"Hashem Elokeinu Hashem Echad"* (Hashem is our God, Hashem is the one and only)? We can only ever find answers when we listen. Only then can we expect others to hear us.

That's why when a Benji talked, when a Benji commanded his soldiers – it wasn't talk – it was doing. It was leading by example. That's why they listened and that's why we listen now.

Benji gave his life defending the People of Israel, but he did far more than that.

When I heard Benji's father Danny speak at his son's funeral in Israel, with the utmost clarity, conviction, pride and courage, I knew that this was a man of Shema Yisrael. This was a man who along with his wife Judy had heard their own Shema Yisrael 30 years ago and listened to it. Everything they did together they did with the utmost honesty, sincerity and modesty. We sometimes think Shema Yisrael means to shout out as loudly as possible so that others can hear us say: "Listen to me, this is the way it should be" and then we wonder why no one is listening. Judy and Danny are doers not talkers. They chose not to pay lip service to Israel, but to 'do Israel.' They chose not to talk about Jewish education, but to do it-for themselves, for their children and for others.

By understanding that education, values and the future of one's family are more eternal than quick ascendancy to business success. By having the courage, conviction and confidence to give up some of those often elusive and transient comforts that never bring true long-term happiness and fulfilment, for the sake of more lasting and eternal investments.

When Danny spoke at the funeral, he stated candidly how he hates speaking, especially in public. But Danny knew what he had to do. Such is the power of Jews who understand Shema Yisrael that when they speak, everyone listens. He knew this was a time to speak. He spoke to Benji, he spoke to the government and leaders of Israel, he spoke to God and he spoke to the hearts of every single one of us. He spoke with his usual unassuming modesty. He was and is so heart wrenchingly torn and broken and yet he spoke with towering strength and power. He spoke with an uncanny depth of belief and trust. He led us all in the deepest prayer. He led us all in the deepest hope. I hope I was listening...

ISRAEL IN 1987

• John Demjanjuk, becomes the second man to stand trial in Israel for crimes perpetrated against the Jewish people during the Second World War.

• The first Intifada, or Palestinian uprising, breaks out

• Meir Ya'ari, leader of the National Kibbutz movement, dies aged 90

In living honour of our grandmothers Raymonde Massri, Ilse Friedmann and Renee Woolf. Dedicated by Rachel and Michael Friedmann, Dovi and Ginat with Shira, Benji and Dina with Dalia, Avi and Yoni and Shoshana.

41 The Jewish Family

Malcolm Herman

During the 1960's Chase Manhattan bank created a popular slogan to draw in more customers "You've got a friend at Chase Manhattan." An Israeli Bank in a very Jewish area of town decided to use the success of the campaign to help itself, they also came out with a slogan. "You may have a friend at Chase Manhattan but with us you're *mishpocha* (family)."

As a nation, we are not only familiar but also familial and we make ourselves at home. We feel a sense of connection to each other that sidesteps the awkward etiquette of strangers.

This intuition has deep roots.

The *Talmud* states, "All Israel are (spiritual) guarantors to one another."[1] This is sometimes presented as though one Jew is responsible *for* another Jew. But this would be to treat the latter as the *object* of the former. The more accurate definition is that which states, "Your responsibility is *my* responsibility and your liability is mine too." This is not simply because I care for you as an outsider, it is more than that. I *am* you and vice versa. We are components of the same organic entity. The term in Hebrew for this is *Arvut*. An *Arev* is a guarantor. If the debtor defaults, the guarantor accepts the debt. In fact the Hebrew term also means an intermingling, a synergy.

This is not just a conceptual idea; it has real and practical *halachic* (legal) ramifications as well. Let's take a typical *Shabbat* morning scene. The host has made *Kiddush* and is settling down to a piece of "it-wouldn't-be-Shabbat-without-it" cake.

There is a knock at the door and an unexpected guest arrives. The guest has not made Kiddush. Despite the normal reservations about making unnecessary blessings and thus unnecessary repetitions of God's name, the host can make Kiddush for their guest and indeed for any number of guests that arrive subsequently. If a Jew comes my way having not yet fulfilled his or her obligation, it remains my responsibility to help them carry it out, should the opportunity arise. This is true for any *mitzvah*.

The exponents of *Kabbalah* talk about the "composite Jewish soul" – a collective spiritual personality. This is not simply a question of unity but unification. Unity is where two or more cooperate together. Unification is where two or more become one. In actuality, this is our natural metaphysical state. We are intrinsically bound.

The *Maharal* (Rabbi Yehudah Loewe 1526 –1609) sees this concept to be at the root of the laws against charging interest to each other.[2] Even if the borrower agrees to the interest payment, the lender transgresses. Ultimately it runs contrary to our togetherness to profit from the financial difficulty of others. This standard of oneness amongst the Jewish community is not a nicety; it is an expression of our quintessential nature. Indeed, at the very moment we accepted *Torah* as a **Nation**, we are referred to in the singular – as **one person**.

The instruction for this reciprocal responsibility was imparted whilst the children of Israel travelled the wilderness. However, the obligation only became operative once the nation had crossed into the Land under the new leadership of Joshua. Six tribes stood on one mountain and six on another while in the valley below, the *Kohanim* and *Levites* stood with the Ark. In a powerful ceremony of renewed allegiance, the tribes pledge their commitment to the Torah and to each other.

The *Maharal* notes that the Land of Israel galvanised this sense of mutual responsibility. Now, they were complete as a nation. No longer a nomadic tribe, the Land would become the binding agent. In the words of one writer "The Land is for Israel what the body is for the soul."[3]

I had the privilege of knowing Rabbi Yehudah Zev Segal *zt"l*, known to many as the "Manchester Rosh Yeshiva." When I first met him he was already an older man with a sagely radiance. He was known throughout the Jewish world for his devotion in prayer and his abiding love for fellow Jews. On one occasion I was in his house, seeking advice and the phone rang. Obviously I could not hear the conversation but it was impossible not to pick up the sound of a woman sobbing uncontrollably. The Rosh Yeshiva was no stranger to such calls, since the efficacy of his prayer was commonly known.

After the call, the Rosh Yeshiva leant his head on his hand and was completely unable to speak for quite a few minutes. Then he looked up and turned to me: "Do you see the pain of our people?" I was deeply moved by his capacity to feel the suffering of another human being. The decades of listening and sympathising had not made him remote nor immunised his ability to feel for others. On the contrary, it had schooled him to identify. Through his constant lens of Torah, the pain and indeed the joys of others became *his* hurt and *his* celebration. He was at one with them.

It must be said that surveying the Jewish world today, we have clearly drifted from our moorings. The Land that once united now divides. We are fragmented and fractious. That is sadly true on the surface. However, perhaps it is the very appreciation of this concept that offers hope. It is vital to know that all too often, to criticise a member of the Jewish community is to damage myself. We are elements of each other. It is enlivening to know that to love another Jew is to invigorate myself. They are my family.

Notes:
1 Talmud Bavli, Shavuot 39a
2 Netivot Olam; Netiv Tzedaka Chapter 6
3 Ascent to Harmony p 84 Rabbi Eli Munk (Feldheim 1987)

ISRAEL IN 1988

- Likud win the elections with Yitzhak Shamir elected as Prime Minister
- A first group of young Israelis participate in the 'March of the Living' from Auschwitz to Birkenau
- Ofek 1, the first Israeli satellite, is launched successfully into space

This essay is dedicated by an anonymous donor.

42 Black Fire on White Fire: The Sanz-Klausenberger Rebbe

Chaim Fachler

Rabbi Yekutiel Yehuda Halberstam, was born in 1905 into one of the greatest dynasties of Polish *Chasidim*: Sanz. At the age of 22, he became Rabbi in Klausenberg, a city on the Romanian – Hungarian border, making him one of the youngest rabbis of his generation. As the community head, he was known for his devotion to the welfare of the poor, so much so, that the lay leaders of the town were eventually forced to give his salary directly to his wife, as he was donating it all to the needy.

By the time war broke out, he had established a reputation as a Torah scholar and was destined for renown, though his true greatness was to come not through peace but through war. Over the next five years, he would suffer the extremes of the fate of European Jewry, losing his wife, all their eleven children, hundreds of members of his extended family and most of his beloved students and community. Yet during the long periods of slave labour and the hell-fires of Auschwitz, he remained an incredible symbol of faith and strength to all those who came into contact with him. His devotion to *mitzvot* earned him numerous beatings from the Nazis, none of which deterred him from his determination to serve his Creator anywhere and everywhere.

The *Rebbe* managed to survive nine months in the Muldorf camp near Dachau, without eating non-kosher food, trading any food for bread, yet it was after the liberation that his greatest hour came. In the displaced persons (D.P.) camps of Germany, rather than allow himself prolonged mourning for his own losses, he went about spiritually and physically rehabilitating young survivors.

In 1947, the Rebbe was still living in the Foehrenwald D.P. camp. On *Erev Yom Kippur* there was a knock on the door to his room. He went to open it, and saw a young girl standing there with tears in her eyes.

"Rebbe, every year my father would bless me before Yom Kippur. My father was burned alive and I have no one to bless me."

The Rebbe, who had lost all his own children, invited the girl to come in and said, "My child, I will be your father."

Holding his hands over her head, he blessed her with emotion and concentration. The girl left the Rebbe's quarters smiling and fortified. A few minutes later a group of forlorn girls came to the Rebbe's door.

"We, too, would like to be blessed, Rebbe," one of them said. "There is no one to bless us either."

Once again, with patience and tears, he blessed each of the girls. The news spread, and soon orphaned girls from all over the D.P. camp were coming in numbers. The Rebbe blessed every single one of them, 87 in all! By the time he had finished, he had little time left for any personal preparation. In reality though, the Rebbe felt there could be no better way of preparing for Yom Kippur than to spend the day comforting broken-spirited orphans.

Two years earlier, the D.P. camp was visited by General Eisenhower, the supreme Allied commander. He was greatly taken by the Rebbe's saintliness. The Klausenberger Rebbe used this opportunity to create a personal connection with the General, which continued for many years, to the benefit of the survivors of the Holocaust.

On one occasion, having been offered new boots by his

Chasidim in the camp, he replied: "When all the survivors here have new boots, you can get some for me."

Though it had been the Rebbe's wish to move to the Land of Israel, he felt that in the aftermath of the war, he was needed in America and went there in 1947. But his heart was always turned toward Israel and in the late 1950s the Rebbe moved there, and founded the Kiryat Sanz community in the coastal town of Netanya. At the inauguration he said, "Many times I asked myself why I was spared... only I remain of my family. Today I know clearly that it happened so that I could lay the foundation stone for Kiryat Sanz in our Holy Land."

After years of planning and fundraising, he also built the famous Sanz-Laniado Medical Centre in 1975, fulfilling a vow made when seriously wounded during the death marches. For the opening he addressed the staff, and said, "Our *Torah* is a Torah of *chesed* (loving kindness). Our hospital is therefore indeed a Torah Institution." He also printed a series of instructions. One was the need for medical staff to be hired not only for their medical competence, but for their warmth and concern, and that they be responsible for fostering an atmosphere of care. A second was the requirement to pay all staff on time and a third was that the hospital see itself as a centre to heal both the wounds of the body and the pain of the soul. Laniado hospital is today a 400 bed humanitarian aid centre of life in the Middle East. As a unique non profit community hospital, it treats more than 50,000 patients annually.

When the Knesset legalised abortion in 1977, the Rebbe told the hospital staff to offer any woman who wished to terminate her pregnancy, that he would adopt their child. In a number of recorded instances, the mothers took up the Rebbe's offer, having been told that their child would be irreparably brain damaged, only to give birth to healthy children, whom they joyfully took home.

The Rebbe also began a wide scale movement, to replace that which had been lost spiritually in the war. He founded Jewish day schools and institutions of higher learning and launched revolutionary programs for comprehensive study of the Talmud, creating a program called Mifal HaShas, in which students would master either 30 or 70 folios of the Talmud each month, for which they would sit a written exam.

Hundreds enrolled in his girls' schools and the Rebbe kept track of each one's spiritual condition, listened to each girl's troubles, and gave them all moral support. In particular, he assumed responsibility for finding them suitable spouses. His attitude toward them was so fatherly and personal that some people regarded his achievements in this area as the pinnacle of his activity.

When the Rebbe died in 1994, so many people attended his funeral, that the city of Netanya was forced to virtually shut down for the day. But his legacy of achievements in Netanya, his writings and his inspiration of faith and prayer live on.

ISRAEL IN 1989
- The resort of Taba is returned to Egypt
- The Tower of David Museum focusing on the history of Jerusalem is established in the David Citadel compound
- Mass immigration of Jews from the Soviet Union begins
- An Israeli Air Force plane is flown to Romania to assist victims of violence and fighting after the revolution

This essay is dedicated by an anonymous donor.

43 Pesach: One Great Jewish Community

Chief Rabbi Dr Warren Goldstein

It is very exciting to discover new treasure. I acquired two new books recently, which contain the recently published writings of one of the founding fathers of the South African Jewish Community: Rabbi Yitzchak Kossowsky, of blessed memory. He came to South Africa from Lithuania in 1933 to take up the position of Head of the Johannesburg Beth Din and all its affiliated congregation, in the then Transvaal. He was a towering rabbinic figure who was famous in Lithuania, a leader who was close to among others the *Chofetz Chaim* zt"l, and *Rabbi Chaim Soloveitchik* zt"l.

The two books of his writings were edited and compiled by his great grandson who lives today in Israel. They are a treasure trove of the vision, thoughts, challenges and ideas of a great rabbinic leader. In there, I discovered the text of a message Rabbi Kossowsky delivered shortly before *Pesach* in 1938, in Johannesburg. The dark shadow of the Nazi threat hangs heavily over his words, although no-one knew at the time of the impending horror of the Holocaust, in which Rabbi Kossowsky was to lose his daughter, son-in-law and three grandchildren.

In that 1938 Pesach message, Rabbi Kossowsky explains what real freedom is. He notes that the festival of Pesach is referred to as a time of our freedom, for which we use the word *cheirut* in our prayers. Cheirut connotes a much more transcendent freedom than the word *chofesh* which also means freedom. It refers to the eternal nature and destiny of the Jewish People, which rises above all adversity to achieve eternal freedom and thereby eternal greatness.

Although, individuals may have perished, often at the hands of our enemies, the Jewish People have defied all the laws of history to survive and thrive when none of the other ancient peoples exist today. This divine miracle is what we celebrate on Pesach: transcendent eternal freedom.

Rabbi Kossowsky cites the *Talmud* that links the word cheirut, freedom, to *charut* which means engraved, referring to the engraving of the Ten Commandments on the tablets of stone that Moses brought down from the mountain, from God. When we are connected to our Divine mission we rise above the here and now and become linked to the generations that come before us.

Exactly 3,320 years ago God revealed Himself and His law to the newly liberated 12 tribes of the children of Israel. Approximately 3 million men, women and children witnessed God's presence, and personally heard His voice at Mount Sinai.

Ethics of Our Fathers states, "Rabbi Yochanan Hasandlar said: Any community dedicated to Heaven will endure forever."[1] *Avot deRabbi Natan*, the classic Talmudic commentary to Ethics of Our Fathers, says that the community referred to, is *Knesset Yisrael*, the paradigm community of Israel at Sinai. So it is that the Jewish community that is dedicated to Heaven, that continues that eternal link, will endure forever, spanning the centuries from Mount Sinai to the present. The Talmudic Sages are teaching us that we, the Jewish people, only survive and indeed thrive, when we are in alignment with the values of the generations of Jews who received and passed on the tradition from Sinai.

Knesset Yisrael, the community of the children of Israel, is what we can term a vertical community, rooted in Sinai. All the generations from Sinai until now form one community.

Anyone who studies *Torah* is in constant dialogue with voices coming from that community – voices that span 4,000 years of our history. Maimonides traces 40 generations of scholars from Moses our teacher, to Rav Ashi, the editor of the Talmud. Through all of them, the truth of Sinai was transmitted to the Rabbis of the Middle Ages – the *Rambam*, *Rashi*, and many others.

Our mission as the Jewish people is to be "a community dedicated to Heaven," to remain part of Knesset Yisrael, the multi-generational community of Sinai. Our moral vision starts with Mount Sinai and ends with the vision of the Prophets for the Final Redemption and a better world. For a time which the prophet Isaiah described in these memorable words, "for the earth shall be full of the knowledge of the Lord as the waters cover the sea … Nation shall not lift up sword against nation, neither shall they learn war any more." It is our task to build our families and communities with loyalty and dedication and so write a proud chapter in the history of the Jewish people, and of humankind.

I speak of writing a chapter because according to the Talmud, even today, the unfolding story of humankind continues to be written, as we continue to journey from Mount Sinai to the Final Redemption. We have the opportunity and the calling to be part of that Book, to write a chapter therein. If we remain loyal to the teachings of Sinai, we shall help to write an illustrious chapter in that Book, and if we do not, God forbid, we will be relegated to a footnote.

On the Seder Night and throughout Pesach we feel an even stronger connection to Knesset Yisrael. The *Haggadah* says that every single Jew should feel as if he or she personally went out of Egypt. We are part of the very same community as our ancestors, who saw with their own eyes the ten plagues, the splitting of the Red Sea and the greatest liberation of all times. It is not a night of fables, but of truth.

As Jews we are only interested in the truth and not in a vague cultural experience. Jews at every Pesach have been remembering the Exodus from Egypt. On a daily basis we have made mention of it in our prayers, as the Torah instructs. But on Seder night we not only remember, we feel. Because that is what it means to be part of the one great Jewish Community which goes back almost 4,000 years to Abraham our father.

On this Pesach, let us sit with family and friends and think of those generations who preceded us, and who sat together on Seder Night speaking about and giving thanks for God's wondrous miracles in Egypt. Let us remember Rabbi Kossowsky and his Pesach message of 1938 – of true *Cheirut*, transcendent freedom. Think about the most wondrous miracle of all – that after thousands of years the Jewish People and its Divine Mission continue to thrive.

Notes:
1 Ethics of Our Fathers 4:14

PESACH IN ISRAEL

*Visit the **Kotel** for the morning service on **Chol Hamoed Pesach** and you will encounter thousands of Jews. At one point in the service, an entire section at the front of the Kotel transforms itself into a sea of white as hundreds of **kohanim** gather to say the priestly blessings. Despite the fact we don't have a temple this gives us a small insight into what Pesach must have been like in biblical times.*

ISRAEL IN 1990

- The Jewish Agency announces a record number of immigrants from the Soviet Union, following the new liberal policies introduced by Gorbachev
- The Israeli Government decides to distribute defence kits against chemical weapons in light of Saddam Hussein's threat of war
- Israel records it's first ever cricket win, defeating Argentina by one wicket in an exiting finish

Day 43. Psalm 106

In loving memory of Anne Leviton, Freda
and Manny Remer a"h.

44 The Kotel and the Gate of Prayer

Sara Yoheved Rigler

What if you could locate a place in this world that is a portal
to a different dimension?

While such fanciful notions underlie several popular
children's novels, in actuality such a place does exist. It is the
portal between this physical world and the world of pure
spirit. To locate this mystical aperture to the highest world, you
don't need a GPS. The location is, in fact, easy to find. It's
located in Israel, in Jerusalem, on Mount Moriah, also known
as the Temple Mount. The point itself is called, "The
Foundation Stone."

According to Jewish tradition, Adam, the first human, was
created at this spot. Later it was the site of the seminal event in
the lives of the Patriarchs, the "Binding of Isaac" by his father
Abraham. Jacob's dream of a ladder with angels ascending and
descending also took place at this point. The First and Second
Temples, which were the vortex that channelled energy and
blessings between this world and the higher worlds were, of
course, located here. The most sanctified section of the Temple,
called the Holy of Holies, was located directly over the
Foundation Stone.

Although the Temple no longer stands, the Foundation Stone
remains the portal to the higher dimension. It is also called,
"The Gate of Prayer," meaning that all prayers uttered anywhere

in this physical world ascend only through that aperture, which is why Jews everywhere in the world, pray facing Jerusalem and Jews in Jerusalem pray facing the Temple Mount.

Because of the tremendous sanctity of the site, Jews today, in our state of ritual impurity, are forbidden from treading on the Temple Mount. The closest we can come to the site of the Holy of Holies is the *Kotel*, or Western Wall. Day and night, Jews from all over the world flock to the Kotel, to pray, to absorb, to recharge. The Kotel is devoid of any religious trappings whatsoever. It has no beautiful architecture, no frescoes, no incense, no rapturous music or choirs and no furnishings except for plastic chairs. But to stand at the Kotel is to stand as close as a Jew can to the portal of the world of pure spirit. This is because in Judaism, spirituality does not require external physical frills, and although we cannot pass through that gate, our prayers can. Every Jew who stops and takes the trouble to touch that reality feels it.

The Western Wall

Soon after Herod became King of Judea in 37CE he decided to renovate the Second Temple. His grandiose building plans included enlarging the area around the actual Temple itself – the Temple Mount. This necessitated constructing four massive walls around Mount Moriah, and filling in the space between the mountain and the walls. Although the eastern and southern retaining walls are still extant and accessible, the Western Wall is most cherished by the Jewish people because it is the closest to the site of the Holy of Holies.

The Temple complex was considered one of the wonders of the ancient world and the construction of the walls – the only remaining part of the Temple area – was a technological feat that still inspires awe. Because Jerusalem was conquered by a series of invaders over the centuries and each one built upon the ruins of the last, the Jerusalem we stand in today, is at times over 50 metres above the ground level of Temple times. This means that almost 90% of the Western Wall is nowadays underground and accessible only through a "Kotel tunnels tour".

The Western Wall itself is 488 meters long (1600 feet). The wall originally stood 60 meters (197 feet) high. Its stones are 4.6 meters deep, and range in height from 3.5 meters to 11.1 meters. Its largest stone, which can today be viewed in the Kotel tunnels, is 13.6 meters long, the largest cut stone ever found from ancient times.

Yet to stand before the Kotel and marvel solely about its engineering wonders would be akin to holding a newborn baby, to be amazed purely by its physical appearance. Rabbi Abraham Isaac Kook, first Ashkenazi Chief Rabbi of Israel, once wrote, "There are men with hearts of stone, and there are stones with hearts of men." He was referring to the Kotel.

The Talmud asserts that the *Shechinah,* or Divine Presence, never leaves the Western Wall and despite the fact that Jerusalem was never without foreign invaders for almost 2,000 years, none of them destroyed our Wall. The greatest wonder of the Kotel today however, is that tourists and travellers of all ages, nationalities, and levels of Jewish observance continue to be stirred by that Divine Presence. One doesn't have to be a mystic to experience that one is standing at the portal to the highest world.

ISRAEL IN 1991

- The International Middle East Conference takes place in Madrid, it is seen by many as the first steps towards an international process for peace
- 'Operation Solomon' airlifts 14,000 Ethiopians to Israel – the largest number of immigrants ever brought to Israel on a single day
- Miriam Ben-Porat, Israel's first woman Supreme Court Justice, is awarded the "Israel Prize" for her contribution to Israeli life
- Every home in Israel creates a sealed room to provide protection, as Iraq launches scud missile attacks

In loving memory of Abraham Israel Samuel.

45 Hide and Seek

Chana Weisberg

One sunny afternoon, I sat watching my two children playing a lively game of hide and seek.

My younger daughter, Shira, was the first to be the seeker and as she counted to 20, the older one, Naomi, ran to hide. Naomi had discovered a creative hiding spot, one that would be difficult for Shira to detect.

Meanwhile, Shira finished her countdown and began to scurry all over the house. She searched and she searched, in small corners and large, to no avail.

The silent moments ticked by, and Shira's search was becoming more desperate. Lines of anxiety were forming on her small forehead. My usually persistent daughter almost seemed ready to admit defeat.

In despair, Shira called out to Naomi, hoping to rouse a response. Silence reigned.

Then Shira turned, as if struck by a new idea, and optimistically headed off, only to get sidetracked along the way by the subtlest sound of shifting legs on the wooden floor. Her ears perked up, and she stopped in her tracks. She made a sharp U-turn darting to search in the opposite direction and seconds later discovered her sister's ingenious location.

Shira leapt at Naomi, and both laughed aloud, reunited. The two shared a moment of closeness, admiring Naomi's ingenuity in thinking of such a location and Shira's in discovering it. For that blithe moment, they enjoyed each other thoroughly, and you would think the two were forever the best of friends, never experiencing the normal squabbling between siblings.

Watching my youngsters play, my mind wandered to You, God. I thought of how, so often, You seem to be hiding Yourself from us. From afar You watch, allowing us to run here and there bereft of direction. The lines of sorrow and anxiety form on our temples as we wonder whether we will ever find you.

Sometimes, despite our perseverance as a nation, we're almost ready to give up. Sometimes we do give up. We trail off in all the wrong directions, despairing of ever making you a meaningful part of our lives.

But always You make some noise. Sometimes it's a slight rustling sound. Sometimes it's louder. Some event in our personal lives, or in our national lives, catches our attention, drawing us back to where we are meant to be. You help us to rediscover You and we feel closer to You.

For those moments in history, we are reunited, surer of our direction.

The sounds of my children reorganising for another round of hide and seek interrupted my reverie. This time my four-year-old son, Yisroel, begged to be included. The round began exactly as before. This time, though, my older children were patronising Yisroel, pretending not to locate him in his obvious hiding spot. Eventually, however, they approached him and laughingly declared, "We found you!"

Yisroel's response? Simple. He put his hands over his eyes and victoriously announced, "No, you didn't. You can't find me!" He stayed like that for several seconds, ignoring their claims. After all, he reasoned, if he couldn't see them, they simply weren't there.

This brought my thoughts back to You again. How often in life do we act like a little child, pretending You aren't there? We cover our eyes, denying You appropriate entry into our lives, even while, deep down, we know that You are right before us. How silly we must appear to You.

Several more rounds of hide and seek were played, and it

was time to call a close to the game. First, though, we all had to even the score.

True, there were times throughout our exile that we acted like a silly child, closing our eyes and denying You access. We pretended that You were not there, feigning ignorance, rejecting You as the guiding force in all that we do.

But then again, You did hide in such difficult, remote spots. Far too many times, these places were impossibly unfair for our limited capabilities. How could You expect us to find you? It has been so long that our Temple in Jerusalem has lain in ruins, so long since Israel was the home of Your entire nation.

So taking all this into account, I think that must make the score just about even now. How about we call it a tie and finally end the game? Then we can be truly reunited, and experience Your presence in our midst, ensuring that our homecoming to Your Land presages the true peace which has eluded us for so long.

ISRAEL IN 1992

- Menachem Begin dies aged 79
- Israel wins its first Olympic Games medals, winning both silver and bronze in Judo
- Jerusalem and New York are declared twin cities
- 29cm of snow brings Jerusalem to a total halt. Snow falls as far north as Haifa and as far south as Be'er Sheva

---

> In memory of Safta Mazal whose mesirut nefesh (self sacrifice) to move to Israel has remained an inspiration for the family and in honour of all members of our families living in Israel today, by Rabbi Andrew and Gila Shaw.

46 Destination and Destiny

David Blackman

The *Haggadah* is the Jewish template, a textbook celebration of freedom. We toast our freedom over four cups of wine corresponding to the four expressions of redemption expressed by God to Moses. It might seem strange that nowhere in the essential text of the Haggadah is mention made of our arrival in the Land of Israel. There is no reference to the Jewish People having conquered or settled there.

The biblical passage in Deuteronomy which serves as the basis of the Haggadah does make specific reference to our arrival and settlement in Israel. So why, asks *Rabbi Soloveitchik*, was the verse discussing the entry into the land of Israel not included in our Haggadah?[1] Why is there no fifth cup of wine in reference to the fifth expression of redemption – that of God bringing us into the Land of Israel? The one line reference in the *Dayeinu* song and the "*Leshana Habba'a Biy'rushalayim*" (next year in Jerusalem) chant do little to satisfy as an effective commemoration to the culmination of freedom, inheriting the Land of Israel.

Rabbi Soloveitchik creatively suggests the purpose pursued by the Almighty through the liberation of our people from Egypt was not just the entry of the Jew into our distant destination, the Land of Israel. Yes, it was our destination, but not our destiny!

There is a difference between destination and destiny. A

difference between destination and purpose. The destination of the Jewish People certainly was the Land of Israel, but this was not the purpose. It was not the ultimate goal. So what was the purpose?

The ultimate purpose of our freedom from slavery was the revelation at Mount Sinai. The Exodus was justified by the receiving of the *Torah* and subsequently the formation of a new community, a "kingdom of priests and a holy nation."[2] The exodus was not just to grant us political and economic freedom, but also to create a sacred people, by becoming servants of God.

Pesach is the festival of the Exodus, but it is also the beginning of the festival of the giving of the Torah. *Shavuot* is really a stay-over from Pesach. But Pesach is not the holiday of receiving the Land. This is not intended to denigrate the importance of settling the Land or the pivotal place the Land of Israel occupies in our religious life. In fact *Maimonides* teaches that the celebration of our entry into and inheritance of the land, its conquest and our eternal right to the land, of our invincible bond and loyalty, is the festival of *Succot*. The four species, the *succah*, the prayer for rain, all these *mitzvot* have a certain link with the Land.[1]

Pesach and Shavuot we observe as a celebration of purpose of destiny, Succot - our destination.

When the crucial distinction between destiny and destination becomes blurred a dangerous mindset begins to emerge, namely: having arrived at our destination is in fact the fulfilment of our destiny; our freedom vindicated and our ultimate purpose fulfilled.

This confusion leads us now as it did in the early years of statehood to rapid secularisation. The Labour Zionist leaders proclaimed that religious values may have been necessary in the Diaspora, but were irrelevant in the new Jewish state. Thus hundreds of thousands of Jews were taught to discard their traditions and to separate themselves from their ethnic and spiritual roots. This was often true in regard to the Sephardic Jews who immigrated to Israel from the Moslem countries of the Middle East.[4] The State of Israel (destination) became a substitute for Judaism (destiny).

This conflict between destination and destiny continues today. Moral relativism, the exaggerated influence of the 'modern' in our state threatens to undermine the integrity of our commitment to our timeless value set. Political secular Zionism alongside its many heroic achievements struggles for air by virtue of one basic error. Secular Zionism asserts that with the founding of the State of Israel, we became a people like all other peoples,[5] our mission accomplished.

Perhaps the greatest challenge assigned to us, is to express our independence but as a declaration of dependence on God. As we stand in celebration 60 years on, we are humbled by the awesome privilege of living in a generation which has witnessed firsthand the greatest miracle wrought by The Almighty on behalf of the Jewish people collectively in 1938 years – a living, vibrant, state in our ancestral home.

Looking to the future we must realise that the qualitative long-term sustainability of our precious State (destination) is inextricably linked to, guaranteed and justified by the commitment to our Destiny (Torah values).

May God's presence continue to rest on the work of our hands.

Notes:

1 Joseph Epstein. 1994. Shiurei Harav, A Conspectus of the Public lectures of Rabbi Joseph B. Soloveitchik, pp.40-42, NJ Ktav

2 Exodus 19:6

3 Maimonides. Guide to the Perplexed, section 3 chapter 43

4 Rabbi Berel Wein. 2001. Faith and Fate, p 215 NY Shaar Press

5 See Rabbi Soloveitchik. Kol Dodi Dofek translated by David Z.Gordon.Yeshiva University 2006, p.81

ISRAEL IN 1993

- The Oslo Accords are signed, seeing the PLO accept Israel's right to exist but Hamas escalates terror attacks killing Israelis
- Michael Jackson and Madonna arrive in Israel, playing to 120,000 fans between them
- The first Kosher McDonald's branch in the world opens in Mevaseret Tzion
- Israel's first commercial television station, Channel Two, begins broadcasting

In fond appreciation of Rabbi Dr Naftali Brawer's 11 years of service to the Northwood community. Dedicated by Meryl, Richard, Daniel and Robert Rosenberg.

47 Rabbi Menachem Mendel of Vitebsk (1730 - 1788)

Dr Naftali Brawer

There was great excitement when the letter arrived from Israel. In it, the *Rebbe* described to his followers in Russia what life was like in the Holy Land for the new pioneers. One haunting passage stood out. The Rebbe confessed that he found it difficult to sleep. "The air in the Holy Land," he wrote, "is pure, and I hear heavenly voices calling out in the night urging me to repent."

The Rebbe was Rabbi Menachem Mendel of Vitebsk, one of the great leaders of the third generation of *Chasidim*. Rabbi Menachem Mendel was born in Vitebsk, White Russia in 1730. As a young man he became a disciple of Rabbi Dov Ber known as the Maggid of Mezrich. After his master's passing he set up his own *chasidic* court in Horodok, not far from Vitebsk. He was regarded as the leader of the chasidic movement in White Russia and thousands of chasidim flocked to his court to spend time with him and to hear his teachings. Amongst his followers were exalted men who would eventually become chasidic masters in their own right; most notably Rabbi Shneur Zalman of Liadi, the first Rebbe of Lubavitch and the founder of Chabad chasidim.

Despite the comfort of his home surroundings, Rabbi

Menachem Mendel thirsted for the Holy Land. So infectious was his love for the land of Israel that when he decided to make *aliyah* in 1777 he was followed by some three hundred chasidim. The journey was long and arduous. On the first leg of the journey across the Black Sea en route to Turkey one of the ships sank. On board were some 80 chasidim who lost their lives. The depleted and exhausted group finally set foot on the soil of Israel on the fifth of Ellul 5537.

The new pioneers settled at first in Tzfat in the north of Israel. Eventually, due to persecution by the Arabs, they were forced to leave for Tiberius. In that ancient city on the shores of the Kinneret they found relative peace. Their material situation however, was far from ideal. To alleviate the crushing poverty of his community Rabbi Menachem Mendel urged his followers back in Russia to send funds to support the fledgling chasidic settlement.

Despite the hardships of poverty and disease Rabbi Menachem Mendel was adamant that he would remain in Israel. His example of devotion to living in the Land was an inspiration to his followers and together they formed the basis of a permanent chasidic community in the Holy Land. They also contributed significantly to the Jewish development of the Galilee.

Ten years after his arrival in the Holy Land, Reb Menachem Mendel passed away as he had lived – in humility and simplicity – at the age of 57. In the ethical will he wrote for his son, he asked that no epitaphs should be engraved on his gravestone, it should simply be inscribed: Rabbi Menachem Mendel.

We began with a story so let us conclude with one as well.

One *Erev Shabbat* when Rabbi Menachem Mendel was visiting Jerusalem some poor fool got it into his head that he was the Messiah. The fellow ascended the Mount of Olives and standing on its summit, proceeded to blow the *shofar*. As there was great messianic fervour at the time, it did not take much to set off the local Jewish population. Hearing the shofar emanating from the Mount of Olives the locals, convinced that the redeemer had indeed arrived began to dance for joy in the streets. Hearing the commotion Rabbi Menachem Mendel inquired as to its cause. When he was told that Messiah had arrived he opened his window and sniffed the Jerusalem air. "No," he said shaking his head sadly, "The Messiah has not yet arrived. The air smells the same as it did yesterday. The world is not yet redeemed. The whole world will change with the Messiah's arrival."

What the two stories about Rabbi Menachem Mendel have in common is that they both reflect his sensitivity not just to his physical surroundings but to his spiritual ones as well. For Rabbi Menachem Mendel, Israel was so much more than a physically beautiful land. It was, for him, a profoundly spiritual place and he was able to sense this spirituality in the very air around him. He was able to instinctively sense the heavenly call to repentance in the clear night air of Tiberius. He was also able to detect in the perfumed air of Jerusalem that despite its holiness, God's city still awaited redemption.

The next time you visit the Galilee step out late at night under the clear star studded sky and reflect on the life of this most remarkable man; Rabbi, communal leader and lover of Israel. As you stand alone absorbed in thought, it is not impossible that you too might hear those heavenly voices ringing out in the night urging you to draw ever closer to your Father in Heaven.

ISRAEL IN 1994

- A peace treaty is signed with Jordan following meetings between Yitzhak Rabin and King Hussein in Washington
- Yitzchak Rabin, Shimon Peres and Yasser Arafat share the Nobel Peace Prize
- An IDF field hospital is flown to Africa by an Israeli Air Force airlift to treat Rwandan refugees

48 Making it happen

Yaacov Haber

In the book of Tehillim (Psalms) created by King David, of the 150 chapters, one of the most famous and most often recited, is chapter 121. This psalm deals with the concept of trust. The central theme is contained in the following words "God is your shadow."

The idea behind this verse is one of the most astounding secrets of the universe, namely that God mimics our every action, our attitudes and passions. If we wave our right hand in the air, so does our shadow and so does God, so to speak. That is the way He wired the world. He set it up in such a way so as to take His cues from us! Clearly if we perform *mitzvot*, we influence the world, similarly in the reverse. However, King David is telling us even more than that. Our attitudes and state of mind shape what happens. If we are positive, we create positivity. If we are negative and despondent, our environment will actually respond in a like way. As Einstein wrote, "Our personal environment is in a state of readiness to respond in a characteristic way to the stimulus we create."

The most classic example of this idea is found in the designer of the Biblical sanctuary that accompanied the Jewish people on their journey through the desert. The Temple of Solomon during the first commonwealth and the Second Temple were all based on the design of *Betzalel*. Why Betzalel? Moses explained that the answer lay in his name. Betzalel was called so because he was *Betzel El* or in the shadow of God.

He understood what we have to do in this world to merit the presence of God in our lives. He understood what the Ark, the Cherubim and the tent should look like. He understood what actions we can do to affect the entire universe.

Shortly after moving to Israel, I was given the opportunity to travel with a group to the city of Mezibuz in the Ukraine. The purpose of the trip was to spend Shabbat in the city of the great *Baal Shem Tov*, the founder of the *Chasidic* movement. I was anxious to use the opportunity of being at such a holy site, to pray at his graveside for the success of my family and myself in our new life in Israel. Although it seemed somewhat ironic to leave Israel to pray at a holy place in the Ukraine, I recalled a teaching of Rebbe Nachman of Breslav, "If God gives one an opportunity to travel, take it! You never know what God has in mind."

It was a spiritually exciting trip. We visited the Chasidic landmarks of Berditchev and Uman, but the jewel in the crown was *Shabbat* in Mezibuz, where the spirituality of the Baal Shem Tov was almost tangible. At some point over Shabbat I found myself alone in the original synagogue of the Baal Shem Tov. My mind wandered to what it must have been like to have prayed in this small wooden room with the founder of the Chasidic movement and his students. On the table before me was a book compiled by his students, which contained a collection of his thoughts on the weekly *Torah* portion. Although the torah portion of the week was *Parashat Beshalach*, I randomly opened the book to what turned out to be *Parashat Behar*.

The Torah there speaks about the mitzvah of the *Shemittah*, the Sabbatical year in Israel. During this year, the Land of Israel must lie at rest and no work may be done on the field. "And what will happen if the people ask: 'what should we eat during this seventh year if we do not sow or gather in our crops? ' (God says) 'I will command My special blessing on the Land and you will have abundance in the sixth year for three years!'"[1]

The Baal Shem Tov comments that in order for one to attract success and abundance in one's life, one's thoughts must be full of faith and positive thoughts of success. The most damaging thing a person can do to their life is to worry and complain. The negativity of worry can, God forbid, attract negativity and remove the blessing from one's life. The message of the Baal Shem Tov resonated in my mind, and I returned to Jerusalem with renewed confidence.

Attitude is so very important. Not only do the mitzvot I perform, affect my life and my world, but in fact every smile and frown makes a difference! The Lubavitcher Rebbe, of blessed memory, once advised me, when I asked him whether he thought I should embark on a huge community project, *"Tracht Gut – un es vet zein gut!"* he said, "Think good – and it will be good!" This is not simply a psychological remedy but a God given formula. This is why when we observe truly spiritual people, we can perceive a sense of inner peace. They are able to live life to its fullest, irrespective of the fact that they are often unable to control events, because they still maintain control of their reaction to events.

If I feel myself to be happy, God will give me happiness. If I fill my life with kindness, God will surround me with kindness – and so it is with many aspects of my life. If I know I can make a difference, then I can become a leader or a scholar.

We can change ourselves, our families, our country and the world! We can make it happen.

Notes:
1 Leviticus 25:21

ISRAEL IN 1995

- Yitzhak Rabin is assassinated while at a peace rally in Tel Aviv
- A forest fire in Sha'ar Hagai becomes one of the most severe natural disasters in Israel
- 'Save a Child's Heart' is created by a team of doctors at the Wolfson Medical Centre in Holon, offering children from the developing world treatment for heart problems
- The Jerusalem Post launches its online news service

In loving memory of Gilad Stiglitz who was killed
on May 28, 2002 while playing basketball at a yeshiva
in Itamar.

49 My Name is Esther Wachsman

Esther Wachsman

My name is Esther Wachsman. I was born in a DP (Displaced Persons) camp in Germany in 1947 to parents who had survived the ovens of Nazi Germany, in which their entire families had perished. My parents, my sister (who had been hidden by a Catholic family during the war) and I sailed to America in 1950.

In 1969 I made *aliyah* to Jerusalem, where I attended the Hebrew University. I was going to be part of the history of our homeland. I would raise proud, independent, believing Jewish children in their homeland after 2,000 years of exile. And so I was married to Yehuda in 1970 and we had seven sons. Our sons were raised on a three-fold love – of their people, their land, and their heritage – the *Torah*. Our lives were complete, my dreams fulfilled, and I felt privileged.

I taught English at a high school for 28 years, my children grew up, attended *yeshivot*, and in time served their country, proudly wearing the uniform of the Jewish army. How proud I was – the Jewish immigrant from Brooklyn, mother of soldiers of Israel!

My two oldest sons served in the Golani Brigade. When the time came for my son Nachshon, to be drafted, he wanted to outdo his two older brothers and volunteered for an elite commando unit of Golani.

Nachshon lived up to his name. He was born on the last day of Passover, when we read the Torah portion about the Jews crossing the Red Sea. God promised the nation, that the water would turn into dry land and Nachshon, the head of the tribe of Yehuda, was the first to jump into the water, thereby expressing complete faith and belief in God, and all of the Children of Israel followed him. It was also on Passover in 1948, that Operation Nachshon took place - the operation that opened the road to Jerusalem. We felt that that name incorporated all of our ideas - faith and belief in God and love of our people and our land.

After having served in the army for a little over a year, he came home on leave, Friday, October 7, 1994 just before *Shabbat*. On Saturday night, he got a call from the army informing him that the following day he was to attend a course up north.

Nachshon got a ride with a friend. He left us late Saturday night and told us he would be back home the following night.

Nachshon did not come home on Sunday night. We notified the military authorities, we traced his movements, we spoke to his army friends. We discovered from one of them that he had been dropped off at the Bnai Atarot junction - where he could either catch a bus or hitchhike (as all soldiers do) to Jerusalem. This friend was the last one to have seen him.

We sent search parties to the area where he had last been seen, to no avail. On Tuesday, we were contacted by Israeli Television, who told us that they had received a videotape showing my son being held hostage by Hamas terrorists.

On that videotape, Nachshon was seen, bound hand and foot, with a terrorist holding up Nachshon's identity card. The terrorist recited his home address, identity number, and then Nachshon spoke at gunpoint. He said that he had been kidnapped by Hamas, who were demanding the release of their spiritual leader, Achmed Yassin, from an Israeli prison, as well as the release of 200 other imprisoned Hamas terrorists. If these demands were not met, he would be executed on Friday night at 8:00pm.

We were all mobilised for the next four days, 24 hours a day, to do everything in our power to save our son's life. We spoke to Prime Minister Rabin, who informed us that as a matter of policy, they did not negotiate with terrorists. We announced Nachshon's American citizenship, and President Clinton intervened. Both Warren Christopher, who was in the area, and the U.S. consul in Jerusalem, Ed Abbington, went to Gaza – where it was believed Nachshon was being held. We appealed to world leaders everywhere and to Moslem religious leaders, all of whom stated unequivocally on the media that they must not harm our son.

And we appealed to our brethren – to the Jewish people throughout the world – and asked them to pray for our son. People everywhere, including schoolchildren who had never prayed before, did so for the sake of one precious Jewish soul.

I asked women throughout the world to light an extra Sabbath candle for my son. From about 30,000 letters that poured into our home, I learned of thousands of women who had never lit Sabbath candles, who did so. Our son became a symbol of everyone's son, brother, friend.

On Thursday night, a prayer vigil was held at the Western Wall and, at the same hour, in synagogues, schools, community centres, street squares ... and, yes, churches throughout the world. People of good faith everywhere hoped and pleaded and prayed for Nachshon.

At the Western Wall nearly 100,000 people arrived. *Chasidim* in black frock coats and long side curls swayed and prayed and cried, side by side with young boys in torn jeans and ponytails and earrings. There was total unity and solidarity of purpose among us – religious and secular, left wing and right wing, Sephardi and Ashkenazi, old and young, rich and poor – an occurrence virtually unprecedented in our fragmented society.

On Friday night, before we ushered in Shabbat, I spoke to my son on the media and begged him to be strong, for all our people were with him. As we sat at the Shabbat table, my eyes were glued to the door, expecting Nachshon to walk in at any moment.

We were unaware that Prime Minister Rabin had located

the terrorists base and had made a decision to launch a military action to attempt to rescue our son.

At the hour of the ultimatum, 8:00 PM Friday night, General Yoram Yair, not Nachshon, walked through our door and brought us the terrible news. The military rescue attempt had failed – Nachshon had been killed and so had the commander of the rescue team, Captain Nir Poraz.

We all sat frozen, unbelieving, shocked and devastated for the rest of Shabbat.

On Saturday night at midnight we buried our son.

That same microcosm of our people who had come to pray for Nachshon's rescue at the Western Wall came to Mount Herzl at midnight Saturday night to attend Nachshon's funeral. My husband's greatest concern when burying his son was that there would be a crisis in faith. That people wouldn't understand

In a eulogy delivered at the graveside – broadcast live to the entire country – Rabbi Mordechai Elon, a friend of the family, related that he came to the house shortly after the terrible news became known, hoping to find the right words to comfort us and my husband said to him:

"There's no need to say anything. Just one thing worries me now. Nachshon succeeded in raising the Jewish people to a high level of faith and prayer. Now we have the responsibility to sustain this level. People will ask, how it is that we were not answered, in spite of all the numerous prayers? But you know, I asked Hashem for many things in my life, and he always granted them, I asked Him for good health and He gave it to me. I asked Him for a family and He granted it to me. So now if they will ask why we did not merit a reply from our Father in Heaven for all the prayers? I will tell them, 'We did receive a response, we did get an answer. The answer was 'No.' Because a Father can sometimes also answer with a 'No.'

The next day on the radio, he said:

"It is clear that all the prayers were not in vain. The terrorists were barricaded behind booby-trapped steel doors! Many soldiers could have lost their lives; the many prayers were a factor in sparing their lives. True, we lost Nachshon, but because of the prayers other lives were spared. I'm telling you again," he stressed, " most of the times that I asked Hashem for something, I received 'Yes' for an answer. This time, the answer to me, personally, was 'No,' but the answer to the prayers in general was a positive one."

The thing that kept us sane and functioning through all this was our faith. We believe that every person has a mission in life. We believe that our years are numbered. When a person fulfils his mission, then that is the end. Our faith was that these were the years allotted to our son and he fulfilled what he was supposed to fulfil.

The entire nation mourned with us. Thousands came to comfort us, though no one can comfort a bereaved parent. Israeli radio began each morning's broadcasts with the words, "Good morning Israel, we are all with the Wachsman family." Food and drink were delivered non-stop to our home; bus and taxi drivers who brought people from all over the country who wished to express their condolences, left their vehicles and joined their passengers in our home. That unity, solidarity, caring, compassion, and love with which we were showered gave us strength and filled our hearts with love for our people.

After the *Shiva*, we all returned to our routines. One son began university, another went back to the army, two others returned to yeshiva, and the two youngest, twins who had just turned eight on the day of the funeral, went back to school.

For that is what the Jewish people have always done – rebuilt after destruction, began new lives from the ashes of the old.

ISRAEL IN 1996

- Mirabilis releases the first version of the instant messaging computer programme, ICQ, playing on the phrase "I seek you": two years later AOL buys Mirabilis for £407 million
- Mount Carmel is declared a biosphere reserve within the framework of the Man and Biosphere Program of UNESCO

Gideon Posner died in a helicopter accident in February 1997 whilst on active service for the IDF. This essay is in honour of Gideon and all JFS Alumni who have died whilst serving in the Israel Defence Forces since 1947.

50 Succot: The Joy of a Restored Relationship

Yossi Michalowicz

The *Torah* tells us that we celebrate the holiday of *Succot* in the autumn to remember, in particular, the kindness that God showed the Jewish people as they left Egypt. During the course of their 40-year journey through the desert, God surrounded them with clouds of glory that protected them from the elements, while at the same time providing them with a climate-controlled and comfortable environment.

The obvious question is: Why do we celebrate this holiday in the autumn when, in fact, the Jews benefited from the clouds immediately when they left from Egypt in the spring?

Another question: God actually provided us with three gifts while we travelled through the desert. In addition to the clouds, He miraculously sent us *Manna* from heaven for food and an endless supply of fresh water from a stone. Why is there only a holiday to commemorate the clouds of glory and not the other two items?

One final question: Each holiday is linked to a particular aspect of time. *Pesach* is called "the time of our freedom," since it was the Exodus from Egypt that gave the Jewish people their liberty. *Shavuot* is labelled "the time of our receiving the Torah," as this was the day in history when at Mount Sinai,

God gave the Jewish people their instructions for life. However, the holiday of Succot is referred to by a more general term "the time of our joy," "*Zman Simchaseinu*". What is uniquely joyous about being accompanied by clouds of glory, more so than receiving our freedom or the Torah?

We can historically answer the first question with the following information. As a result of the Jewish people sinning by worshipping the Golden Calf three months after the Exodus, God withdrew the clouds of glory. [He could not withdraw the Manna or water – for then we would have died.] The Jews lived for nearly three additional months without those clouds until Moses returned to the Jewish people on *Yom Kippur*, the 10th day of Tishrei. He brought with him the second set of the Ten Commandments, inscribed on two tablets of stone, and informed the Jews that God had forgiven them for their sin. Five days later, on the 15th day of Tishrei, the clouds returned. It is for these restored clouds of glory that we commemorate the holiday of Succot – which begins on the 15th of Tishrei.

However, this answer begs the question: if the Jews were forgiven on the 10th of Tishrei, why didn't the clouds return on that day? Why was it delayed until the 15th?

The answer to this is based on a fundamental principle in relationship building. If a person wrongs someone else, the relationship has been damaged and is in danger of never being able to return to its original state. Three things must happen in order for the relationship to be restored. First, the violator must sincerely seek forgiveness and appease the victim. Second, the victim must accept the overture of the offender and grant forgiveness. But that is not nearly enough. Often people will say, "I forgive you for what you did, but I no longer wish to have a relationship with you. So stay out of my life, because anything you would do for me would be a painful reminder of your past activities."

That may be the human response – but it is not the Godly response. Even though the Jews violated their relationship with God in the worst way by sinning with the Golden Calf,

He did more than just forgive them and not punish them. He was willing to continue the relationship at the same level as before the Jews sinned. To forgive, to forget, and to act as if it never occurred.

What was the litmus test of this relationship? The clouds of glory! They weren't just a protective shield providing a mere utilitarian service. They were the manifestation of God's desire to create a secluded home in which He would dwell with us – His nation. It was our intimate relationship with God that was represented by those clouds. When the Jews violated the relationship by worshipping the Golden Calf, the clouds retreated in response. However, when the Jews repented, God firstly forgave them as evidenced by Yom Kippur, but that was not all. The day after Yom Kippur, God told Moshe to ask the Jews to donate towards the building of a *Mishkan*, a tabernacle, where they could serve God – a miniature home.

For the next three days the Jews were busy contributing until they were told that there was enough and on the following day, the 15th of Tishrei, God gave the people the green light to begin construction of the Mishkan. God, in effect, was saying, "I am interested in your gifts and the renewed display of your affection towards Me, in building a house where we can live together. As a sign of our renewed relationship, I will demonstrate to you how much you mean to Me and will bring back the clouds of glory!" This was truly a joyous moment for us.

Every year we go through this process. All year long we make mistakes in our relationship with God. Eventually we come to Him during the High Holiday period and ask for forgiveness. By the end of the ten days of repentance, we hope to have achieved that forgiveness once again. But our greatest concern is: *Is my relationship with God as intimate as it once was? Does He want me in the same way?* The answer plays itself out when we build a *Succah*, commemorating those clouds of glory that came back. It is God's response to us that says: "I want your *mitzvot* – these mitzvot will bring you closer to me." When we sit in our cosy Succah on a starry night, performing this *mitzvah* alone, secluded, and intimately with God – there can be no greater "time of joy" than that – knowing that the feelings of love, once lost, have returned to their former glory!

SUCCOT IN ISRAEL

*Visit Israel in the days leading up to **Succot** and you will see streets filled with trestle tables selling the **arba minim** (the four species) as well as posters and decorations for the **succah**. People all over town are busy putting up their succahs outdoors. On Succot itself, the real sounds of celebration are heard as communities celebrate the **Simchat Beit Hashoeva** with live music and dancing. Each night the fun is at a different venue. However, perhaps the best part of Succot in Israel is the weather; you never worry about rain, even at night!*

ISRAEL IN 1997

- Israel sends aid to Mexican hurricane victims
- A survey of 5,000 Israeli men and women over 60 carried out by Hebrew University finds that adults who attend synagogue regularly live longer than their peers who do not
- The FDA approves Copaxone, a drug for multiple sclerosis developed at the Weizmann Institute

51 Aliyah: Making the Move

Gideon Sylvester

Early one morning in August, the Prime Minister, dignitaries and well-wishers travelled to Ben Gurion Airport to witness five planes from Britain and America touch down. With music and great fanfare, they greeted the hundreds of people who were arriving on *aliyah* – to make their homes in Israel.

There are many reasons why people make aliyah: some just like the sun and the sea, others come because they feel uncomfortable with the rising antisemitism in their home countries or in search of a better standard of living.

These are all valid reasons, but my heroes are the idealists – the people who make their homes in Israel because they believe that it is a *mitzvah* and an expression of their Jewish identity, because Israel is the place to perform *mitzvot*.

These people point to the Biblical verse, "and you shall inherit the land, and live in it; for I have given you the land to possess it,"[1] explaining that it is incumbent on all Jews to make their home in the Land of Israel. Is this commandment given to our ancestors in the desert, thousands of years ago, still binding upon us? In medieval times, the rabbis debated the question at length; some explained that it remained obligatory for all Jews to come and live in the Land of Israel,[2] while others argued that it was no longer binding since it was too difficult and dangerous to make the journey there.[3] In modern times, when aliyah has become very easy, the debate continues. Some rabbis describe it as one of the most important demands of the *Torah*[4] while others argue that although it is a positive act to make your home in Israel, it is not obligatory and depends on individual circumstances.[5]

Many Jews believe that there is a religious dimension to aliyah which goes beyond the legal requirement. They argue that living in Israel is central to the message of the Torah. Throughout the Torah, we read of God's covenant with our forefathers in which he promised that he would give them and their descendants the Land of Israel. Occasional crises forced them to leave the land, but they always longed to return to it. The Torah relates at length the story of the Jewish people leaving Egypt and spending forty years wandering through the desert in order to reach the Promised Land and build a just society there. The later books of the Bible continue this narrative describing the conquest and settlement of the land. They warn of exile as the punishment for sin and promise the return to the land as the reward for repentance.

Perhaps all of this led Rabbi Abraham Isaac Kook, the first Chief Rabbi of the Land of Israel, to see aliyah in mystical terms. He felt that life in the Diaspora meant constantly apologising and justifying why we were different from our neighbours and this damaged the psyche of the Jewish people. Only a return to our own land would enable Jews to have the dignity of a sovereign nation and experience the spirituality of living on the holy soil of the land that God chose for us.[7]

I find it thrilling to live in the land where so much of our history and so many of the events of the Bible took place. I will never forget my first *Chumash* class in *yeshiva*. We were examining the story of the binding of Isaac when my teacher, Rabbi David Walk, pointed out of the window. "Look over there," he said, "that's the road that Abraham and Isaac walked along on their way to the *Akeida*." Living in the land brought a whole new dimension to studying our ancient texts.

But making aliyah is not about living in the past. Each time I walk through the streets of Jerusalem and see the walls of the

Old City looming up on the horizon, I feel affirmed in my Jewish identity. I particularly love strolling through the streets on *Shabbat*, and absorbing the serenity borne of a national day of rest. Just a brief walk through my neighbourhood is guaranteed to bring me into contact with one of the many Jewish heroes who live here. Next door lives a man who fought bravely in Israel's wars; around the corner is an Ethiopian who trekked through the desert to come to Israel; the former refusenik Natan Sharansky lives up the road and there are many world renowned rabbis and scholars who live locally. Life in Israel is an ongoing seminar in Jewish living and Jewish thought. It is the problems and achievements of the Jewish people that make the newspaper headlines every day and when the Knesset debates moral issues, the discussion is passionate with Jewish texts central to it.

Most exciting of all, the decision to take out Israeli citizenship gives one a chance to participate in the national debate about how to build the Jewish future. In Israel, we delve into our tradition to find authentic Jewish responses to difficult questions: What are the rules governing a modern, conscientious Jewish army? How do we run an ethical Jewish national economy? These are tough issues, but as a new immigrant, I relish the fact that they open up new vistas of Jewish thought that expand our Jewish consciousness and engage Jewish Law in some of the most sensitive issues on the world agenda.

It is wonderful to immigrate to a country where the Prime Minister meets you off the plane because he values the fact that you and other Jews have chosen to come and live here. Life in Israel may not always be easy, but each difficulty reminds us that aliyah in itself is not enough. Our challenge is to come to live in Israel and build a just society based on the values of the Torah, and by living an ethical life, become a light to the nations.

For thousands of years, Jews have prayed every day to God saying, "Bring us in from the four corners of the earth to our land." Now, every day, we can go to Ben Gurion airport and witness the miraculous fulfilment of this prayer as Jews arrive from across the world to make their homes in the State of Israel.

Notes:
1 Numbers 23:53
2 Ramban Commentary on the Bible Numbers 13: 53
3 Tosafot Ketubot 110b s.v. *Veayn*
4 See for example Rav Ovadiah Yosef, Yehave Da'at, IV:49 and Rav Chaim David Halevi, *Aseh Lecha Rav*, I:17
5 Rabbi Moshe Feinstein, *Iggrot Moshe, Even Ha Ezer* I:102
6 Talmud Bavli, Ketubot 112b
7 See for example Rav A I Kook, *Orot* p.17

ISRAEL IN 1998
- Israel celebrates its 50th anniversary
- Tel Aviv named by Newsweek as one of the ten most technologically influential cities in the world
- Work starts on building a state of the art terminal 3 at Ben-Gurion airport
- The International Centre for the Study of Bird Migration opens, to study the 500 million migrating birds that fly over Israel twice a year

Dedicated to Grandma Sadie
and Grandpa George Albaster zt"l.

52 Mezuzah: Faith and Conciliation

Daniel Levy

In Israel, the vast majority of homes, offices and public buildings proudly display a *mezuzah* on their front door. The mezuzah has become to the home what circumcision has become to the body - a *mitzvah* integral to the Jew. But what is the meaning behind this small parchment scroll?

Mezuzah incorporates some of the essential aspects of our belief and practice. Firstly, the text written on the scroll is the *Shema,* the prayer fundamental to our Jewish beliefs. This is the essence of the mezuzah. It spells out our faith in God and how we are committed to serve Him. The Shema was recited by martyrs throughout history. When they were forced from their homes and had to abandon their *mezuzot,* the words accompanied them - engraved on their hearts and taken with them to the grave.

The mezuzah's text is also a reminder of our Covenant with the Almighty. If we keep His commandments then the seasons will function properly and we will receive the blessings of food and peace. Furthermore, the wording of the scroll must be carefully and precisely written, with no mistakes. This symbolises that our practice and belief in the *Torah* should be steadfast and uncompromising.

In addition to this, the positioning of the mezuzah at a specific height on the doorpost shows us how we must position ourselves correctly in the world and not in a way that may dilute our values and ethics. On a school visit, the world famous American rabbi, Rabbi Yaakov Kamenetsky (1891–1986) *zt"l* once noticed that the mezuzah had been placed half way down the doorpost. Rabbi Kamenetsky approached the teacher and gently asked the teacher why the mezuzah was not as it should be – in the top third of the post. The teacher replied that it was too high for the children to reach and had been placed lower down, so that the children would reach it in order to kiss it.

Rabbi Kamenetsky explained that *halachically* the mezuzah must be placed in the top third of the doorpost. When the teacher asked, "How will the children kiss the mezuzah?" he smiled warmly and answered, "Let them stand on a chair to reach it. Otherwise they will grow up thinking that a mezuzah can be put anywhere you wish. One does not raise children with untruths."

Rabbi Kamenetsky believed passionately that when educating children in the performance of mitzvot, we cannot lower the standards to meet them. Rather they should be encouraged to raise their standards. This is because *chinuch* (the mitzvah of educating children) is to prepare children for the fulfillment of commandments in adulthood. If they are used to adhering to the correct halachic requirements in their childhood, they will continue to do so when they become adults.[1]

The mezuzah also helps us understand the concept of conciliation in *halachah*. Two views are expressed about how to affix the mezuzah, one is that it should be in a vertical position; the other that is should be horizontal. The halachah takes both views into account; since we affix it at an angle. Few of our practices convey so starkly this idea.[2] The angling of the mezuzah reminds us that we must attempt to find a path of compromise where possible whilst still remaining firmly within the realm of halachah. This approach allows us to embrace others more easily.

It is customary to kiss the mezuzah when entering and leaving the home.[3] When we do this we are mindful of the protection that God affords us, and this act reinforces our faith in His protection. In fact, the outer side of the Mezuzah, contains one of the divine names of God.[4] This provides a reminder that He is the Guardian of the Jewish people.

But perhaps when entering a building, we should also be aware of the art of co-operation that is symbolised by the mezuzah. Imagine returning home from a hard day's work and entering the home kissing the mezuzah, mindful not of how hard our day has been, but how difficult our spouse's day may have been. Or going into a business meeting and kissing the mezuzah of the boardroom, mindful of the need to find a middle path amongst board members. As such, we would be more understanding and willing to compromise with others, be they parents, spouse, children or associates.

These ideas go to the heart of Israeli society. Unfortunately, different religious and irreligious groups in Israel are often portrayed as being at each other's throats. However, this is not actually as the media would have us believe. I could cite many examples, but I will just share a personal one. In 2003, I had the *zechut* of leading a solidarity trip from Leeds UK to Israel. We visited Kfar Bialik in the North and went to a farmer's field where food that had been donated from local businesses and factories, and purchased through charitable donations, was being prepared for needy families. Chicken, meat, eggs, cheese, bread, fruit and vegetables, were being bagged up by groups of volunteers comprised of religious Jews and secular Israelis, who then arranged the deliveries together. What we beheld then, was what we rarely see reported: religious and irreligious people engaging in what Abraham the father of our faith engaged in: *chesed* (acts of loving kindness).

Despite the sometimes fractious relationship between different groups in Israeli society, there are a considerable number of Jews who have made huge efforts to co-operate and work together. They have learnt from the message of the mezuzah and have internalised that message so that barriers have been overcome and progress made. Yes, more work may be required and will continue to be done, but as the *Mishnah* says, "The work is not for you to complete but neither are you free to desist from it."[5]

The mezuzah teaches us fundamental lessons both about our relationship with God and with people – this is something for us to think about next time we enter our homes.

Notes:

1 For a full discussion of this principle see Rabbi Kamenetsky's halachic analysis in his book *Emet Le'Yaakov on Shulchan Aruch*, Orach Chayyim 689

2 Shulchan Aruch YD 289:6.

3 Shulchan Aruch YD 285:2.

4 The 3-letter acronym Shin-Daled-Yud stands for Shomer Daltot Yisrael: God is the Guardian at the entrances to our houses

5 Ethics of the Fathers 2:21

ISRAEL IN 1999

- Ben Gurion University builds the world's largest solar-concentrating dish, able to generate thermal energy at an intensity 10,000 times stronger than normal noontime sunshine.
- After a massive earthquake hits Northwest Turkey, Prime Minister Ehud Barak sends a medical team to assist local authorities. The Israeli team rescues 12 people, treats 1,200 people, performs 40 operations, and delivers 15 babies
- Israel's Pentium III chip, developed by their Israel company, is released.

53 Chesed and Gemachs

Yoni Sherizen

Sarah lived in a crowded Jerusalem neighbourhood and as news of her recent engagement spread she had never been happier. The close-knit community showered her with joyous wishes, but with the wedding plans progressing, Sarah became increasingly distraught. Her family simply didn't have the money to pay for a wedding nor did her bridegroom. As the prospect of collecting communal funds for the wedding appeared the only way forward, Sarah was feeling increasingly distressed and embarrassed.

Sarah was in desperate need of what the *Rambam* classified as the one of the greatest forms of *tzedakah*[1]: a gift both given and received anonymously. But how would an anonymous donor know of her plight and how would she receive the funds without being shamed by uncovering the severity of her need?

Thankfully, Sarah benefited from a brilliant system devised to help people in situations like hers: the *Gemach*. The impetus behind these Gemachs is the emphasis placed by the *Torah* on extending a helping hand to those who are in need. What she received was a great deal more than simply tzedakah, it incorporated *chesed* / loving-kindness too.

The word tzedakah comes from the root *tzedek* - justice. However, it cannot be translated as simply justice because tzedakah is also charity. Our charitable gifts are an act of justice because we are taking that which has been given to us by God and allocating the necessary amount to those in need. We must do our share as just people by giving charity. But beyond that there is chesed, giving of one's self. Chesed goes further than tzedakah, as illustrated by the *Gemara*[2]:

The rabbis teach: Acts of loving-kindness (chesed) are greater than charity (tzedakah) in three ways:

Charity is done with one's money but loving-kindness may be done with one's money or body.

Charity is given to the poor but loving-kindness is done for both rich and poor.

Charity is given to the living but loving-kindness is done for both the living and the dead.

Sarah's wedding didn't depend on tzedakah in the form of a donation. Instead, a system known as Gemach provided most of the necessary resources. Based on the Hebrew acronym for *Gemilut Chassadim* (acts of loving-kindness), a Gemach is a source for borrowing everything from wedding dresses to prayer books, tables and chairs to medical equipment and baby clothing to free short-term loans.

These societies receive gifts donated by private individuals that they in turn lend to those who require them. All donations become gifts that keep on giving, because the item is used over and over again. But more importantly, the Gemach takes away the embarrassment of taking tzedakah by hiding who gives and who takes from its resources. It also promotes itself to the entire community - rich or poor - and having more people taking from the system reduces any embarrassment associated with receiving. This even transforms taking from the Gemach into a good deed because it establishes it as normative - a living example of the Rambam's "tzedakah in action", with the added touch of chesed. Gemachs have now developed in the service and volunteer sector, in areas such as free legal and financial advice and there are even ones that provide emergency baby-sitters!

Historically Gemachs have been a mainstay of Jewish communities. Over the last 60 years this system has flourished in Israel - a state that was born with limited resources. Its new members cared for one another like family; sharing your belongings was a natural habit and disposing of them seemed a crime. Today the Jewish community in Jerusalem alone runs over 1,000 Gemachs and a look at Jerusalem's Yellow pages will reveal 40 pages devoted to these societies!

Another facet of Gemachs is the connections between communities: most are initiated and staffed by religious Jews but serve the spectrum of society. Internationally this has replicated itself in many Jewish communities. This means that thousands of Jewish families, including my own, have benefited and contributed to one of these organisations at some point, with no shame involved.

With time some Gemachs have expanded beyond all expectation. Yad Sarah - a medical facility - is a typical example of this. Founded by Rabbi Uri Lupoliansky, the current mayor of Jerusalem, 30 years ago, it started when he lent a simple hot-steam vaporiser to a neighbour with a sick child. Others asked to borrow the device too, and Lupoliansky - using a small sum left by his grandmother Sarah - purchased additional vaporisers. Today, with over 6,000 volunteers and 90 branches around the country, Yad Sarah has assisted one out of every three families in the country. This Gemach saves the economy some $250 million a year in hospitalisation, as well as lending out tens of millions of dollars worth of equipment.

Many significant events, like Sarah's wedding, would be crippling without the resources of a Gemach. By building and maintaining communal institutions like these, which promote self-sufficiency and maintain a basic standard of living, we can hope to fulfil the teaching in the Book of Psalms (*Tehillim*), "*Olam chesed yibaneh* - You shall create a world of loving-kindness." A world where both tzedek and chesed shine.

Notes:
1 Laws of Gifts to the Poor, 10:7 where the Rambam classifies the single greatest form of 'tzedakah' as providing someone with a livelihood
2 Sukkah 49b
3 Book of Psalms 89:3

ISRAEL IN 2000

- The Ayalon Highway launches a traffic control system, the first of its kind in Israel, and one of the most advanced in the world
- Pope John Paul II visits Israel
- Israel withdraws from the Security Zone in Southern Lebanon
- Kodak purchases Israeli startup, Picture Vision, for $90 million
- The 2nd intifada breaks out

In memory of Gad Yaakov ben Yehudah zt"l who died
in July 1970 while on IDF duty.

54 Behind the Mask

Dr Akiva Tatz

We can gain access to the spiritual world only through the mask of the physical. To do so however, we need to know the rules. The world of nature hides the spiritual, by appearing to be self-sufficient, reliable and predictable. Yet, intrinsically, a miracle is no more wonderful than the natural – it is simply that the miraculous breaks the expected pattern.

There is an allusion to this during the Exodus – at the splitting of the sea. After the Jewish people had crossed over, Moshe was commanded to stretch his staff out over the sea to bring the waters back to their original, natural position. But why was an act necessary for this? To split the sea an act was necessary because that was miraculous; nature had to be set aside. But surely, as soon as the Jewish people were safe and the need for the miracle was over, nature should have re-asserted itself automatically. The answer is that nature is *miraculous* every day, whether the natural act is commonplace or rare. It is no less the express wish and manifestation of the Creator for the sea to manifest in the way that we are used than the once-in-history splitting of that sea. The only difference is that we are accustomed to the one whereas the unexpected, rare occurrence makes us take notice.

We are lulled into insensitivity by the routine of nature. The Hebrew word for nature is *teva*, the root of which means "to drown". If the world of natural cause and effect is not carefully and perceptively studied for its clues to depth, it drowns awareness of the spiritual. But the word *teva* is also the root of *matbea*, meaning a coin which has an embossed image stamped on its surface. The world is a stamped-out image of a higher reality. If one studies the world with the knowledge that it accurately reflects its Source, one can perceive the features of that Source. The choice is entirely the observer's, to look at the world with the tired eyes of habit and see only the mechanical, or to look with eyes of wonder and see the image of a higher reality.

Moreover, each detail of the world teaches us something about its source in the spiritual world. Each detail here is an exact parallel of that which exists there. This is perfectly logical. If we were commanded to study and understand the spiritual realm and yet had no avenue of access to that understanding, what would be the sense of such a command? The pathway is clear. We are, in fact, enjoined to look more deeply, to look into those depths that cannot be seen by human eyes, and the access is by means of a close and sensitive study of that which *is* revealed. Just as a person observes the physical body of his friend in order to relate to the person or the inner being of that friend, so too, we study the structure and movements of the physical world in order to perceive its root. There is simply no other way; a person never sees the inner being or *neshama* of another person – we have no sense organ which can perceive a soul. All we can do is observe the person's bodily expression and gain insight into what they are. Subtle movements of the body, a flicker of expression on the face, the slightest gesture of tension in bodily posture – all of these speak worlds.

All communication between people occurs in this way. Speech itself is none other than the physical moving of tongue and lips generating sound waves which cause a physical response in the ear of the listener. Yet amazingly, subtle and refined ideas can be translated from their native medium in the mind and reduced to these physical forms. But there is no other way – the only access we have to the thoughts and personality of another human being is through the vehicle of the concrete, the physical.

In relating to people, that switch from outer body to inner person is achieved effortlessly: while relating intensely to another person one is usually unaware of the interface provided by the body, one simply perceives the inner reality *as if* directly. This natural ability to use the body and yet see its core is a Divine gift which teaches us that such perception can be achieved. Our challenge is to use the entire world in this way; to study all aspects of the physical world for what they reveal about their Creator.

This is a remarkable and inspiring view of the world. Every object and phenomenon contain a Divine lesson, a *mashal* relating to the Creator. He, so to speak, clothes Himself in a body which is the Universe and asks us to study it. And from each flicker of movement in that cosmic body we learn about that which pertains to Him. He, in His essence, is unfathomable to us. While we inhabit physical forms we cannot perceive the transcendent directly, just as we cannot perceive the soul of a human directly. But just as we can perceive the human soul by means of its vehicle, the body, so too, can we begin to perceive the Divine root of the world by means of that vehicle, that body which we call the world.

A parable for this is to consider images projected on a screen. The forms and figures moving on the screen are no more than light dancing in two dimensions. They may look very convincing and one may even forget for a while that they are only pictures. But in fact, those images are very distant versions of the people and places photographed. However, and this is the critical point to remember, *they are exact replicas of the original.* They may be entirely illusory compared to their sources, but one who carefully studies that light dancing on that screen *will recognise those people and places when he meets them in the future.*

The analogy is clear. One who studies this world well, is studying that which is a distant representation of a source – one that cannot be seen from here. But one day in the future, on that inevitable day when the transition must be made from this world to another, the one who has studied well will recognise every detail of reality. Then it will become apparent that this world, for all its beauty and sense of reality, is in depth a *mashal* for the Divine Source of that reality.

(This essay is an edited extract from the author's book Worldmask *published by Targum / Feldheim.)*

ISRAEL IN 2001

- First clinical trials take place for a miniature video camera that once swallowed transmits real images of areas of disease
- The new central bus station in Jerusalem opens
- Israel's number one export becomes flowers
- Ariel Sharon (Likud) is elected prime minister and forms a broad-based unity government
- Ikea's first Israeli store opens in Netanya

In memory of Yoni Jesner of Glasgow, Scotland, one of five people killed in a suicide bombing on a bus in Tel Aviv. A remarkable young man whose good work continues through the Yoni Jesner Foundation at www.yonijesner.org

55 Chevron: Connecting Heaven and Earth

Holly Pavlov

That city of our forefathers, the city in which our patriarchs and matriarchs are buried, the city of King David's coronation, the first capital of Israel before the conquest of Jerusalem, a city of spirituality, a city that bridges Heaven and earth: Chevron.

Every city in the Land of Israel is connected to a Heavenly sphere and the name of the city indicates the spiritual essence of that city. Chevron comes from the Hebrew word *chibur*, connection. Chevron, then, is a place of ongoing connection.

But what is this connection? The *Zohar* tells us an interesting story regarding the Biblical story of the three angels who visit Abraham. Abraham did not know that these three visiting messengers of *Hashem* were angels. Instead, he thought them to be pagan nomads. Abraham welcomed them into his tent, and began preparing a sumptuous meal for his guests. Abraham then ran to the cattle and chose a tender young animal from which to prepare the meal, but the calf he chose ran away.

Abraham tried to catch the animal, but the calf ran into a cave. Chasing it, he followed into the cave and witnessed the most amazing sight: Adam and Eve, sleeping on funeral biers, candles lit all around them and the smell of sweet incense filling the cave. It was because of this encounter that Abraham acquired this cave as a family burial plot in Chevron.

What was this vision? Ancestors, departed from this world, yet seemingly, not dead, merely sleeping. Lit candles, burning bright, like the menorah in the Temple, the sweet smell of incense, like the incense brought daily in the Temple. Abraham understood that this cave was not an ordinary cave, but one that, like our Temple, connected worlds; the world of physicality and the world of spirituality, this world and the next world.

The *Ramchal* teaches that when a person sleeps, part of their soul leaves them and rises to a more spiritual place, whereas when they die, the soul leaves the body altogether. In Chevron, however, part of the soul remains in this world, even after death. It is then, a place of eternal connection, a place where life does not end.

This is further seen in the Hebrew letters of the word Chevron – which when transposed read as Churban: Destruction. The teaching behind this idea, is that even when the Jewish people are in a state of desolation – when Jerusalem and the Temple are not built – there exists a connection to God through Chevron, through the prayers of our Patriarchs and Matriarchs.

There is another name associated with Chevron: The Cave of Machpelah. Machpelah derives from the Hebrew word *kaful,* double. The Talmud teaches that the cave is called the "Cave of Doubles" because couples are buried there: Adam and Eve, Abraham and Sarah, Isaac and Rebecca, Jacob and Leah. Couples are doubles.

On a deeper level, we learn that couples who build their marriages properly are connected in two ways: physically and spiritually. Our Rabbis teach that in marriage, "A man and a woman merit the Divine Presence between them."

The Hebrew word for man is *ish,* and for woman *ishah.* The words contain two common letters that together spell, *aish*, fire. Part of marriage is the physical connection, the fire and passion.

Conversely, the words for man and woman contain two different letters. *Ish*, man, contains the letter *yud,* while *ishah,* woman, contains the letter *heh*. Together *yud* and *heh* spell one of the names of God. This signifies the spiritual aspect of marriage through giving, love and stretching to meet the other person's needs.

Marriage brings couples great potential for spiritual growth, with both husband and wife contributing to each other. In *Kabbalah*, the letter *yud* in the word *ish*, man, indicates connection to the spiritual source, to Hashem. On the page, the letter *yud* hangs in the air, without touching the line, so a *yud* stands for raw spirituality without grounding in the physical world. On the other hand, the *heh* in *Kabbalah* is spirituality as it is used in the physical world, practical spirituality, with two feet on the ground.

When husband and wife live a life of harmony, they each share their ability with the other. A husband is connected to Heaven, the spiritual source. This often expresses itself as ideas and theories, a vision of the bigger picture, but not in practical application. A wife, on the other hand, knows how to translate vision into practical reality. A conversation between them might go something like this: He: "I have an idea," She: "How are you going to do that?"

A woman is often the practical partner, knowing how to create spirituality in the physical world, how to translate the ideas of *Torah* into facts on the ground. Yet, she can sometimes get stuck in the practical and lose sight of the bigger picture. In a marriage of sharing, the husband can hold on to the vision while the wife creates the reality.

Of course, stereotypes don't always work, as people differ and each marriage has its own internal rules. However, the essential idea remains: Marriage should be a union of mutual help and giving, and when it is built on this premise, *Hashem* - the *yud* and *heh* - dwells within the relationship.

The Cave of Machpelah is called by its name the "Cave of Doubles" for this reason; it is a burial place of partners that were each helpers to their mate, creating union, harmony and connection. Having lived a life of connection, they are buried in a place of connection, Chevron.

Chevron represents the Jewish idea that the physical world and the spiritual world are connected, not two mutually exclusive realms. The Torah teaches us how to use the material world to achieve spiritual aims. And Chevron contains that energy that fuels the process.

Chevron is a place of doubles. Chevron is a place of connection, a place that bridges heaven and earth.

ISRAEL IN 2002

- Daniel Kahneman receives the Nobel Prize in Economics for his work in Prospect Theory
- 1.9 million Israelis now have mobile phones
- A geneticist at the Hebrew University of Jerusalem breeds a featherless chicken

Dedicated to Jeremy Jacobs in recognition of his
outstanding dedication to Tribe UK and Tribe Israel.

56 Kids: A Public Commodity

Yaffa Ganz

Israel is a land of babies and it's quite obvious why. The *Torah* tells
us in a perfectly plain and forthright fashion that if, in the Land
of Israel, we walk in God's ways, carefully keeping His statutes,
laws, and commandments, He will turn His face towards us,
make us fruitful, multiply us, and establish His covenant with us.
Even though we haven't quite learned how to 'walk' properly in
His ways as yet, fortunately for us, God is patient and merciful
and very generous about advancing us credit.

So throughout the country, wherever you go, you see a world
of children. Women with children and women about to have
children. Women pushing buggies and strollers, and stores which
sell them - together with cribs and dressers and bassinets and
potties. Children's clothes, toys and shoes are big business, even
when business is slow. And the busiest municipal departments are
always the pre-kindergarten / kindergarten divisions. There are no
two ways about it. Israel is a child-orientated society. Thank God.

It does, however, take some getting used to, because your
baby isn't only yours in the Holy Land. Once you've had it, it
becomes communal property, a fact you will discover as soon
as you walk out the front door. Did the little darling squeak?
Someone will comment. Did he cry? Someone will
investigate. Is it hot out? Or cold? Don't worry. Someone will
instruct you and tell you what to do.

"Give him a drink."

"Put his hat on."

"Take his hat off."

"He's tired, hungry, thirsty, teething."

"Give him water."

"Give him juice."

"Take his sweater off; he's hot."

"Put the sweater on; it's cold."

"Doesn't he have a hat? It's windy and his ears will hurt."

They'll ask who your doctor is, how much the baby weighs, if he sleeps through the night. And you're expected to answer.

Even an outing with a smiling baby is a public affair. On a quick, fifteen-minute walk to the neighbourhood drugstore with her six-month-old daughter, one young woman I know was stopped a total of nine times. Four times by neighbours; three times by elderly people she did not know; and twice by kids. All stopped her to comment on how adorable the baby was. Admittedly, hers is cute, but nine times in fifteen minutes shows an enormous amount of public interest in the younger generation!

Once, on a bus ride in Jerusalem, a screaming baby refused to be comforted. The resulting chaos had to be seen to be believed. Old men and women from all parts of the bus gave advice and directions; people passed food and drinks to the mother; the bus driver wanted to turn the radio up ("Maybe some music will soothe him?"); teenagers were willing to walk the infant up and down the aisle. So what did you expect from a busload of Jewish grandparents and parents and kids? Cool and detached we aren't.

I personally know of four separate emergency cases where people were flagged down and ended up taking expectant mothers to the hospital – women they had never seen before. Having deposited their uninvited passengers at the door of the delivery room, each one parked his car, went into the hospital and waited patiently to find out if he had "delivered" a boy or a girl. If it was a boy, he came to the *brit milah* as well.

The Israeli government participates in births. *Bituach Leumi* (the Israeli version of Social Security) gives a gift of several hundred shekels to each new baby, plus a monthly sum for each child until the age of 16. The Jerusalem municipality sends a colourful certificate for a tree planted in honour of each baby. Many stores, organisations, community centres, and schools take the number of children in a family into consideration when billing a client.

In our neighbourhood, elderly men going to or from synagogue in the morning are regularly accompanied by neighbourhood kids on their way to school. Conversation ensues; smiles are exchanged; and a bit of candy or gum is passed into eager hands. A little love and communication between the generations is a nice way to start the day, both for the elderly and for the young.

The most heart-warming display of children, however, is during *chol hamoed* when Israeli families turn out en masse. The majority are either hiking or driving or picnicking or visiting with their kids. In the religious neighbourhoods you can see long strings of handholding brothers and sisters helping each other to cross the streets or to see the animals in the zoo or to kiss the *Kotel* or to buy an ice cream cone.

Just as the Prophet Zechariah promised, our children - the offspring of our father Abraham - are filling the streets of Israel. "And the streets of the City shall be filled with little boys and girls playing... and if it be a marvel in the eyes of the remnants of the people in those days, it shall also be a marvel in My eyes, says God."

(Reprinted by kind permission of the author from her book, All Things Considered. *Copyright Yaffa Ganz.)*

ISRAEL IN 2003

- Israel accepts the roadmap for peace
- Colonel Ilan Ramon is the first Israeli astronaut in space, sadly, he is also the first to lose his life on such a mission
- Professor Yoel Margalith develop a natural occurring vaccine against the mosquito-borne West Nile virus which has killed thousands and infected many around the world, used to control malaria

In loving memory of Jeanne and Jack Hall zt"l.

57 A Modern Day 'Dayeinu' Song

Laurence Perez

The *Dayeinu* song that we say on *Seder night* immediately after the recital of the story of the Exodus from Egypt contains praise and gratitude for our miraculous escape from slavery. However, a closer look at the song reveals that it seems to make no sense at all. It describes the 14 stages of redemption from Egypt, beginning with the Exodus itself and ending with the building of the Temple in Jerusalem many years later. After each of the 14 stanzas, we sing the chorus, consisting of the Hebrew word *Dayeinu* (meaning *"It would have been enough"*). If *Hashem* would have brought us out of Egypt and not split the sea, "*Dayeinu.*" If Hashem would have split the sea and not given us food and water to drink in the desert, "*Dayeinu.*" These are two examples, which capture the essence of the song.

But these statements seem ludicrous. After all, if Hashem had brought us out of Egypt and <u>not</u> split the sea, surely we would have all died at the hands of the advancing Egyptian army? Similarly without being given food and water, we would have died of starvation and heat exhaustion in the desert. Clearly each single stage is incomplete without the continuation and realisation of the stage which follows, and had the process of redemption got stuck at any one of the earlier stages, it most certainly *would <u>not</u> have been enough*; The purpose of the redemption from Egypt would not have been achieved.

The answer to this question, explains *Rabbi Soloveitchik*, lies in understanding the very essence of what gratitude is all about. If our only focus in life is goal orientation then we will never be able to feel appreciation for anything until we have achieved that goal. If we focus incessantly on the final purpose of any process, we will find it exceptionally difficult to appreciate each stage of the journey itself.

The *Dayeinu* song is about a different frame of mind: *the mindset of gratitude and appreciation.* When we focus on each stage of the process itself, we are able to appreciate every small step. When we see how far we have come as opposed to how far there is to go, what we have as opposed to what we still lack, we are able to feel deep gratitude irrespective of whether we have achieved our final aim or not. The word *Dayeinu* in this song means "it would have been *enough reason to say thank you.*" If Hashem had brought us out of Egypt but not split the sea, this miraculous act of freedom and liberty would have been enough for us to thank Him for a taste of freedom against all odds. If Hashem would have split the sea but we would have died shortly after, we ought still to thank Him for the miraculous act of splitting the sea, for the opportunity of seeing God's glory.

This song forms the basis of the *Hallel* prayer (praising and thanking God), and it is only with the mindset of *Dayeinu* that we are able to begin to appreciate all God does for us in our personal and collective lives.

The State of Israel is, for many, very far from the spiritual State that it could be. There is no question that there is still a long journey ahead and so much more to be achieved. At the same time this should never cloud our ability to appreciate the enormous accomplishments at every step of the way since the beginning of the endeavour. The purpose of the modern day *Dayeinu* song which follows, is to arm ourselves with the mindset of appreciation, in the spirit of the *Haggadah*. By doing so, we will be able to appreciate, as we approach our 60th anniversary, the incredible achievements within the State of Israel.

IF Hashem had brought us back to the Land of Israel
BUT not given us a sovereign State
DAYEINU it would have been enough

IF Hashem had given us a sovereign State and allowed us a taste of freedom and dignity for but a moment
BUT we would have lost the War of Independence
DAYEINU

IF Hashem had helped us be victorious in the War of Independence
BUT we would not have succeeded in building a viable country
DAYEINU

IF Hashem had helped us build a viable country
BUT not brought back hundreds of thousands of Jews from Sephardic and Yeminite backgrounds
DAYEINU

IF Hashem had brought back hundreds of thousands of Jews from Sephardic and Yeminite backgrounds
BUT not allowed us to win the Six Day War
DAYEINU

IF Hashem had allowed us to win the Six Day War
BUT not allowed us to liberate the Old City of Jerusalem
DAYEINU

IF Hashem had allowed us to liberate the Old City of Jerusalem
BUT not allowed us to rebuild her ruins
DAYEINU

IF Hashem had allowed us to rebuild His Old City
BUT not implanted a deep spirit of self sacrifice in the hearts of our young Israeli soldiers
DAYEINU

IF Hashem had planted a spirit of self sacrifice in our young Israeli soldiers
BUT not allowed us to live with dignity in secure borders
DAYEINU

IF Hashem had allowed us to live in secure borders
BUT not created a strong and sustainable economy
DAYEINU

IF Hashem had built for us a strong and sustainable economy
BUT not ingathered the exiles from almost a hundred countries
DAYEINU

IF Hashem had ingathered the exiles from almost a hundred countries
BUT not allowed us to rebuild the Torah World in Israel with thousands of students in Yeshivas and Seminaries, perhaps the most in Jewish History
DAYEINU

IF Hashem had rebuilt the Yeshiva World
BUT not produced so many outstanding Torah leaders
DAYEINU

IF Hashem had produced so many outstanding Torah leaders
BUT not opened the gates of freedom to the oppressed Russian and Ethopian Jews
DAYEINU

IF Hashem had gathered in the multitude of exiles
BUT not made Israel's number of Jews soon to be larger than that of World Jewry for the first time in two and a half thousand years
DAYEINU

ISRAEL IN 2004

- Israel sends doctors and supplies to aid Tsunami victims
- MineGuard Medical Devices develops the diverter, a filter implanted in the neck to reduce the risk of strokes by 40%
- Avraham Hershko and Aharon Chachnover receive the Nobel Prize in Chemistry for their groundbreaking work on ubiquitin and its role in cancer
- Gal Fridman wins a gold medal in windsurfing at the Olympics in Athens, the first gold for the Jewish State of Israel

Dedicated in memory of Yetta Bat Yehoshua Shmuel,
by Karen and Jeremy Jacobs.

58 Listening to our Inner Voice

Tziporah Heller

I have a friend who married rather late in life. She is still waiting for that special moment of unabashed elation. Her husband is, by her account, a person who matched her wish list, which is identical to the one my mother would have written for me and to the one her mother wrote for her. He is an orthodontist; tall, and religious (in that order). The problem is that while her life revolves around moving out of their small, antiseptic suburban box and into a home with a yard, large living room and original décor, he has a huge student loan debt, and is unwilling to incur more debt for the time being. The day she moves is the day she plans as being her happiest.

Until then, each day is tinged with a subtle shade of grey despair. Whatever voices she hears, the one that tells her, "Life has cheated me," is the loudest. Of course whenever she does move, she will inevitably have to face the day when the loudest voice is asking, "Is that all there is?"

At the ripe old age of 18, I was sure of one thing: I didn't want to marry a man for the sake of financial security, for gaining status or as a refuge from loneliness. I didn't want to marry a man who had no vision of what we would build. Throughout the years of our marriage, with all of the dramatic ups and downs that are inherent to a relationship based on growth, nothing ever eclipsed the sheer joy of the moment that my new life began. I chose that moment then, and a million times since then.

I am not any better than my friend, just luckier. I also have voices. Others had visions for me, but in the end, I let my own voice be the loudest, the strongest.

Each of us is unique. We were all created with a specific mission, one that no one else has ever done or will ever do. Real joy comes from the good feeling of knowing that you are on target, that your life is not being lived in vain.

We must constantly ask ourselves who we are, where we are going and what we will need to get there. These questions are inherent to leading a happy and meaningful life. Most of us have a life script submitted by our parents, our peers, or our community which answers these questions. But are these answers right for us?

Shraga Eizenstark never planned to be a hero. When he met the Heilbrun kids, something happened. Due to life circumstances, their father was unable to be much of a hands-on parent. Their sweet, fragile, soft-spoken mother was no match for three adorable savages. Shraga entered their lives. Being a primary school teacher carries with it many responsibilities. They don't usually include making wake up calls to be sure that the kids actually got out of bed on Jerusalem's cold mornings, or calling at night to ask them whether they were in pyjamas and had brushed their teeth. This was just part of Shraga's daily ritual.

Two weeks ago Mrs. Heilbrun was killed in a tragic car accident that also took the life of her youngest son. Shraga dropped everything and has hardly left the other boys' sides. If he were asked how much time he needs to get them through this, the minimum would include seeing them through to adulthood. He was made for this and he is wise enough to grab the opportunity and run.

You don't need to think too deeply to realise how enduring his influence on the boys will be. It will affect their entire lives. What is less clear to those of us who don't look beyond the surface is that the affect on the young teacher is no less real and enduring. He discovered the heroic, compassionate, and transcendent part of himself that could have easily remained hidden, even to his own eye, had he failed himself at this time by taking refuge in complacency.

We are all here for something. The neighbour who is here to open her house to anyone who needs a meal for any *Shabbat* of the year, the friend who is here to love his son despite the disappointment of having a child who rejects everything that he holds to be sacred, the colleague who is here to use her words to bring a smile to those who need a lift. These people live with the sense of purpose and fulfilment that so many of us find elusive.

In order to find our way in this world, we must stay clear of the major pitfalls that make it almost impossible to actualise ourselves.

Learn to hear your voice. We may confuse what we need to do with what others have made us think we must do to validate our lives. Although pleasing others is important, this is only in the context of living a meaningful life.

Reaching your potential takes ongoing effort. We admire people who work hard to make things happen. Sometimes their investment involves things that we just don't have: their talents, charisma or money. However, when we look further, we see that there are others who invest their most prized possession, their very essence, which is far more precious than their resources; meaning that self-actualisation is always within our grasp, irrespective of our belongings.

Don't be afraid of failure. We fail and try again. We give it one more chance, this time with all of the passion and energy we can muster. Guess what? We fail again. When this pattern repeats itself enough times, we stop trying. When we hear about other people's spiritual journeys, we rarely hear about all of the stops along the way. Painful detours are opportunities for growth, and they are inevitable. Eventually, even a long and winding path will get us where we need to go, but only if we stick to it.

I envision myself having a conversation with an angel, an accuser, a lifesaver. The angel of death appears to me in a dream.

"I've come for you, Tziporah," he says gently.

"No! Not now, I'm not ready."

There is a moment of silence. He is being kind, giving me time to think about what I really want to do with the years, if I have them. The moment feels like eternity.

"What is it that you still want to do, and how long will it take?" he persists.

The words finally tumble out. "Building. Guiding. Learning. The kids. Their kids. It would take years. Give me life! I'll use it."

But will I? One of the easiest questions to answer is: "What time is it?" One of the most difficult questions to answer is: "What is time?"

So I flinch when I imagine my older, married friend saying, "You mean I'll never move out of this tiny house? I'll die before I get out of the suburbs?"

ISRAEL IN 2005

- Israeli-American economist Robert J. Aumann wins the Nobel prize in economics for developments in game theory, used to explain conflicts
- Israel's top ice skating team captured the silver medal at the Cup of Russia
- Israelis grow a date tree from a 2,000 year-old seed
- Commander Shahar Ayalon, traffic police chief and speaker to foreign delegations compiles a new tool that will prove invaluable to Israeli law enforcement: a Hebrew-English pocket-size dictionary

> In memory of Benji Hillman who was killed in action at the beginning of the second Lebanon War on 20th July 2006.
> May his memory be blessed.

59 Doña Gracia: An Inspiring Example

Aubrey Hersh

In a 16th century that produced famous and powerful women including Elizabeth I and Catherine of Medici, Doña Gracia stands out; her heroism, loyalty and faith easily eclipsing any epic legend.

Widowed at the age of 26, and forced for many years to live a dangerous double-life: outwardly a Catholic, secretly a Jewess, she dined with the most powerful rulers of her day, including Queen Maria of Hapsburg, Maximillian II and the Sultan of Turkey. She also oversaw a financial empire, whilst clandestinely providing sanctuary for thousands of *Marrano* (secret) Jews.

She faced imprisonment and death on numerous occasions for her beliefs, but managed to thwart the all-powerful Inquisition and defy her enemies. Doña Gracia was one of the most outstanding figures in Jewish history, yet amazingly is virtually unknown - even to Hollywood, despite her life being fully documented.

It is almost impossible to describe the plight faced by the Jews across Europe at the turn of the 16th century, a plight made up in equal measures of fear and defencelessness. Many countries had been emptied of their Jews for centuries and it was now the turn of the Iberian Peninsula. Spain expelled its Jews in 1492, and tens of thousands died in exile looking for a refuge. As many as 150,000 more, outwardly converted to Christianity. These included Doña Gracia's parents, who had lost most of their family to the Inquisition.

However, at best, this would prove a temporary solution. New Christians as they were known, were the target of suspicion from the Church and informers were everywhere. Arriving in Portugal as Marranos, no month went by without some unfortunate family being discovered furtively practicing Judaism and being burnt publicly at the stake.[1]

Doña Gracia was born in 1510 and in 1528 she married a fellow Portuguese Marrano – who had created a banking empire. Knowing that to live as Jews in any Christian country, made them liable to imprisonment for renouncing their 'new faith', they made plans to flee. These plans were accelerated in 1536 when Doña Gracia was suddenly widowed.

Leaving the country however, was far from simple; travel was in its infancy, and emigration was forbidden to all non-Christian countries. Displaying an ingenuity that would serve her well, she created an intricate plan with an interim destination of Antwerp, a trading port, which although under Spanish Catholic rule, was geographically safer. Her brother-in-law Diogo Mendes, had established tenure there, making it possible to convince suspicious church officials that her move was economically and not religiously motivated, and allowing her to transfer her wealth.

In Antwerp she was clandestinely able to observe *Shabbat*, *Matzah* and *Yom Kippur* with less fear, as rulers needed their trade too much for the Inquisition to be allowed to probe too deeply. However, she made sure to attend mass and all public church proceedings.

Their financial status can be gleaned from an episode in 1532, when her brother-in-law was arrested on direct orders of the Holy Roman Emperor Charles V, for helping Jews, and released on the testimony of King Henry VIII!

Once established, Doña Gracia became extraordinarily helpful to other Marranos. Using her trading contacts, she, together with Diogo, created an underground network all over

Western Europe (which included Daniel Bromberg, the famous non-Jewish Italian printer), to spirit Jews into safe harbours. These actions were exceptionally dangerous and though they find some parallel in the post–WWII Breicha movement,[2] the danger for the Mendes' wasn't arrest but execution.

In 1542, her brother-in-law died and she became adept at navigating the twin worlds of finance and politics, only to confront a new danger. Young and attractive, she and her daughter found themselves the objects of unwanted attention. This attention came to a head in May 1544. The Queen Regent (a sister of Charles V) invited her to the palace, to inform them that the Emperor had decided to marry off Doña Gracia's daughter to Francisco d'Aragon, a Spanish nobleman.[3] A refusal would have brought into immediate question, her true faith.

Flight however, would incur great difficulties: where to go, how to move her wealth and how to explain away their sudden departure without subsequently being accused of the ever-present charge of heresy.

In secrecy she liquidated many of her assets, although being forced to abandon all her landed interests, and fled to Venice, a gateway to Turkey and freedom. Once there, she avoided arrest by putting about the story that her nephew had eloped with her daughter (they actually married ten years later!)[4], which had precipitated her sudden departure. She resumed outward life as a Christian, settling outside the ghetto, but her ordeal however was far from over. In 1548 she was imprisoned on the orders of the King of France, who – seeing an opportunity to obtain her fortune – accused her of religious dissent, and had her daughter placed in a convent to prevent their escaping to Turkey.

However, France had not counted on the strength of Jewish connectedness. Moshe Hammon, the Turkish Sultan's Jewish physician, influenced his sovereign to intervene, and Turkey, now at the height of its power, placed the family under its protection, resulting in their eventual release and departure.[5]

At last Doña Gracia was able to throw off the burden of

double-life that she had been living for decades. Her true love for Torah study came to the fore and she created close associations with Rabbi Yosef Karo - author of the Code of Jewish Law - and other rabbinic leaders, to whom she accorded tremendous honour. She supported hospitals and synagogues as well as the poor (historian Cecil Roth writes of 80 paupers being fed at her table every day). But above all, she valued and financed both Jewish education and the rescue of fellow Jews. Salonika - home to 10,000 Marranos and to the *yeshiva* she established in the Lisbon synagogue - stood as testimony to these.

The scene of her next skirmish was the Papal city of Ancona. Having initially offered its protection to the Jews, the city was subsequently obligated to hand them over, by the new pope, Paul IV.[6] 25 Jews were tortured and publicly executed and a further 30 were sent as slaves to row in the galleys.[7]

Having personally helped many of these Jews escape from Portugal, the news horrified Doña Gracia. She rallied the Sultan, who demanded that the Pope release the rest of the captives. Faced with trade threats, Paul IV freed those who had ties with the Ottoman Empire, but unsatisfied, Doña Gracia called on the Ottoman Empire and all Jewish merchants to boycott the city. Rabbi Yosef Karo and Rabbi Yosef Ibn Lev signed a declaration endorsing this idea, which was an audacious and unheard of act of Jewish defiance for the times.

In the twilight of her life, Doña Gracia embarked on a dream, the first serious attempt to found a Jewish settlement and rebuild *Eretz Yisrael*, in a thousand years. She obtained from the Sultan, a lease to the Tiberias region, which at that time lay desolate. In exchange she promised an annual payment of 1,000 gold ducats; to be increased tenfold after 10 years! Behind this move was the sorry state of the many Spanish refugee Jews and Doña Gracia made a fleet of her ships available, to transport new settlers to the region.

A yeshiva was founded there and Jews from Tzfat, Italy and even Yemen began to be drawn to the city. Doña Gracia herself, was unwell by then, and a move to another country beyond her strength. Unfortunately with her death, the Jewish settlement in the city dwindled. Even today though, some houses remain, as a reminder of this honourable mission of *aliyah*.

In 1554, she brought about the transfer of her husband's remains from a Christian cemetery in Lisbon to the Valley of Jehoshaphat, just outside Jerusalem. How she achieved this and at what financial cost, remains unknown, as does paradoxically, the final resting place of this noble woman.

Doña Gracia could have lived a fairytale existence, surrounded by the princes of Europe, but opted instead for the more difficult and often dangerous route: living for and by the truth. In our 21st century democracies, we would do well to reflect on her courage and integrity and on her absolute commitment to her People, her Judaism and her Land. She was truly a Jewish heroine.

Perhaps it's fortunate she is unknown to Hollywood, no film could ever do her justice.

Notes:

1 The Inquistion was only abolished in 1810 and spread in the 1500's, to the Iberian colonies in South America.

2 The Breicha was created to smuggle Jews into Palestine and to rescue Jewish children from monasteries in Europe.

3 In a letter dated April 28th 1544, the Emperor explained that he'd been promised 200,000 ducats for a successful conclusion to the match and that he was willing to pay a quarter to his sister.

4 Joseph Nasi's life was as incredible as his aunt's. He became a favourite of the Turkish sultan - enobled as the Duke of Naxos - and played a leading role in peace negotiations with Poland in 1562, even influencing the election of the Polish King. He won Cyprus from Venetian rule and in 1569 encouraged the Netherlands to rebel against the Spanish. He

also took revenge against the French for their treatment of the House of Nasi, by confiscating all French ships in the harbour of Alexandria and selling their goods, with the Sultan's permission. Unfortunately Joseph and Reyna had no children and the family line died out with her death in 1599.

5 The French ambassador to Venice wrote in 1549: "…the principal reason for the despatch of the special envoy [from Turkey] is to ask them, in the name of the Sultan, to hand over Doña Mendes and her daughter." Since France were in alliance with Turkey at the time, they reluctantly withdrew the charges.

6 He rigorously enforced anti-Jewish laws: confining Jews to ghettoes and enforcing the wearing of the badge of shame. These were to last in Italy until the 19th century.

7 Cecil Roth, *History of the Jews of Italy*, p301. In his book *House of Nasi* Roth writes how the martyrs withstood all pressures to embrace Christianity and died *Al Kiddush Hashem* and how Solomon Jachia, having recited aloud on their behalf, the blessing of martyrdom, jumped into the flames.

ISRAEL IN 2006

- Israel sends aid to help refugees from the Darfur massacres
- The Pensioners party gains six seats in Knesset at its first attempt
- The world's first underwater museum opens in Caesarea
- Warren Buffet buys the Israeli car company Iscar for $4 billion, the biggest foreign buy-out in Israeli history
- Andy Ram becomes the first Israeli tennis player to win a Grand Slam event (mixed doubles at 2006 Wimbledon and the 2007 French Open)

This essay is dedicated in loving memory of
Alexander Rosenzweig zt"l, by Mark
and Melissa Shooter and boys.

60 Our Israel: A Youth Perspective

Judith Flacks, Gideon Glass & Ben Gross

Judith Flacks

The first time I visited the *Kotel*, I knew I was at a place that could give me hope. I knew that, even amidst security checks in a country constantly suffering the threat of attack, I was safe. I had reached that place you dream about when you are little.

At the Kotel, I prayed for guidance in my life. At 16 years old, to some, this may have seemed like a strange thing to ask for. Though at the time, no prayer seemed more appropriate, no wish too great and no thought too trivial. I prayed to make the right decisions so that things would work out best for myself and all the people I cared about. I believe my prayer that day was heard. Without being able to make that prayer, without being able to visit that site, I honestly believe my life would have taken a different direction. For the past 60 years, I am certain that countless others have felt the same way.

When I saw the sun rise at the top of Masada, I felt that nothing could beat me and that I could achieve whatever I wanted to. To stand and see the view and to remember its history, I felt that no task in my life would be too small. I do not believe that anywhere else in the world would give you the same feeling.

Israel is a country of many things to many people. Indeed,

it has been a land filled with struggle, conflict and division from its very establishment. But to me, 60 years since its declaration as a state, it remains a land of hope, diversity, comfort and security. Just look around and see its achievements in academia, medicine and culture and appreciate the things it has given the world. Life would be so different without them.

Almost more than anything, being in Israel gives you a sense of responsibility. One day, I was sitting in a family friend's home about 20 minutes outside Tel Aviv, and I admired all the trees, flowers and plants he had filled his garden with. When I complimented him on this, he turned to me and said something I will never forget. He told me that, "Other people have worked and fought so we could have the right to live here, I didn't want to live on the land and take from it, without giving anything back". Without even living in Israel, I felt as though I was taking without giving. From then on I told myself that I would give back to it in any way I could and have tried to do so ever since.

My Israel is my home, my hope, my heart.

Gideon Glass

Yad Vashem, the most solemn reminder of the Jews' history and heritage, shows us just how destructive man can be. The Holocaust was one of the most terrible oppressions, but it was not the first time that the Jews had almost been destroyed. Whether it be the pogroms in Russia or the destruction of the second temple by the Romans, there has not been a period in history where the Jews have lived in peace, without the shadow of a force intent on destroying them. In 1948, the UN gave us Israel, thinking they would be able to end the oppression, but within minutes of the state being declared most of the Middle East declared war on us.

In the past 60 years, we have fought more wars than most other countries have in the past 600. We have also had to contend with the constant threat of terrorism but have managed to keep the most important thing, our identity as the Jewish state and a land in which we, as Jews, are safe. The biggest challenge of the next 60 years will be to keep it this way.

We must stand shoulder to shoulder with our brothers in Israel and keep it as the Jewish land, as promised to Abraham.

Ben Gross

Israel has been the land of the Jews for thousands of years. Now entering the 60ᵗʰ year of the establishment of the State of Israel, what does Israel mean to me? Obviously this goes beyond words, and it delves into the emotional and spiritual realm that can only be experienced after gaining a connection to the Land.

There are the obvious superficial benefits, such as a climate which can only be dreamt of in dreary London. The fact that I can find a synagogue not further than a 10 minute walk away (as I live in Jerusalem this is not hard, admittedly in places such as Dimona it might be a slightly longer walk).

But then come the 'only in Israel' experiences; when you're driving down the motorway and it's starting to get dark, you see more and more cars on the hard-shoulder with people praying, all facing towards Jerusalem. On Friday afternoon there's the mad panic to get ready for *Shabbat* with shopkeepers shaving while they serve you your goods' (some will like this more than others!) Or when a taxi driver stops next to a shop and he gives you some money to go inside and buy him some Kiddush wine. All these experiences, which put a smile on your face, very soon reach your heart.

Nowhere else in the world can you walk the land and feel the major characters in history walk with you. Traveling to Mitzpe Yericho, where you look upon the place where Joshua crossed the Jordan and conquered the city of Jericho. In Be'er Sheba we felt where our forefathers dug the wells and cultivated the land. And the experience which struck me most: when I was hiking in the North, I passed through the Druze village of Peki'in and came to the cave where Rabbi Shimon Bar Yochai hid for 11 years, fleeing from the Romans. Later that the night we reached Meron where we slept on the roof of the building where his tomb lay.

It doesn't matter whether you're secular or religious, you feel a special difference when it comes to Shabbat. When all types of people gather together to support the people of Sderot or to demand that our captured soldiers be released you then feel true unity with your fellow Jews. This is what Israel is really about: Jews coming together from the most diverse backgrounds heading towards a common goal and striving for a united future.

L'Shana Haba B'Yerushalayim (Next year in Jerusalem).

ISRAEL IN 2007
- Shimon Peres is elected president
- Thomsonfly announces it will fly regularly scheduled flights to Israel making it the first low-fare European airline to serve Israel
- Israel launches a two shekel coin
- 75% of Israel's water is now recycled after use, well ahead of any other country

Afterword

Rabbi Andrew Shaw

On May 26th 1991 I was invited to a hotel in Jerusalem. My invitation was not your normal invite for dinner. This invitation was to help look after the 500 guests who had just arrived after a long and arduous journey. Their journey had taken them many hours, some would say many centuries. These were not paying guests but were still welcomed with open arms. They had come from Ethiopia to Jerusalem – as one of them said to me – they had come home.

I cannot describe what I saw when I arrived that afternoon. There I was in my western clothes confronted by hundreds of people in white robes. We didn't speak the same language, we came from completely different cultures and yet we were together in the Land of Israel. What did we have in common: the student from Britain and the refugees from Africa? We shared one crucial thing – we were all part of the Jewish people, in the Jewish homeland.

Operation Solomon, on May 24 and 25, 1991, flew 14,310 Ethiopian Jews to Israel in 34 hours and 4 minutes. In addition to being an act of mercy, it was an act of courage in a dangerous world, an act of generosity in a selfish world, and an act of diplomacy in a belligerent world.

Think about it. What other country would spend millions of dollars to not only rescue 14,000 poor and destitute refugees but to help make them a part of their society. And what other country's populace would celebrate such an event rather than campaign for the overthrow of the government. That day I saw one of the things that makes Israel special.

For thousands of years Israel has represented much more than a piece of territory; Israel is home. It is a focus for the Jewish heart, a haven for the Jewish People and a sanctuary for the Jewish soul.

Today is Yom Ha'atzmaut – the 60th anniversary of that

historic day when Israel became a State. Over those last six decades Israel has experienced some incredibly demanding and testing times but it continues nevertheless to be a beacon of light in an ever darkening world. So please, celebrate today. Celebrate the wonder that is Israel, the country for which we prayed, for almost 2,000 years.

However, this Yom Ha'atzmaut we have even more to celebrate, we can collectively celebrate the finishing of this book and the start of further exploration into the fascinating world of Judaism and Israel. For 60 days we have observed a period of commemoration and celebration. 60 days later, we hope that each of us has a greater understanding and deeper appreciation of Israel, of their Judaism today and of the role they want to play in the next 60 years, both in terms of Israel and personally. As a Jewish Nation we still await and pray for the ultimate fulfillment of our Destiny: the rebuilding of our Temple in the Messianic era and the peace that will come to the world as a result.

Thank you for taking part (wherever in the world you live) in a project which I hope has been a fitting commemoration to those who lost their lives in defence of Israel and a fitting celebration of the country we all love and pray for.

I will finish this book with the words that began our state – the last words of the Declaration of Independence, May 15th 1948, 5th Iyar 5708:

"We appeal to the Jewish people throughout the Diaspora to rally round the Jews of Eretz-Israel in the tasks of immigration and building and to stand by them in the great struggle for the realisation of the age-old dream – the redemption of Israel."

ISRAEL IN 2008

- The State of Israel celebrates its 60th anniversary
- For the first time in 2,000 years, Israel is the country with the largest Jewish population in the world

Prayer for the Welfare of the State of Israel and its Defence Forces

May He who blessed our fathers, Abraham, Isaac and Jacob, bless the State of Israel, its leaders and advisors in the land which He swore unto our fathers to give us. Put into their hearts the love and fear of You to uphold it with justice and righteousness, and may we be worthy in our days to witness the fulfilment of the words of Your servants, the prophets: "For out of Zion shall go forth the Law and the word of the Lord from Jerusalem". Heavenly Father: Remember the Israel Defence Forces, guardians of our Holy Land. Protect them from all distress and anguish, and send blessing and success to all the work of their hands. Grant peace in Your Holy land and everlasting happiness to all its inhabitants, so that Jacob shall again have peace and tranquillity, with none to make him afraid. Spread the tabernacle of Your peace over all the dwellers on earth. May this be Your will; and let us say, Amen.

Prayer for the Missing Soldiers

He who blessed our forefathers, Abraham, Isaac and Jacob, Joseph, Moses, Aaron, David and Solomon, may He bless, preserve and protect the captive and missing soldiers of the Israel Defence Forces including:

Gilad ben Aviva Shalit
Ehud ben Malka Goldwasser
Eldad ben Tova Regev
Yakutiel Yehuda Nachman ben Sara Katz
Zecharya Shlomo ben Miriam Baumel
Zvi ben Penina Feldman
Ron ben Batya Arad
Guy ben Rina Hever

May the Holy One, blessed be He, rescue them from captivity and speedily restore them in peace, in the merit of this prayer.

May the Holy One, blessed be He, show them mercy, increase their strength, remove their pain and send them a recovery of body and recovery of spirit. May He return them to their families swiftly and soon.

Supporting Israel

As part of this important project some of the proceeds from the *60 Days for 60 Years: Israel* project are earmarked for three initiatives closely associated with the personal and spiritual needs of Israel's soldiers.

HABAYIT SHEL BENJI (BENJI'S HOME)

The late Major Benji Hillman, killed in the second Lebanon War, had an unstinting sense of responsibility toward the soldiers under his command in the Egoz Unit and Golani Brigade. He was especially sensitive to the needs of the 'Lone Soldiers' from overseas and from broken homes who had nowhere to stay whilst on leave. Benji's Home, in Ra'anana, is a home providing Lone Soldiers with a warm bed, good food, a room of their own away from the army, and of course all the love, care, attention and help that they need.

BEIT MORASHA OF JERUSALEM (BMJ)

BMJ runs educational courses for a variety of groups including youth groups, the Police and members of the Israel Defence Force. Their innovative programmes and courses enhance the Jewish and Israeli identity of those participating. These courses empower a committed leadership to engage in contemporary religious, cultural and social challenges. Beit Morasha of Jerusalem integrates intensive study of Talmud, Halacha and Jewish philosophy with formal academic scholarship, and promotes a bold intellectual exchange of ideas between all Jews, across the spectrum of society, through educational programming.

CUSTOM-BUILT SYNAGOGUE ON IDF BASE

The Friends of the Israel Defense Forces (FIDF), the Diaspora partner of the Association for the Wellbeing of Israel's Soldiers (AWIS), supports the social, educational and recreational needs of the young men and women soldiers defending the Jewish homeland. FIDF is planning to build a custom-based synagogue on a major IDF base, aimed at serving the spiritual needs of all soldiers, observant or not.

For more information

For suggested further reading or for websites on the topics discussed in this book visit www.60for60israel.com

If you have any feedback on the *60 Days for 60 Years: Israel* project, please email us at info@tribeuk.com

Biographies

Alan Dershowitz: Professor of Law at Harvard Law School, he is one of the nation's foremost appellate lawyers and a distinguished defender of individual liberties. He appears frequently on television and writes for the New York Times as well as other newspapers and magazines.

Sir Martin Gilbert: Leading historian and author of 79 books including *The Holocaust: The Jewish Tragedy* and many others on Israel and the Jewish People. He is an Honorary Fellow of Merton College, Oxford and was awarded a knighthood in 1995.

Lady Jakobovits: A child in war-torn Europe, she fled for her life with her family from Paris to the South of France and was then smuggled into Switzerland. She married Rabbi Immanuel Jakobovits, the former Chief Rabbi and later Lord Jakobovits. She also developed in her own right into an inspiring speaker on issues of faith, morality and the sanctity of the family. She is a luminary of many charities and is affectionately known to all as Lady J.

Chief Rabbi Sir Jonathan Sacks: Chief Rabbi of the United Hebrew Congregations of the Commonwealth since 1991. The Chief Rabbi is widely recognised as one of the world's leading contemporary exponents of Judaism. A gifted communicator, the Chief Rabbi is a frequent contributor to radio, television and the national press. He is also a prolific author.

Dr Raphael Zarum: Chief Executive and Senior Lecturer at the London School of Jewish Studies. He is a graduate of the Mandel Leadership Institute in Israel and has an MA in Adult Education and a PhD in Theoretical Physics. He is a sought-after international Jewish Educator.

Rabbi Mordechai Ginsbury: Rabbi of Hendon United Synagogue and the Principal of Hasmonean Primary School. He is the Chairman of the United Synagogue Rabbinical Council and former Rabbi of Prestwich Hebrew Congregation in Manchester.

Sara Yoheved Rigler: Author of the bestseller *Holy Woman* and the recently published *Lights from Jerusalem*. She is a featured writer on aish.com. She resides in the Old City of Jerusalem with her husband and children.

Simon Goulden: Formerly the Executive Director of Jews' College (now the London School of Jewish Studies). In 1995 he took up his present position as Chief Executive of the United Synagogue Agency for Jewish Education.

Rabbi Yehudah Silver: Senior Lecturer at seed UK. Founder and director of Gateways, an outreach organisation dedicated to the continuity of the Jewish people. He also worked previously at Aish HaTorah in Jerusalem where he designed and directed the Discovery Program.

Shalom Verrilli: Works for Hazon Yeshaya in Jerusalem.

Rabbi Mordechai Becher: Senior lecturer for the Gateways Organisation in the USA. He taught at Ohr Somayach in Jerusalem for 15 years and was also a chaplain in the IDF. His latest book, *Gateway to Judaism* is a comprehensive introduction to Jewish concepts.

Dr Kenneth Collins: A general medical practitioner and medical historian. He writes on Jewish medical history, Jewish medical ethics and the Jews in Scotland. He has been President of the Glasgow Jewish Representative Council and Chairman of the Scottish Council of Jewish Communities. He is a member of the Chief Rabbinate Trust.

Rabbi Joel Zeff: Rosh Yeshiva of Yeshivat HaMivtar-Torat Yosef of Ohr Torah Stone Institutions in Israel. He holds a BA from UCLA in Hebrew Language, an MS in Jewish History and Rabbinic Ordination both from Yeshiva University.

Rabbi Dr Abraham Twerski: Descended from a long and distinguished rabbinic ancestry. Rabbi Twerski is recognised as an international authority in the chemical dependency field and is also a resident psychiatrist and an Associate Professor of Psychiatry. He is a prolific author on topics such as stress, self-esteem and spirituality.

Rabbi Binyamin Tabory: Rabbinic Scholar in Residence at London School of Jewish Studies 2007-08 and rabbi of the Alei Tzion Synagogue. He is the Rosh Kollel of the new Torah MiTzion Kollel, London. He has a MA in Jewish philosophy from Yeshiva University and semicha from Rabbi Soloveitchik.

Rabbi Zev Leff: Rabbi of Young Israel in North Miami Beach for 11 years. He moved to Israel in 1983 settling in Moshav Matityahu where he serves as Rabbi and Rosh Yeshiva of Yeshiva Gedolah Mattisyahu.

Sarah Shapiro: Author of *A Gift Passed Along* and *Wish I Were Here*. She is the editor of the *Our Lives Anthology* of Jewish writers of which volume III, *The Mother in Our Lives,* was published in 2005 and volume IV is now being compiled. She lives with her family in Jerusalem and teaches writing in Israel and the United States.

Rabbi Ari Kahn: Received his rabbinic ordination from Yeshiva University, as well as a BA in psychology and an MS Degree in Talmud. He is Director of Foreign Student Programs and Senior Lecturer in Jewish Studies at Bar-Ilan University. Rabbi Kahn is also Vice President of Migdal Ohr Institutions in Israel.

Rabbi Dr Dovid Gottlieb: A senior faculty member at Ohr Somayach in Jerusalem. An author and lecturer, Rabbi Gottlieb received his Ph.D in Mathematical Logic at Brandeis University and later become Professor of Philosophy at John Hopkins University. Author of *Ontological Economy: Substitutional Quantification and Mathematics*, 1980 and *The Informed Soul*, 1990.

Yehuda Avner: Married to Esther Cailingold's younger sister, Mimi. He is an Israel Prize winner and acclaimed writer and diplomat. He served on the staff of five Israeli prime ministers and has represented Israel in the United States, Ireland, Australia and Britain, where he served as Ambassador of Israel to the Court of St James's. He is also author of the book, *The Young Inheritors*.

Professor Cyril Domb: Emeritus Professor of Physics at Bar-Ilan University in Israel. Formerly a lecturer in mathematics at Cambridge University and Professor of Theoretical Physics at King's College, London, and Academic President of the Jerusalem College of Technology.

Samuel Y Agnon: Born in Eastern Galicia in 1888 and emigrated to Israel in 1907. He was one of the most celebrated Hebrew authors of the 20th Century. He died in 1970 and has become an Israeli icon.

Rabbi Yitzchak Schochet: Rabbi of Mill Hill United Synagogue and a member of the Chief Rabbi's Cabinet. He was ordained in New York and has a MA in Jewish Studies from UCL.

Rabbi Chaim Kanterovitz: Rabbi of the Yeshurun Hebrew Congregation in Manchester and formerly the Senior Rabbi of the Kenton Synagogue in North London. He holds several semichas and a degree in psychology and international politics.

Rabbi David Mason: Rabbi of Kingston United Synagogue in London and represents the Chief Rabbi on issues of world aid, debt and trade. He has also worked as an educator for the Lauder Foundation in Poland. He has two degrees in economics and is studying towards qualification as a family therapist.

Rabbi Dr Shlomo Riskin: Internationally renowned educator, speaker and author. He founded and serves as Chancellor of Ohr Torah Stone Colleges and Graduate Programmes. He is also the founding Chief Rabbi of Efrat.

Rabbi Aubrey Hersh: Studied at Gateshead Yeshiva and in Jerusalem. He worked in media and advertising until 1997, when he joined the JLE, in London. Currently he is their Projects Director, as well as the tour leader for Eastern and Central European trips. A regular *Muchni* lecturer, he was the associate editor for both the '60 for 60' book projects.

Rabbi Shaya Karlinsky: Co-founder and Dean of Yeshivat Darche Noam/David Shapell College and the Midreshet Rachel v'Chaya College of Jewish Studies for Women. He studied at UCLA followed by Yeshivat Kerem B'Yavneh and the Mir Yeshiva. He has a MA in Educational Psychology and is a widely published photojournalist.

Samuel Green: Educated at the City of London School before graduating from Trinity College, Cambridge, with a degree in Oriental Studies. In 2006-7 he held the post of *mazkir* at the Federation of Zionist Youth.

Gila Manolson: Author of *The Magic Touch: A Candid Look at the Jewish Approach to Relationships, Outside/Inside* and *Head to Heart: What to Know Before Dating and Marriage.* She graduated from Yale University and currently teaches and lives in Jerusalem.

Danya Ross: Born and educated in Israel, where she graduated with a degree in special needs education – a field in which she worked for many years in Jerusalem. In 2002, she and her husband moved to London, where she taught at the JLE. Currently she runs a text studies programme at JFS as well as being a relationships counsellor and full-time mother to her 5 children.

Rabbi Yitzchok Reuven Rubin: Rabbi of Bowden Synagogue in Manchester. He is also a member of the Chief Rabbi's cabinet. He is an author and columnist, and his interest in mental health led him to become the first elected Chairman of the Maimonides Hospital's Outpatient Facility.

Yitta Halberstam: Author of numerous books including the *Small Miracles* series. The first volume of this series was a national bestseller in the USA. She has appeared on many radio and television shows.

Rabbi Harvey Belovski: Rabbi of the Golders Green United Synagogue in London. New chaplains' mentor for Jewish Chaplaincy, a relationship counsellor and the author of two books, as well as numerous articles for the *Jewish Chronicle* and *Cross-Currents*. Received his ordination from Gateshead Yeshiva, and graduated in mathematics from University College, Oxford.

Rabbi Jason Kleiman: Currently Rabbi of the Beth Hamidrash Hagadol Synagogue in Leeds. He is a graduate of Leeds University and Jews' College. Former Rabbi to the Reading, Catford and Clayhall communities, teacher of Jewish studies at City of London School for Girls and Jewish Chaplain to the Royal London Hospitals NHS Trust.

Rebbetzin Esther Jungreis: Came to the USA after surviving the Nazi's Bergen-Belsen concentration camp. She founded Hineni, a pioneering outreach organisation that reconnects Jews to their Jewish Heritage. She writes a weekly column for *The Jewish Press* and her weekly Hineni programme is the longest running Jewish broadcast in America.

Rabbi Daniel Rowe: BA in philosophy from University College, London. He is a former tank driver in the 401st Armoured Brigade of the IDF. Awarded an "Outstanding Soldier" award. Currently part of the UK Aish team.

Rabbi Emanuel Feldman: Rabbi in Atlanta, Georgia, USA for 40 years. He was ordained by Ner Israel in Baltimore and has B.S., M.A. and PhD degrees from Johns Hopkins University and Emory University. He is the former editor of *Tradition* magazine, has written nine books, and taught at Emory and at Bar Ilan University.

Rabbi Paysach Krohn: A fifth generation *mohel*, affiliated with major hospitals in New York. Author of a book on *Brit Milah*, six "Maggid" books, 500 stories and a DVD series on Central and Eastern Europe.

Rabbi YY Rubinstein: Regular broadcaster on UK TV and radio as well as writing for *Hamodia* and teaching at various seminaries and yeshivot. He is the current Jewish Student Chaplain for Manchester, serving over 2,000 Jewish students, and author of *Dancing Through Time*.

Rabbi Menachem Leibtag: One of the pioneers of Torah education via the internet. He has 25 years of experience as a teacher at Yeshivat Har Etzion. He is the founder of the Tanach Study Center [www.tanach.org]. Rabbi Leibtag also lectures at Yeshivat Shalaavim, Yeshivat ha'Kotel, Midreshet Lindenbaum, and Orot College for Women.

Rabbi James Kennard: Educated at Oxford University. He is a former Jewish Student Chaplain in Leeds and Head Teacher at King Solomon School in Essex. Currently, he is the principal of Mount Scopus Memorial College in Melbourne, Australia.

Dayan Yonason Abraham: Dayan of the London Beth Din. He is the former Rabbi to a community in Melbourne, Australia and is currently the rabbinic consultant to Tribe.

Rabbi Naftali Schiff: Studied at Yeshivat HaKotel in Jerusalem prior to joining Givati IDF combat unit. He has been the Director of Jerusalem Fellowships Programmes since 1994 and Executive Director of Aish UK since 1999. He is also the Founder and President of jGIFT a grassroots young volunteer organisation.

Rabbi Malcolm Herman: Programmes Director of seed UK. Seed specialises in the interests of parents of young children, working with primary schools and synagogues throughout the UK.

Chaim Fachler: Grew up in Letchworth and studied at Carmel College before attending various yeshivot in Israel. In 1980 he joined the staff of Laniado Hospital, serving as Director of International Fundraising until 2003.

Chief Rabbi Dr Warren Goldstein: Chief Rabbi of South Africa. Co-author of "African Soul Talk" with Dumani Mandela, a dialogue on the values for the new South Africa. An advocate of the South African High Court.

Chana Weisberg: Author of four books including the best-selling *Divine Whispers* and the newly released *Tending the Garden: The Unique Gifts of the Jewish Woman.* She is associate editor for Chabad's website and an international lecturer.

Rabbi David Blackman: During more than a decade at Yeshivat Har Etzion, Rabbi Blackman became a close pupil of Rabbi Aharon Lichtenstein. He also has a degree in Education and Jewish Philosophy. Rabbi Blackman served in leadership roles in Bnei Akiva as well as serving in the Infantry of the IDF. He is married to Deborah and they have 6 children.

Rabbi Dr Naftali Brawer: Spiritual leader of Borehamwood and Elstree United Synagogue. Member of the Chief Rabbi's Cabinet with responsibility for Jewish-Muslim relations. He is a regular columnist for the *Jewish Chronicle*. Dr Brawer is an honorary research fellow and lecturer at the London School of Jewish Studies. He holds a PhD in Hebrew and Jewish Studies from UCL.

Rabbi Yaacov Haber: Founder and driving force behind TorahLab. Rabbi Haber is the former National Director of Jewish Education for the Orthodox Union, founder of the Australian Institute of Torah. He is also one of the founding members of the Association of Jewish Outreach Professionals.

Esther Wachsman: The inspirational mother of Nachshon Wachsman.

Rabbi Yossi Michalowicz: Received his *semicha* from Telshe Yeshiva and his MA in Education from John Carroll University. He has been the Rabbi of the Westmount Shul and Learning Centre in Thornhill, Canada for the past 10 years.

Rabbi Gideon Sylvester: Rabbi of Tribe Israel and Executive Director of Yeshivat Hamivtar – Torat Yosef in Efrat where he also teaches. Previously, he was the Rabbi of Britain's fastest growing community, Radlett United Synagogue. Following his aliyah three years ago, Rabbi Sylvester served as an Advisor at the Office of the Prime Minister of Israel.

Rabbi Daniel Levy: Rabbi of the United Hebrew Congregation, Leeds. Previously, he was Rabbi in Cardiff and an associate lecturer at Cardiff University. He has *semicha* from Gateshead Yeshiva and BA and MA degrees from Jews' College.

He is the Chairman of the Rabbinical Council of the Provinces and a member of the Chief Rabbi's Cabinet. He has recently written a book *The Fox, the Foetus and the Fatal Injection*.

Rabbi Yoni Sherizen: Chief Executive of University Jewish Chaplaincy, the organisation behind the Jewish Chaplains on UK campuses. Prior to this, he was the Jewish Student Chaplain in Oxford for three years. He has been involved in social action projects around the world and is currently working on a project that brings Jewish students from Britain to developing countries to strengthen community infrastructure.

Rabbi Dr Akiva Tatz: Qualified as a Doctor in South Africa and served as an army medical officer on the Namibian border during the conflict there. Studied in Yeshiva in Jerusalem and founded the Jerusalem Medical Ethics Forum. He has authored books on Jewish philosophy. Currently, he is a senior lecturer at the JLE in London.

Rebbetzin Holly Pavlov: Jewish educator and author. She is the Founder and Director of She'arim, College of Jewish Studies for Women in Jerusalem.

Yaffa Ganz: Has written more than 40 books for Jewish children (and two for Jewish adults!). In 1990, she was awarded the prestigious Sydney Taylor Book Award. The Ganz family made aliyah in 1964 and live in Jerusalem.

Rabbi Laurence (Doron) Perez: Rabbinic Leader of Mizrachi South Africa. He also serves as the senior Rabbi of the Mizrachi Yeshiva Community Centre in Johannesburg. Rabbi Perez has recently been appointed the Managing Director of the Yeshiva College schools, the largest Torah school system in South Africa. He lives in Glenhazel with his wife Shelley and children.

Rebbetzin Tziporah Heller: International lecturer and faculty member of Neve Yerushalayim College in Jersusalem. She specialises in Biblical literature, Jewish philosophy, Maimonides, the Maharal and the role of women in Judaism. She is a weekly columnist in *Hamodia* and the author of numerous books.

Judith Flacks: Ex JFS student, she was a participant in the 2006 Ambassador competition. Judith now studies at Sussex University.

Gideon Glass: Currently a year 12 student at JFS School in London.

Ben Gross: A finalist in the JFS 2006 Ambassador competition, he is now a yeshiva student at Hakotel. He has been involved in Tribe Teens and is active in Tribe Israel.

Glossary of Jewish Terms

Abraham: The founder of Judaism and the physical and spiritual ancestor of the Jewish people. The first of the three Patriarchs of the Jewish People.

Akeidah: Word used to depict Abraham's binding and intended sacrifice of his son, Isaac (Genesis 22:1-19).

Aliyah: Immigrating to Israel.

Amidah: (The Silent Prayer) one of Judaism's central prayers. Recited 3 times a day, it is made up of 19 blessings.

Ari–zal: Lit. "the lion of blessed memory". Rabbi Isaac Luria (1534-1572), one of the leading luminaries of the Kabbalah.

Avodah: Lit. Service, generally in reference to the Temple service, especially the part performed by the High Priest on Yom Kippur.

Baal Shem Tov: Rabbi Israel ben Eliezer,(1700-1760), the founder of Chasidism.

Bar Kochba: Aramaic for "Son of a Star". Simeon ben Kosiba, the leader of the last Jewish rebellion against Rome in 132-135C.E.

BCE: Before the Common Era

Beit HaMikdash: Holy Temple (twice destroyed) in Jerusalem.

Brit Milah: The ritual circumcision of a male Jewish child on the 8th day of his life or of a male convert to Judaism.

CE: In the Common Era.

Chafetz Chaim: (1840-1933) Considered one of the greatest leaders of his generation. Most famous for his commentary on the Shulchan Aruch, called the Mishnah Brura.

Challot: Bread traditionally used on Shabbat and Festivals, often braided.

Chanukah: An eight-day festival celebrating the rededication of the Temple in Jerusalem after it was defiled by the Greeks.

Chanukiah: A eight-branched candelabra lit on Chanukah.

Chasidism (adj. Chasidic): Lit. "pious ones". May refer to a medieval German sect, but usually used in reference to a particular Orthodox movement founded by Israel Baal Shem Tov in Poland in the mid 18th century. There are various sects each of which follows their own *rebbe* as their leader.

Chesed: An act of kindness.

Chol Hamoed: The intermediate days of Pesach (Passover) and Succot. In Israel this starts on the 2nd day of the festival and in the Diaspora on the 3rd.

Chumash: The five books of Moses (the written Torah).

Davening: Praying.

Elokim: A Holy Name of God.

Eretz Yisrael: The Land of Israel.

Erev: Lit. evening. The evening part of a day, which precedes the morning part of the same day because a "day" in the Jewish calendar starts at sunset.

Erev Shabbat: Lit. eve of shabbat, but in common usage: the hours before Shabbat.

Gehinam: A place of spiritual punishment and/or purification after death.

Gemara: Commentary on the Mishnah. The Mishnah and Gemarah together form the Talmud.

Haganah: Underground military organisation in Palestine. It operated until 1948 when its members transferred to the Israeli army.

Haggadah: The book read during the Passover Seder, telling the story of the holiday.

Halachah (adj. Halachic): The complete body of rules and practices that Jews are bound to follow, including biblical commandments, commandments instituted by the rabbis, and binding customs.

Haman: Formulated a plot to kill the Jewish Nation in the story of Purim.

Hashem: Lit. "The Name"; God

Kabbalah: Jewish mystical tradition.

Kashrut: Jewish dietary laws.

Kedushah: Holiness.

Kibbutzim: Collective villages, generally run on socialist lines. The kibbutz movement played a large role in the economic and political activities of the country.

King David: Famous for killing Goliath, becoming King of Israel and writing the book of Psalms.

Kiddush: The prayer that is recited at the beginning of a festive meal on Shabbat and festivals, over a cup of wine.

Kiddushin: Lit. sanctification. The first part of the two-part process of Jewish marriage, which creates the legal relationship.

Kittel: The white robes in which the dead are buried, worn by many married men during Yom Kippur services.

Kohen (pl. Kohanim): Priest. A descendant of Aaron (brother of Moses), charged with performing much of the Temple service.

Kollel: A Yeshiva (a place of learning Torah) for married men.

Kotel: The Western Wall.

Lehitraot: Goodbye in Modern Hebrew.

Levite: Someone from the tribe of Levi (one of the twelve tribes of Israel).

Ma'ariv: The evening prayer service, said after sundown every evening.

Maccabees: A name for the family of heroes of the story of Chanukah, derived from the title of one of his sons, Judah the Maccabee.

Machzor: A special prayer book for the High Holidays of Rosh Hashanah and Yom Kippur and for the three Festivals (Pesach, Shavout and Succot).

Matzah (pl. Matzot): Unleavened bread traditionally served during Pesach.

Megillat Esther: Lit. "Scroll of Esther". One of the five prophetic books, read in the synagogue during the year. Megillat Esther tells the story of Esther and the events of Purim.

Mezuzah (pl. Mezzuzot): Biblical passage on a parchment scroll placed in a case and affixed to a doorpost.

Midrash: (pl. midrashim) Stories elaborating on incidents in the Bible, to derive a principle of Jewish law or provide a moral lesson.

Mishkan: Tabernacle. The Temple used by the Children of Israel in the wilderness, which was portable.

Mishnah: A written compilation of the oral tradition (c.200CE), the basis of the Talmud.

Mitzvah (pl. Mitzvot): Any of the 613 commandments that Jews are obligated to observe; it can also refer to any Jewish religious obligation, or more generally to any good deed.

Moshiach: The man who will be chosen by God to put an end to all evil in the world, rebuild the Temple and usher in the world to come.

Mot'zai Shabbat: Saturday night, after Shabbat is over.

Muchni: A mechanism designed to lower the laver into contact with the water table. A term used to describe an in-depth educational talk.

Nachmanadies: *(1194-1270)* Leading Spanish Talmudist, Kabbablist and biblical commentator. Known as Nachmanadies, his Hebrew name was Moses ben Nahman.

Oral Law: Jewish teachings explaining and elaborating on the Written Torah, handed down orally until the 2nd century

CE, when they began to be written down in what became the Talmud.

Parashat: Torah portion of the week.

Pesach: A festival commemorating the Exodus from Egypt; also known as Passover.

Poskim: Religious scholars who interpreted the meaning of the law in practice and thus contributed to its codification.

Purim: A holiday celebrating the rescue of the Jews from extermination at the hands of the chief minister to the King of Persia (4th century BCE) as related in the Book of Esther.

Rabbi Akiva: One of the greatest Rabbis recorded in the Talmud. Died a martyr for the Jewish People.

Rabbi J.B. Soloveitchik: (1903 to 1993) Rosh HaYeshiva of Yeshiva University, New York. Father figure of Modern Orthodoxy in the United States.

Rabbi Yehudah HaNasi: Lived in 2nd century CE and was the person who compiled the *Mishnah*. He is also known as Rebbi throughout the Mishnah.

Rabbi Yochanan ben Zakai: Leader of the Jewish people at the time of the destruction of the *Second Temple*.

Rambam:(1135-1204) His full name was Rabbi Moshe ben Maimon and is known as Maimonides. He was one of the greatest medieval Jewish scholars, and is renowned for his codification of Jewish Law and the *Guide to the Perplexed*.

Rashi: (1040-1105) His full name was Rabbi Shlomo Yitzchaki, the most famous Jewish Commentator on the written Torah and the Talmud.

Rav: Term of endearment for Rabbi.

Rebbe: Means Grand Rabbi. This person is the leader of a Chasidic community, often believed to have special, mystical power.

Rosh Hashanah: The Jewish new year.

Rosh Yeshiva: The spiritual head of a Yeshiva.

Seder night: Lit. night of order. The family home ritual conducted as part of the *Passover* observance.

Sedra: The Torah Portion

Sefirot: Lit. "emanations". In Jewish mysticism, the 10 emanations from God's essence that interact with the universe.

Semicha: Essentially, a rabbinical degree, authorising a person to decide questions in Jewish law.

Sephardi: A Jew who's origins are from Spain, Portugal, North Africa and the Middle East. Jews from Egypt and the Middle East are sometimes described separately as Edut Hamizrach.

Shabbat: The Jewish Sabbath.

Shavuot: Lit. weeks. One of the three pilgrimage festivals. The festival occurs 50 days after Pesach and commemorates the giving of the Torah and the harvest of the first fruits.

Shema: One of the fundamental Jewish prayers, taken from verses in the Torah and inscribed in the mezuzah and tefillin.

Shemittah: Sabbatical year for the land of Israel.

Shiva: Lit. seven days. Period of mourning for family and close relatives of the deceased, in order to mourn their loved one.

Schlepp: A Yiddish word to Drag, carry or haul.

Shofar: A ram's horn blown on Rosh Hashanah, as a call to repentance.

Shtender: A stand or lectern, where books are placed during learning, or a prayer book during prayer.

Shtetl: A small Jewish town or village formerly found throughout Eastern Europe.

Shtibel: Yiddush for small synagogue.

Shul: Yiddish for synagogue, house of prayer.

Shulchan Aruch: A code of Jewish law written by Rabbi Joseph Caro in the 16th century, and one of the most respected compilations ever written.

Simcha: A happy occasion.

Succah: The temporary dwellings lived in during the festival of Succot.

Succot: A festival commemorating God's protection in the wilderness and also the final harvest; also known as the Feast of Tabernacles.

Tallit: A shawl-like garment worn during morning services with tzitzit (fringes) attached to the four corners as a reminder of the commandments. Sometimes called a prayer shawl.

Talmud (Babylonian): The most significant collection of the Jewish oral tradition interpreting the Torah (late 5th century CE).

Talmud (Jerusalem): A companion to the Babylonian Talmud but written in Israel 150 years earlier (4th century CE).

Tanach: The 24 books of the written Bible. Referred to by non-Jews as the Old Testament.

Tehillim: The Book of Psalms.

Teshuva: Lit. return. Repentance.

Tisha B'Av: The 9th of the Jewish month of Av. The destruction of both Temples, as well as much other Jewish suffering, happened on this day throughout history.

Torah: In its narrowest sense, the first five books of the Bible: Genesis, Exodus, Leviticus, Numbers and Deuteronomy, sometimes called the Pentateuch; in its broadest sense, Torah is the entire body of Jewish teachings.

Tzaddik (pl. Tzaddikim): Righteous people.

Tzedakah: Means righteousness. Generally refers to charity.

Vilna Gaon: (1720-1797) Rabbi Eliyahu ben Shlomo Zalman of Vilna leader of Lithuanian Jewry and one of the most influential Jews in the last 300 years.

Yarmulka: Lit. "Fear of King". Circular piece of material worn as a head covering by men.

Yehudah Halevi: A great Talmudic scholar, poet and philosopher. Born in Spain in the 11th century.

Yeshiva (pl. Yeshivot): An academy of religious study for men.

Yom Kippur: The Day of Atonement; a day set aside for fasting, depriving oneself of physical pleasures and repenting from the sins of the previous year.

Zechut: Merit.

Zohar: The primary written work in the mystical tradition of Kabbalah, written by Rabbi Shimon bar Yochai and brought into public study during the 13th century.

Zt"l: Abbreviation for *"Zecher Tzadik Livracha"* – may the memory of the tzaddik serve as a blessing. Added as a suffix to the name of someone who has died.

If you have enjoyed this book you might like to know more about the first 60 Days project in memory of the victims of the Holocaust: *60 Days for 60 Years: Remember the Past to Build the Future.*

Visit **www.60for60.com** where you can find out more and order a copy.